W9-AMS-524

THE PICTORIAL HISTORY OF FOOTBALL

12
32

THE PICTORIAL HISTORY OF FOOTBALL

ROLAND LAZENBY

Published by Gallery Books
A Division of W H Smith Publishers Inc.
112 Madison Avenue
New York, New York 10016

Produced by
Bison Books Corp.
15 Sherwood Place
Greenwich, CT 06830

ISBN 0-8317-6890-8

Printed in Hong Kong

1 2 3 4 5 6 7 8 9 10

Part III
The Golden Age of Pro Football, 1946-1959

Part IV
Thoroughly Modern: The NFL from 1960

INTRODUCTION

In 1892 Pudge Heffelfinger, a former Yale University star, accepted $500 to play for a Pittsburgh athletic club, thus sewing the first recognized seed of professional football. From that meager beginning, the game has grown over the past nine decades into a major preoccupation of American society. By the 1980s more than 13 million fans were passing through stadium gates each season. The game's championship, the Super Bowl, has become a media extravaganza, attracting well beyond 120 million television viewers worldwide each year. As would be expected from such a spectacle, the business of football generates hundreds of millions in revenues, making wealthy men of the players, coaches, owners and agents involved.

Often forgotten is the fact that the game endured decades of low esteem, small crowds and virtual anonymity before blossoming with the cloudburst of money from television in the 1950s and 1960s.

In the 1920s, the Chicago Bears' Red Grange, the first of the bonus babies, and his coach George Halas, met President Calvin Coolidge, who greeted them. 'How are you young gentlemen?' the president asked. 'I have always admired animal acts.' The world of sport, particularly pro football, has traveled far since then. Modern presidents, of course, often collect a bushel of political currency by phoning their congratulations to championship teams.

The game, however, reaches beyond politics and money. Its sublime moments occur on the field and involve nothing more grand than blocking and tackling, running and passing. 'Football is blocking and tackling,' Vince Lombardi once said. 'Everything else is mythology.'

In another sense, blocking and tackling have *become* mythology, the substance of metaphor for modern American society. Pro football players of the 1980s are the most watched athletes in history, perhaps the most watched *people* in history. Because of that, they are important threads in the fabric of our value system. Fans follow their heroes closely, exalting when they achieve, suffering when they fail, often finding similarities to athletic struggles in their own lives.

England's King Henry II, who banned 'futballe' in the twelfth century, would certainly shudder if he knew the exalted position the game holds in modern life. Yet, it's just that essence that makes pro football so valuable. Beneath all the media and money and spectacle, it's just a game. Nothing more, nothing less. For all the high drama and pretended seriousness, the outcome of each Super event brings no real consequences. The strugglings up and down a football field, up and down the league standings, hold importance only in their measurement of human achievement, in their chronicling of a group striving for a common goal. As Vince Lombardi said, winning is everything. It is also nothing.

Television ratings and poll after poll have shown that pro football long ago replaced baseball as America's national pastime, an endeavor to occupy us and relieve us of the hassles of life. It is primarily an item for the present. At the hour of the game, nothing on earth seems so important as the outcome. Yet two weeks later, it has been erased from our minds, a thing of mild interest at best. The reliving of old sports events sometimes does nothing more than remind us of their absurdity. Other times the reliving brings back personalities, smells and sounds, hopes and disappointments that summon a vanished moment with all its attendant emotion and drama. On the following pages we offer you a pictorial history of professional football – the grand moments, the wins and losses, the dynasty teams, the outstanding players and colorful coaches. We hope that we've recaptured some of it for you, that you, too, will find something to treasure.

PART I

Early Times

ORIGINS OF THE AMERICAN GAME

The game of football has grown from roots wound centuries deep into the psyche of civilized man. The ancient Greeks called their version of the sport *harpaston*. Typical of their cultural plagiarism, the Romans played *harpastum*. The Italians in the Middle Ages dubbed their game *calcia*. Across the world, the Polynesians shredded bamboo to make a ball for kicking, while the Eskimos stuffed moss into a leather hide.

Whatever the culture, whatever the implements, the phenomenon of football has struck a chord of pride and manhood in young men across the ages. Even better than war, it has appealed to the rakishness of their egos, to the baseness of their desire for power and physical prowess.

Its promoters have touted it as a test of toughness and character. Its detractors have decried it as an expression of violence, a glorification of brute force.

Its analysts suggest that while the game feeds on aggression, football has become an effective release valve for modern man, giving him the opportunity to vent the dark side of his nature in a controlled, almost sanitized, setting. Perhaps there's some merit to that opinion. As militaristic a genius as Vince Lombardi was, he never ordered his troops to march on Moscow. Yet that line of thinking is a bit too esoteric for football, a wonderfully uncomplicated pastime. The simple essence of the game is contact. Hitting. Ringing an opponent's bell, so to speak. Ask an 18-year-old linebacker his feelings on the greater issues of the sport, and he'll tell you he just wants to knock somebody's jock off.

Any number of theories have been advanced on the origins of modern football. One of the more interesting traces the American professional game to the Danish invasion and occupation of England between 1016 to 1042. It seems that a number of Danes were killed and buried on the field of battle, only to be disinterred during ploughing a number of years later, after the English had driven the Danes from their island. As Danish skulls were turned up by the plough, the farmhands made quite a game of kicking them about the field. It's a gruesome story, yet it does seem suited to the territorial urge that pervades modern football. The whole game, in fact, is built on protecting one's home goal from invaders.

Kicking games played by crowds of unruly youths were much in evidence in England throughout the ensuing centuries. The object kicked was usually an inflated cow or pig's bladder, usually procured immediately after butchering in late fall. Some enthusiasts went so far as to cover the bladder with leather hide.

The game knew few boundaries, with any landmark serving as a goal. There was no limit to players on a side. In fact, the game of 'futballe,' as it was called in twelfth-century England, often drew large crowds, which, once caught up in the movement of the game, were known to wreak havoc on communities, trampling gardens, breaking down fences and creating a general mayhem.

Often the competition raged between villages, pitting the youthful population of one locality against another. It is no surprise that authorities considered the game a nuisance. Fearing the games would distract the population from the archery practice needed for England's military preparedness, King Henry II, who reigned from

"DRIBBLING" IN ASSOCIATION FOOTBALL.

ABOVE: *Association football, a name that was abbreviated to soccer, was one of the parents of American football. This line drawing shows a nineteenth-century player 'dribbling' the ball out of the crowd.*

LEFT: *Rugby, the other parent of American football, evolved at the Rugby school for boys in England in the 1820s. This line drawing was published in 1870.*

RIGHT: *This woodcut from 1885 shows what was considered to be a 'low' tackle for the period. Tackling around the legs and ankles would eventually become a distinguishing characteristic of the American game.*

LEFT: *At Eton College in England, a rugby style of competition evolved known as 'the Wall Game.' Because of the limited playing area at the school, the Wall Game employed 11 players on a side, which became another factor in the development of American football when a player from Eton enrolled at Yale University.*

BELOW: *By the late nineteenth century rugby football was well established, as evidenced by this match between England and Scotland at the Athletic Grounds in Richmond, England.*

1154 to 1189, banned the sport. 'No more futballe,' Henry is said to have declared.

Edward II did the same when he was king from 1307 to 1327, as did Henry VI in the early fifteenth century. In 1314 Edward's laws forbade 'hustling over large footballs, from which many evils arise, which God forbid.'

Like a weed, the game persisted and flourished, wrapping itself like a vine in the English cultural heritage, capturing the fancy of generation after generation of schoolboys and ruffians. By Shakespeare's time, football was described as a 'friendlie kind of fyghte . . . a bloody and murthering practice.' By the seventeenth century, the town fathers of Manchester railed against 'a company of lewd and disordered persons using that unlawful exercise of playing with the football in the streets . . . breaking many men's windowes and glasse at their pleasure and other great inormyties. . . .'

Its rambunctious seed was carried to New England during the Colonial period, beginning a cross pollinization between cultures that would result in the flowering of the American hybrid in the late

RIGHT: *Football at Princeton, as shown in this 1877 drawing, was a roughhouse struggle between freshmun and sophomore classes.*

LEFT: *The Flying Wedge, shown here in an 1892 version, led to widespread complaints that football was a violent, deadly sport. Eventually, the formation was outlawed.*

nineteenth century.

In the early nineteenth century, schoolyard football had evolved to a game called 'association,' a word that was promptly corrupted to soccer. Although the game was similar in both countries, the English were infuriated and disgusted by the American affinity for 'offsides' play, or the running of interference.

The two major developments of the period came at English schools. At Rugby in 1823, a schoolboy named William Webb Ellis shocked his fellows by picking up the ball and running with it, in blatant disregard of the rules. Although Ellis was reviled for his unsportsmanlike behavior, the sudden burst of action caught the fancy of his mates and the game of rugby was born. The kicking game suddenly had a ball-carrying cousin. Within four decades a network of clubs had sprung up, and in 1863, the London Football Association was organized, bringing the game a code of organized rules. During this period, the boys of Eton adjusted to their limited playing area by allowing only 11 players per side, a development that would play a large role in the evolution of the fledgling sport in America.

Colonial authorities had expressed the same irritation with the game as their English counterparts, but by the nineteenth century the game was soundly imbedded in the college scene. It was nurtured on the fields of the Ivy League, not so much as an intercollegiate sport but as a class competition, pitting freshmen against sophomores. Internecine struggles at Yale in the 1840s led to the development of the flying wedge, the particularly bloody form of interference. And football day at Harvard came to be known as Bloody Monday, bringing college authorities to abolish the game in 1860. Harvard students held a mock funeral for the game. The effect of the abolition, alas, was the same as in merry England centuries earlier. Football flourished.

On 6 November 1869, Princeton (then known as Nassau Hall) and Rutgers engaged in the first intercollegiate competition, featuring 25 players to a side and a black rubber ball that could be kicked or butted with the shoulder. The Rutgers boys hoped to avenge a 40-2 baseball defeat by Nassau Hall in 1866, and did so with a narrow win. The game, however, was a soccer match.

The first shoot of modern football didn't appear until 1874 when the rugby team from McGill University in Canada played a match against Harvard, which left the Americans infatuated with the new rules. The climate for change warmed further when a football student from Eton, David Schaff, enrolled at Yale.

On 13 November 1875 Harvard and Yale played a game with variations of rugby rules at New Haven, marking the true birth of American football. More than 2000 spectators paid 50 cents each to watch Harvard trim Yale, four goals to none.

The following year, Harvard, Yale, Columbia and Princeton formed the Intercollegiate Football Association with a mix of rugby and soccer rules, setting the evolution of the game spinning off at a new pace over the next two decades.

CAMP

Walter Camp entered Yale University in 1876 as a 17-year-old freshman intent on becoming a doctor. Instead, he immediately fell in love. His sweetheart was the rough-and-tumble game, the bastard child of chance, American football. To the good fortune of the modern sports world, what began as youthful infatuation stretched into a lifelong love affair for Walter Camp.

Over the next five decades, he provided much of the vision and leadership that freed the sport from its uncertain past. He installed rules that uncluttered the play and set the framework for football's dynamic evolution. He selected college All-America teams and set standards for performance. Above all, he championed the intelligence and character of competition. For that, Camp is known as 'the father of American football.' Seldom has a title been more fitting.

Perhaps the most amazing part of the story is that Camp sired his offspring while still a Yale undergraduate. Beginning in 1878, his junior year, and lasting until his death in 1925, he sat on the amateur rules committee, a position from which he commandeered the philosophy of football toward sophistication. 'When it comes to the football field,' he said, 'mind will always win over muscle and brute force.' That was the precept to which he dedicated his life.

The Ivy League was the cradle of football in the United States in the 1870s, and Camp happened there at the cusp of the game's development. He was just the right person in just the right place. He not only loved the game, he was good at it. As a 6-foot, 157-pound freshman, he made the Yale varsity and went on to play seven years for the Elis, serving as captain three years. Later, from 1888 to 1892, Camp reigned as Yale's first football coach (with his wife Allie as assistant).

ABOVE: *Walter Camp was Yale's captain in 1878. He went on to become the driving force behind the evolution of American football rules.*

RIGHT: *Pudge Heffelfinger (left) graduated from Yale and became America's first professional football player. He is pictured here with Yale teammate Tom McClung, who later became Secretary of the Treasury. Both were All Americans on Yale's undefeated 1891 team.*

ABOVE: *The 1888 Yale team scored a total of 698 points in 13 games. Their opponents scored none. Amos Alonzo Stagg, who went on to fame as one of the game's great early coaches, is on the far left of the front row.*

LEFT: *The brawling atmosphere of nineteenth-century American football is captured in this 1881 depiction of a goal-line struggle.*

In the 1870s and 1880s, only a visionary could have seen through football's mass confusion to its promise. The early version of the game was played on a wide, long field (140 by 70 yards), which was unmarked save for the goal and midfield stripes.

The participants were known for their rakish toughness. They disdained padding as something for sissies and wore instead sweaters or canvas jerseys (and were often called canvasbacks). There was no headgear, so players grew their hair long to pad their skulls when they smacked heads. The art of tackling was in its rudimentary stages. As a result, the games were often rough affairs of pushing and punching. Noses were broken, teeth were knocked out, heads and limbs bruised – all badges of courage to be worn proudly after the game.

Frederic Remington, the great American painter, captured the essence of early football in his first published works. Remington played for Yale in 1878 and submitted a drawing to the Yale *Courant* showing an injured player in his room. The drawing was accompanied by a caption: 'The doctor says I'll be all right by Thanksgiving, and that's all I care for now.' The next year his depiction of Yale and Princeton players straining for position was published in *Harper's Weekly*.

Football's roughneck image had persisted for centuries, since its schoolboy days of mayhem in merry England. If anything, that image had become even rougher by the late nineteenth century, acquiring the central elements of blood and leather.

'It was some bloodbath . . . ,' Pudge Heffelfinger, an Ivy Leaguer,

said of the 1889 Yale-Harvard game. 'One of the Harvards suffered a broken collarbone, and a Yale teammate had one eye nearly blinded. Practically all of us were bleeding from cuts or from kicks or from smashes. Another one of our players was unconscious for five hours afterward in a Springfield hospital.'

The early games were marathons, consisting of two halves, 45 minutes each, with substituting allowed only for injury. There was no line of scrimmage, only the rugby scrum, where the players locked shoulders and necks and heads to struggle about, kicking at the ball with their feet, until it popped out to be put into play.

The officiating crew consisted of a referee and one umpire for each team. The umpires readily assumed the role of lawyers, arguing each rules case for their respective sides. The players would quickly jump into any dispute, creating a rowdy, turbulent atmosphere that led an Englishman, Stephen Leacock, to remark: 'The Americans are a queer people. They can't play football. They try to, but they can't. They turn football into a fight.'

In this atmosphere, Walter Camp emerged as a leader, a natural strategist, not just on the field, but in the game's planning sessions as well. He led the Yale effort to have the number of players on a side trimmed to 11 from 15, a change that was finally approved by the rules committee in 1880. The size of the field was also decreased to 110 by 53 yards.

Another refinement attributed to Camp was the establishing of the line of scrimmage. By perfecting a method that allowed the center to step on the ball to snap it to the backfield, Camp eliminated the mass confusion of the rugby scrum.

'Walter Camp's scrimmage plan gave the ball into possession of the center,' the legendary coach and former Ivy Leaguer John Heisman said, 'and he alone could put it into play with a snapback. This control of the ball made it possible for the offensive team to plan plays in advance.'

LEFT: *This engraving from the 1880s shows a player breaking free on an end run, leaving would-be tacklers sprawling.*

BELOW: *The 1890 Harvard football team went undefeated, including a 12-6 victory over Yale's powerhouse team.*

RIGHT: *This 1884 woodcut shows the good-natured fisticuffs exchanged during a Yale-Princeton match. Such depictions boosted football's free-for-all image.*

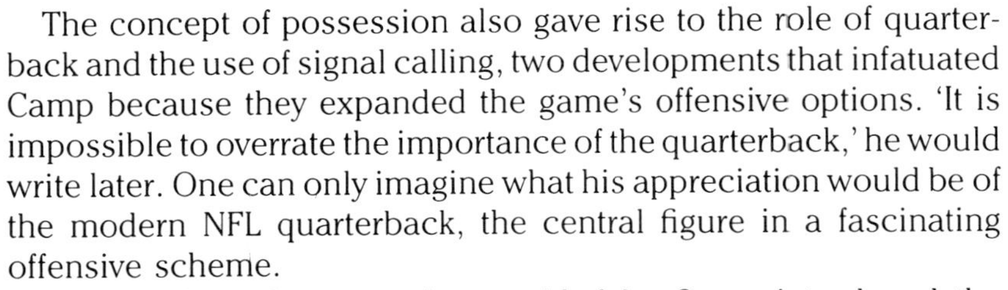

LEFT: *Walter Camp coached the Yale team from 1888 to 1892 with his wife Allie.*

ABOVE: *Helmets had come into limited use by the 1889 Yale-Princeton game.*

The concept of possession also gave rise to the role of quarterback and the use of signal calling, two developments that infatuated Camp because they expanded the game's offensive options. 'It is impossible to overrate the importance of the quarterback,' he would write later. One can only imagine what his appreciation would be of the modern NFL quarterback, the central figure in a fascinating offensive scheme.

In 1882 the rules committee guided by Camp introduced the concept that a team would have three downs to gain five yards. At first, opponents of the rule complained that there would be no means of measuring gains and losses. The field, Camp said, would have to be marked with chalk lines every five yards.

Ned Peace, the rules committee member from Princeton, exclaimed, 'Gracious. The field will look like a gridiron.'

'Precisely,' Camp replied.

Having established the idea of downs and yards, Camp and the committee turned to tinkering with signal calling and scoring over the next few years. In 1883 Camp introduced a point system allowing one for a safety, two for a touchdown and five for a field goal. The system was adjusted the following year to allow four for a touchdown, two for a conversion after and two for a safety.

The lifeblood of Camp's ideas spurred growth on other college campuses across the East, South and Midwest. Schools began organizing teams, adopting colors and attracting the attention of alumni.

The spreading craze alarmed university presidents. 'Football today is a social obsession,' Shailer Mathews, dean of the Chicago Divinity School, remarked. 'Football is a boy-killing, education-prostituting, gladitorial sport. It teaches virility and courage, but so does war. I do not know what should take its place, but the new game should not require the services of a physician, the maintenance of a hospital, and the celebration of funerals.'

Such railing stirred rather than killed interest. The crowds, small at first, increased as the action became more discernible to the fans. By the Gay Nineties, football was on its way to becoming an American fixture. It would be only a matter of time before two-bit promoters cast their dreams of profit on this game of scruffs and scrapes.

EARLY PROFESSIONALS, EARLY RIVALRIES

THE GASLIGHT ERA

As the early players graduated from college and moved on to business and working careers, they retained their love for football and expressed it in the forming of athletic association teams.

The earliest of these teams sprouted in Pennsylvania, around Pittsburgh, Latrobe and Greensburg, and Philadelphia, and later they appeared in Ohio and around Chicago. As the teams spread, the demand for players increased, and competition being what it is, not much time passed before the managers of the athletic clubs were offering pay to top players.

Playing for pay was somewhat scandalous to Gaslight Era sensibilities, although for years many college players had been earning stipends. In fact, it was not uncommon for college athletes to suit up with athletic club teams under assumed names on Sundays, after playing with their college teams on Saturday.

The situation led a London newspaper to comment: 'Amateur standing in American football is like virginity – highly prized but difficult to ascertain.'

The very first professional player, or at least the first to acknowledge it, was William W 'Pudge' Heffelfinger, the Yale guard who had been named to Walter Camp's very first All-America team in 1889.

Heffelfinger, who graduated from Yale in 1891, was the beneficiary of a keen rivalry between the Pittsburgh Athletic Club and the Allegheny Athletic Association. The AAA managers offered Pudge $500 to play for them in the 12 November 1892 game against the PAC. It proved to be a wise move for the AAA, as Pudge picked up a PAC fumble and ran for a touchdown, the game's only score, to give his team a 4-0 victory. The payment from the AAA was no big thing, Heffelfinger remarked years later. 'Until then, they usually paid us with silver pocket watches.'

FAR RIGHT: *Pudge Heffelfinger graduated from Yale in 1891 and was paid $500 to play a game with the Pennsylvania athletic club.*

BELOW: *Another early professional, Lawson Fiscus, was dubbed the 'Samson of Princeton.'*

The celebritity of that first victory pushed him off on a barnstorming football career that lasted several decades. 'Whoever said football is a tough game?' Heffelfinger told sportswriter Grantland Rice during a 1939 radio interview. 'I played it for 50 years. I know I was better at 45 than I was at 20. But I'll have to admit I slowed down a little when I was 66. Not much. But a little.'

The next year, 1893, the nearby Greensburg Athletic Association purchased the services of a strong, fleet former Princeton halfback, Lawson Fiscus, whose bushy hair brought him the title 'the Samson of Princeton.' His price per game was $20 plus expenses.

If nothing else, Fiscus heated up the rivalry with nearby Jeannette Athletic Club by kicking a prone Jeannette player and shattering his jaw, an incident that stirred for years in the memories of players and

ABOVE: *A depiction of a nineteenth-century goal-line struggle.*

LEFT: *John K Brallier, quarterback for the Latrobe, Pennsylvania professional team, began earning $10 per game at age 16.*

LOWER RIGHT: *One of the early professional teams, the Duquesne Country and Athletic Club footballers of 1898.*

fans, bringing the need for extra deputy sheriffs at subsequent meetings of the two teams.

Latrobe's first effort at professional recruitment was a 16-year-old quarterback, John K Brallier, from the town of Indiana, Pennsylvania, who was hired for $10 per game plus expenses. Brallier quarterbacked Latrobe as well as his high school team and went on to play for Washington and Jefferson College and West Virginia University. He later returned to play for Latrobe after his college teams had trouble meeting their payrolls.

Latrobe's lineup later featured such All-Americans as Walter Okerson, from Lehigh, and Doggie Trenchard, from Princeton. The remainder of the squads in this era were a mixture of young businessmen and roughnecks from the mill and mining communities of western Pennsylvania.

To the public, it was a game fit for crazy men. 'Football!' said John L Sullivan, the heavyweight boxing champ from 1888 to 1892. 'There's murder in that game. Prizefighting doesn't compare in roughness or danger with football. In the ring, at least, you know what you're doing. You know what your opponent is trying to do. He's right there in front of you. There's only one of him. But in football, there's eleven guys trying to do you in!'

Certainly, the game was rough but undergoing a steady refinement. The rules reform movement of the 1890s established the line of scrimmage and the concept of offsides. Theretofore, line players engaged in contact before the snap of the ball, keeping for American football the appearance of a rugby scrum. The line of scrimmage, however, made complete the separation of the new and old game.

The reforms of 1894 again attacked the flying wedge and other dangerous forms of mass interference, and they also required that a kickoff travel 10 yards, ending the practice of the kicker merely brushing the ball off his toe and then running with it.

Blocking had been changed to prevent the use of hands and extended arms. The early Carlisle Indian teams contributed the innovation of the rolling block to take an opponent's legs out from under him. A player removed from the play by such a block was said to have been 'Indianized.' Also, the rugby rule forbidding tackling below the waist was repealed. Ball carriers' legs became a target.

Most offense was structured on an old-fashioned variation of the T-formation, with the fullback a step behind the two halfbacks that flanked him. The quarterback squatted low several yards behind the center so that he could peer into the center's upside down face, for improved communication on signals.

The closest thing to a forward pass was the swift, short kick by the quarterback to his streaking end, or a quick lateral pitch to a running back. The ball was much too fat and rounded for effective passing. In fact, the kicking game dominated strategy and was essential under rules that allowed only three downs to make ten yards. Ed Abbatticchio was a great early kicker for Latrobe and went on to honors as a baseball infielder with the Pittsburgh Pirates.

Frederic Remington, who played for Yale in 1878, captured the essence of football in his early works. This Remington woodcut illustrates the straight arm.

Padding remained scant, although canvas pants began featuring protection for the knees. The decade also marked the appearance of ribbed shin guards, similar to those worn by hockey players. The only headgear were small knit caps, worn mostly by fullbacks. (Asked about head protection, Pudge Heffelfinger replied, 'None of that sissy stuff for me. I just let my hair grow long and pulled it through a turtleneck sweater.' Extensive use of headgear did not begin until 1897 when Pop Warner outfitted his Carlisle Indians with them.) In fashion were bushy hair and a mustache, which became the sign of a hearty football lad.

The professional game was actually semi-professional, with most players requiring outside jobs to pay their bills. Quite often college players were better paid, simply because they played the more popular game. The pro sport was on tenuous economic ground, but it survived because old players loved football and wanted to keep playing it. They played for pride more than anything.

On that strength, the professional game spread. In 1898 the Morgan Athletic Club was founded on Chicago's south side, later to become the Chicago Normals, then the Racine (Racine was the name of the team's street address) Cardinals, after that the Chicago Cardinals, and finally the St Louis Cardinals, pro football's longest running operation.

In 1899 the Duquesne Country and Athletic Club spent goodly sums signing players returning from duty in the Spanish and American War. But the expenditures led to financial trouble, and the club's managers sought the help of Pittsburgh businessman William C Temple. Upon purchase of the team, Temple became football's first real owner, a position of dubious distinction in that early era of high expenses and low income.

The next century lay waiting in the path of this young, uncertain sport, pro football. Yet, for all its poverty, the game would work its way into the hearts and minds of America. Not overnight, mind you. There were still more sandlot games to play, more bankruptcies to face, more dreams to be deflated.

But what a century it would prove to be.

TURNING THE CENTURY

For pro football, the first decade of the twentieth century was marked by more uncertainty and head scratching as the game's early promoters tried to figure out the economics of the sport. Too often, they were struggling with elements beyond their control, and their efforts were punctuated by failure.

Yet, the glowing coal of enthusiasm for professional football was somehow kept alive, despite the very dampening effect of scandal and bankruptcy.

The game of professional baseball was flourishing, and for a time, pro football attempted to hitch a ride. But the two sports moved at a different pace and worked on a different logic. Baseball was leisurely and organized and easily dissected by the spectator. Football was full of the wildness of young bucks.

That wildness fueled the flaring up of small, ill-fated semiprofessional clubs throughout Pennsylvania, New York, Ohio and Illinois. For the most part, these teams were run by part-time managers seeking to continue their playing days beyond their college careers.

Still, there were those who wanted to accomplish something on a big-time scale. In 1901 William C Temple formed his Duquesne club into a new team with baseball man Barney Dreyfuss of the Pittsburgh Pirates. Their intention was to arrange a cross-state rivalry with a team in Philadelphia. The competition was a football version of the Phillies. Also the Philadelphia Athletics' baseball manager Connie Mack organized a gridiron edition of his baseball Philadelphia Athletics, featuring one of his baseball stars, Rube Waddell.

In Pittsburgh the team owners briefly lured Christy Mathewson, the baseball Hall of Famer with the New York Giants and former Bucknell football star, into uniform for the Pittsburgh Pros. Although he would later referee football games, Mathewson served his stint with the Pros on the bench.

Connie Mack's interest in the game proved to be passing. But he was responsible in part for a new wrinkle, the first night game, played on 21 November 1902 in Elmira, New York and won by the Athletics, 39-0, over the Kanaweola Athletic Club.

Among other things, that 1902 season marked the brief appearance of the original National Football League, which was little more than an attempt to organize the efforts of Mack, Temple and Pittsburgh Pro owner David J Berry into league competition.

Berry, a newspaperman who had been a central figure in the Latrobe team in the 1890s, had moved to Pittsburgh by the turn of the century and become a successful printer. He was a tremendous source of energy and spent much of that currency trying to make the NFL successful. From recruiting players to organizing games with teams throughout the East, Berry tried everything.

The first league game, played in Pittsburgh on Thanksgiving between the Pros and the Athletics, resulted in a scoreless tie. But the crowd was sizable, and Berry persuaded Connie Mack to hold his team in town to play a second game two days later, in hopes they might attract a crowd of 10,000 or more.

The draw for the second game was substantially less than that, and because of a large payroll, Mack refused to allow his team to take the field until he could have his money. The fans became restless, and Berry was in a fix, until one of the top managers at

LEFT: *Baseball star Christy Mathewson (third row up, second from the right) played briefly with Pittsburgh's professional football team in 1901.*

ABOVE: *The Philadelphia Athletics of 1901-02 were owned by Connie Mack, owner of the baseball Athletics. His team played pro football's first night game – in 1902.*

Carnegie Steel who was in the stands asked about the delay. The businessman produced a check for the Athletics' share, and the game went on. The Pros scored twice that day and defeated the Athletics.

For all Berry's effort, the 1902 season was reduced to a smattering of games. The Athletics won the championship by compiling a 2-1 record against the Phillies and a 1-1-1 record against Pittsburgh. The other teams in the East, mostly in Pennsylvania's steel and mill towns and in upstate New York communities, simply could not generate the capital to compete for the 300 or so professional football players available at the time. The uniform costs, travel expenses and payrolls were too much. Each team held a variety of fundraising events – opera shows, wrestling matches, weightlifting competition – but the revenue generated wasn't nearly enough. Even as pro football grew, parts of it were dying, its firmament of small town franchises snuffed one by one by financial failure.

The Athletics were invited that December to the 'World Series' of pro football, an indoor tournament played at Madison Square Garden in New York. The other three teams were the New York Knickerbockers, the Watertown (New York) Red and Blacks, and the Syracuse Athletic Club.

Although the field was only 70 yards long and 35 yards wide, promoter Tom O'Rourke managed to attract a collection of cab drivers and bartenders to the Garden by promising them blood and action. Attempting to have the atmosphere simulate college spirit, the promoters handed the crowd slips of paper with cheers printed on them and colored streamers to wear in their lapels. The members of the press found the results laughable.

As an extra touch, O'Rourke dressed the referees in high silk hats, white gloves and patent leather shoes. Early in the tournament, the players couldn't resist the urge to run a play at the official and give his outfit a turn in the loose soil of the indoor stadium. The crowd roared and hooted in approval.

Syracuse was the team to beat with Glenn 'Pop' Warner at guard and two big Indian brothers from Carlisle, Bemus and Hawey Pierce and Phil Draper, a star from Williams College. Syracuse beat the Athletics 6-0 in the first game, which was shortened by five minutes when someone shouted from the stands that time was up and the crowd rushed onto the field. With that momentum, Syracuse went on to win the tournament.

The World Series, complete with its fancy dress referees, survived to 1903, when the Franklin (Pennsylvania) Athletic Club claimed the title over Watertown, Syracuse and the Orange, New Jersey Athletic Club. But the event died after that. There was no money in it.

From there, pro football wavered and declined in the East as its backers grew tired of watching it drain their cash away. The enthusiasm for the sport shifted to Ohio, where a new round of promoters and financiers were ready to boost the teams they had nursed along. Where the money was, the players went also, to places with names like Canton, Massillon and Akron.

In the Midwest, the young sport added to its growing list of troubles a new enemy: scandal. That alone was nearly enough to kill any promise of the future of football.

OHIO

The East seemed to be saying it had carried its share of the burden, now it was someone else's turn. So the scene shifted a few hundred miles west, where, fortunately for the orphan sport, the young men in the mining and mill towns south of Cleveland wanted a rowdy entertainment.

On an impulse, Eddie Stewart, a reporter for the *Massillon Independent*, purchased a number of used uniforms in 1903. The jerseys were striped, so Massillon's team was the Tigers, the first professional team in Ohio.

By the following season, 1904, there was a collection of eight struggling teams in the state. They quickly developed as their own worst enemies by engaging in talent bidding wars, driving their high operating costs even higher. Some attempts were made to organize to end the bidding. But the efforts failed, and the cutthroat atmosphere nearly killed the competition.

Stewart's Tigers survived into 1905, when he challenged his friend, Bill Day, in nearby Canton to set up a team. Suddenly pro football had regained its lifeblood, an intense rivalry – the Canton Bulldogs versus the Massillon Tigers. And what a rivalry it proved to be, strong enough to survive scandal and a grave lack of sportsmanship. But that's getting ahead of the story.

Day hustled to find talent. His big acquisitions were Blondy Wallace as coach and captain and Michigan's big running star, Willie Heston, who joined the Bulldogs for $600, which he promptly spent on liquor and good times, a development that weighed heavily on his training.

Stewart, meanwhile, busied himself by preparing a light, toy football for the first game in Massillon. He tricked Day into signing an agreement allowing the home team to select the ball. The Bulldogs traveled the eight miles from Canton by train ready for a rough one. Upon their arrival, they found a ridiculously light ball, almost impossible for kicking. They protested loudly but sullenly took the field after being reminded of their agreement.

Financially, the game was a success. The stands were filled, and betting was heavy. Many had come to see Christy Mathewson serve as umpire.

On the first series, Heston, Canton's big ball carrier, was slammed to the ground for a loss and went to the sidelines. He later returned to play defense but was never a factor running the ball (he broke his leg in Canton's next game and ended his pro career). Having had time to practice with the lighter ball, the Tigers seized the advantage

BELOW: *The Massillon (Ohio) Tigers of 1906 played the Canton Bulldogs in a game marked by allegations of gambling and score-fixing.*

and won, 14-4, which only stirred the coals for the teams' meeting the next year.

The rivalry intensified when just before the season Canton hired away four of Massillon's best players. Massillon countered by taking advantage of the new forward pass rule. The Tigers lured a hired gun down from Cleveland, Peggy Parratt, who had a reputation as a passer.

Two games were scheduled for 1906, and the newspapers hyped the first event in Massillon. Betting was reported to be heavy. With its passing attack, Massillon won, 12-6, then captured the rematch in Canton by the same score.

The *Massillon Independent* published a story charging that Bulldog coach Blondy Wallace had attempted to bribe several Massillon players into throwing the game. Failing at that, Wallace had arranged with several of his own players to tilt the outcome, the newspaper said. The hitch appeared when Wallace was unsuccessful in placing bets with several hundred dollars he had collected from his players. Wallace threatened to sue the paper for libel. But the *Independent* asserted that it had evidence, and Wallace swiftly left town.

The news stirred considerable anger in Canton, where the betting losses had been heavy. The evening after the second game a brawl erupted in the Courtland Hotel Bar, where several Canton players were nursing their injuries over drinks. The brouhaha broke out when Victor Kaufmann, a Canton fan, openly and loudly declared, 'I think that game was crooked!'

'Tables were overturned,' recalled Jack Cusack, a teenager who witnessed the event and went on to become a pro football promoter, 'and the surging crowd crashed through the plated glass window and continued the battle on Court Street until the coppers arrived, with their night sticks, to quell the rioters and haul some of them away to the pokey.'

In that single incident, the public's confidence in pro football was shattered. Wallace went on to become a well known bootlegger in Atlantic City, New Jersey. And pro football went to the backlots. Teams such as the Cantons, the Simpson Tigers, the Nutshell Indians, the Petersburg Nationals and the Cohen Tigers, survived by passing the hat on the sidelines.

But the crowds were small and the enthusiasm lacking. The game lived in that meager hibernation for nearly a decade until a new star could rejuvenate it.

LEFT: *Willie Heston, a renowned ball carrier for the Canton Bulldogs, offered this profiled pose for a photographer in 1903.*

BELOW: *This graphic from* The Canton Morning News *captured the atmosphere before the controversial 1906 game between Canton and Massillon.*

PASSING AND TEDDY'S REFORM

The reform of football, as it is known, began in 1905 when President Theodore Roosevelt happened to see a photograph of a bloodied Swarthmore player being led from the field. His anger properly stirred, the president told college footballers to clean up their game or face its abolition.

The immediate result was a White House conference between Roosevelt and representatives of the Ivy League's Big Three – Harvard, Princeton and Yale. From there, the football powers of the East agreed to form a new rules committee with a goal of opening up the game, taking it out of the rowdy rut it had fallen into.

Walter Camp, who had lobbied long to remove football's nastiness, said, 'We have lost the Homeric thrill of human action, the zest of out-of-doors, the contest of speed, of strength, of human intelligence, of courage. Unless steps are taken to reform the sport, we shall discover that our precious football is being relegated to the ash heap of history. Brutality has no place in this sport. This is a game that must train its followers, its players and its spectators in the qualities of successful character.'

The committee met in 1906 and offered several new rules, the most memorable being, of course, the forward pass, although its immediate impact wasn't great. The pass had been used irregularly in games for years, and the rules members agreed it was time to make it official. They also strapped it with enough restrictions to chill its major impact. As a result, the early pass was only remotely related to its modern offspring. The first version was little more than a variation of the kicking game.

First, the ball could be thrown forward only when the thrower had moved laterally five yards from the center of the line of scrimmage, thus the field was marked off with hash lines to show the throwing zone.

Once it had been touched by a receiver, an incomplete pass, like a kick, resulted in a loose ball that could be recovered by either side. If the pass went out of bounds, it was given to the defense where it went out, which gave the pass the same use as a coffin-corner punt in the modern game.

The earliest passes were hurled end over end. The passer would

cup a hand over the blunt nose of the ball, brace it against his forearm, and fling it. Downfield, the blockers would gather around the receiver to protect him from defenders while he attempted to catch the punt-like toss. Although the pass proved its usefulness and eventually caught on at colleges across the country, it was viewed for years as a sissified thing.

To offset its impact, the rules committee increased the number of yards needed for a first down from five to ten. With only three offensive downs allowed, the throwing of a pass was more of a gamble than many coaches wanted to take.

The real contribution the 1906 rules committee made toward lessening the violence in football was the establishing of a 'neutral zone' on the line of scrimmage. Theretofore linemen had battered each other before the ball was snapped, which led to much fighting and slugging. But the neutral zone forbade offsides contact until the ball was put into play.

The rules committee, however, might as well have tried to stamp out the male ego as to eliminate brutal toughness from football. In 1908, before Harvard's legendary mentor, Percy Haughton, coached his first game against Yale, he was said to have brought a bulldog into the locker room at Yale Field, where, as his players watched aghast, he strangled the animal.

'There,' he said after ridding his hands of the lifeless creature. 'That's what I want you to do to those Yale bastards out there this afternoon.'

The failings of human nature aside, the 1906 rules had introduced a revolutionary element to the game in the forward pass. In time, colleges across the country were using it, as coaches had a new toy

ABOVE: *Walter Camp grew to prominence in American football, overseeing rules changes and selection of college All-American teams.*

LEFT: *Depictions of college football's violence led to numerous calls for reform in the early twentieth century.*

FAR LEFT: *President Theodore Roosevelt saw a photograph of a bloodied Swarthmore player in 1905 and demanded that college football adopt rules to curb violence or face abolition.*

ABOVE: *Harvard's famous coach, Percy Haughton, shown leading his team onto the field. Haughton was said to have strangled a small dog in the locker room before a Yale game to motivate his players.*

RIGHT: *Glen 'Pop' Warner, the legendary coach and football innovator, who coached the Indians of Carlisle School in Pennsylvania to greatness.*

with which they could experiment. By 1908 the first spiral was thrown in a Penn-Michigan game. That same season, Pop Warner, football's great innovator, directed his Carlisle Indians to pitch spirals underhanded.

In 1910 the rules were further amended to add a fourth offensive down, a factor that increased the use of the pass. Third down quickly gained recognition as the passing down. The new rules also disallowed linemen lining up in the backfield, unless they were positioned five yards behind the line of scrimmage. This eliminated the hurtling, smashing interference that caused so many injuries.

Better yet, the 1910 rules stopped the practice of pushing or pulling the ball carrier. In the 1903 'World Series' game between Franklin, Pennsylvania and Watertown, New York at Madison Square Garden, a giant Franklin guard had picked up his teammate carrying the ball and hurled him into the end zone for a score. The elimination of such behavior went a long way toward reducing injury.

Begrudingly, the oldtimers recognized that an offshoot of the improved forward pass was the opening up of the game, which in turn added a new defensive wrinkle. The center in the defensive line was forced to begin hanging back to defend passing plays. The evolution of the game is no better exemplified than by the center rising from all fours to a crouch that allowed him to read offenses.

It wasn't long before coaches and players identified the position as a 'roving' element in the defense. The modern linebacker had been born. And now the defense had a factor to counter this new threat, the passer.

THE PRO RENAISSANCE
CUSACK AND THORPE

Jack Cusack liked to think of 1912 as the Renaissance year of American professional football. Cusack should know. He was the game's Leonardo da Vinci. His gifts were the arts of bookkeeping and management. To them, he added a touch of promotional flair. He brought pro football a strong helping of business sense when it needed it most. Beyond that, he brought pro football Jim Thorpe.

Perhaps someday pro football will get around to settling an old debt and name him to its Hall of Fame.

Buried by scandal six years earlier, the coals of hope for a professional football network flared up again in Ohio, Michigan and Pennsylvania in 1912 with an array of teams – the Akron Indians, the Cincinnati Colts, the Cleveland Erin Braus, the Toledo Maroons, the Columbus Panhandles, the Elyria Pros and the Pittsburgh Lyceums. In Canton, promoters considered calling their team the Bulldogs but feared it would stir memories of the 1906 scandal and decided instead on the Canton Professionals.

'The spirit of pro football was on the march again,' Cusack once recalled of the period, 'even without formation of an official league.'

Cusack, then 21, accepted the post of secretary-treasurer of the Canton team, which consisted mostly of stout local boys who played for a percentage of the gate. Big name college talent was too expensive for the club to afford. By the next season, Cusack had gained a share of the ownership and persuaded the local players to accept salaries rather than a gate share.

Cusack then used the gate share to add players with college experience. But for the second year in a row, Canton lost to its chief rival, the Akron Indians, managed by the former Canton star quarterback, Peggy Parratt. Still, Cusack put aside the urge to engage in rampant talent buying because he believed it would destroy the business balance in the league again. Instead, he quietly worked out an agreement with the other team managers not to allow players to jump teams.

Canton and most of its competitors flourished with business stability. Cusack received the support of a local brewery for the 1914

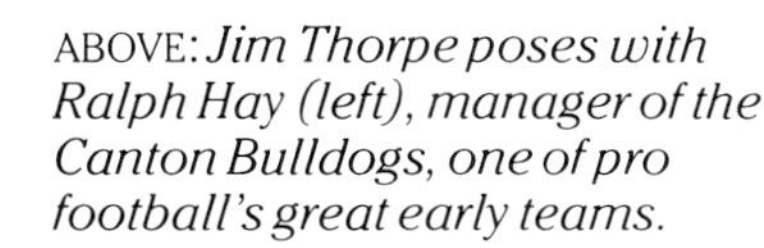

ABOVE: *Jim Thorpe poses with Ralph Hay (left), manager of the Canton Bulldogs, one of pro football's great early teams.*

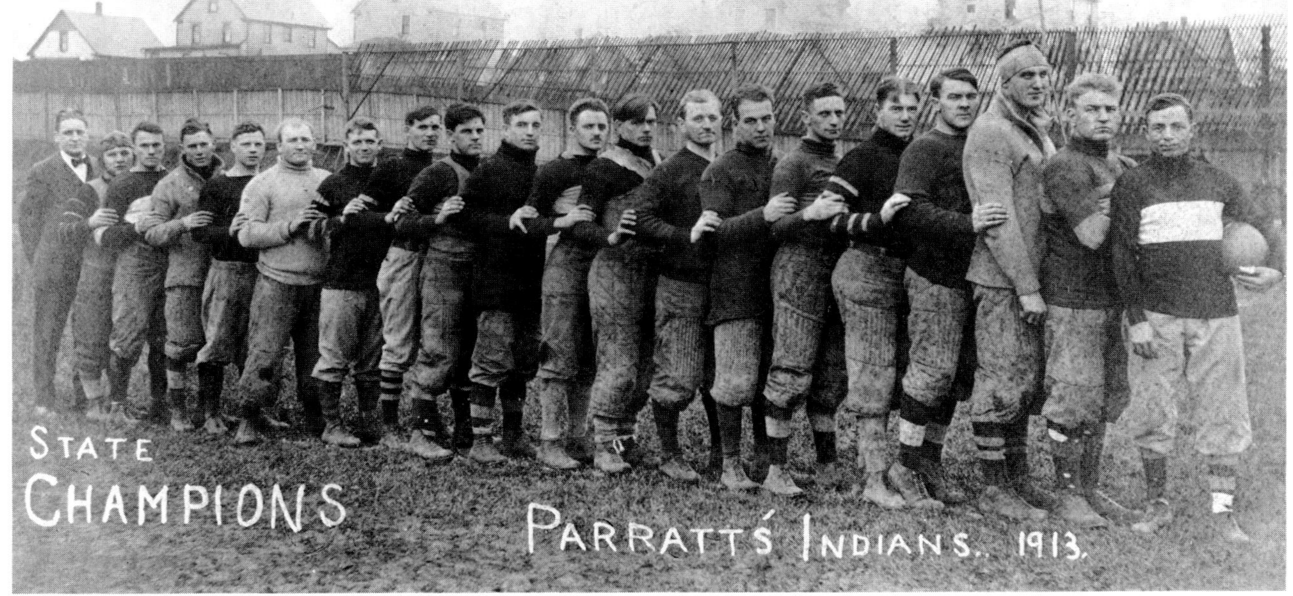

LEFT: *Peggy Parratt's Indians were in the thick of Ohio-area competition in 1913. Parratt, a quarterback, is holding the ball.*

season, yet found the team could prosper on its gate receipts. Just when good business translated into victory, the Canton Pros were struck by tragedy. Harry Turner, a center from Canton, sustained a broken back playing against Akron and died of his injuries. Canton finally beat the Indians that day, but the win held little joy for Cusack and the community.

Turner's death and a narrow victory over the Shelby Blues cut deeply into the Pros' gate draw. Fortunately, the early season's receipts had been good enough to allow Cusack and his partner to hang on for the 1915 season, when Cusack left his job as a gas company clerk to give his full attention to the team.

The horizon brightened greatly for pro football that next season,

1915, when businessmen in Massillon succeeded in organizing a team there and renewing the strong Canton rivalry. After running through a successful 1915 schedule, Cusack was preparing for the last two games, both with Massillon, when he came up with his grand idea: sign to a contract the great Jim Thorpe, who had dominated the college game while playing for Pop Warner and the Carlisle Indians.

Thorpe, then 27, was working as a backfield coach at Indiana University after two frustrating years with the New York Giants baseball team. Cusack sent Bill Gardner, a Canton tackle who had played for Carlisle, to ask Thorpe to play. The odds seemed small.

Thorpe, a Sac and Fox Indian from Oklahoma, was perhaps the world's best known athlete, having dominated the 1912 Olympics in Sweden by winning the decathalon, pentathalon, the shot put, the 1500 meters, the high hurdles and the high jump. He placed fourth or higher in six other events and was called 'the greatest athlete in the world' by Sweden's King Gustav. But before the year was out, he would have to return all his Olympic medals after it became known that briefly during the summer of 1909 he had played baseball professionally in Rocky Mount, North Carolina.

Thorpe's prowess on the football field was just as renowned. In 1912, his final college season, he scored 25 touchdowns and 198 points, frequently on long runs. He was as multi-faceted at football as he was at track. He was a brutally powerful defensive player, yet his offensive skills were more varied. He ran with both power and speed and could be elusive when he wanted to (usually he preferred running over tacklers). He was also an excellent thrower and kicker and was said to have turned in at least one game where none of his punts traveled less than 70 yards.

The average salary for a pro in those days was between $75 and

$100 per game. Cusack sent Thrope an offer of $250 per game. The Canton manager was pleased and surprised when Thorpe accepted it, although several business advisers told Cusack he would wreck the finances of the club spending that much for one player.

Instead, it proved to be just the right move for the atmosphere. The newspaper reporters had taken to calling Canton the Bulldogs again. And with Thorpe as a draw, the crowds surged. Having averaged 1500 paying spectators for each game, the Bulldogs were delighted as Thorpe attracted 6000 to the first Massillon game and 8000 to the second. As Red Grange would do a decade later, Thorpe's magnetic presence brought in the revenues to strengthen the business of football.

The Canton-Massillon series of 1915 was memorable for several reasons. First, the Bulldogs acquired the services of Michigan A&M tackle Charlie Smith, thought to be pro football's first black player. Second, the games set up a clash between Thorpe and Knute Rockne, then a Notre Dame assistant coach who played end for Massillon. On the first series, Rockne broke through the Canton line and tackled Thorpe for a loss. Then he did it a second time.

Legend has it that Thorpe became angry and told Rockne, 'You shouldn't do that to Jim. All these people came out to see Jim run.'

'Well, go ahead and run,' Rockne replied, 'if you can.'

In a burst of power on the next play, Thorpe trampled Rockne on his way to a long run. As Rockne was being helped up afterward,

LEFT: *The 1914 Canton Bulldogs marked the resurgence of football in Ohio following the gambling scandal of 1906.*

ABOVE: *Jim Thorpe's appearance in a Canton uniform proved to be a major gate draw for the struggling business of pro football.*

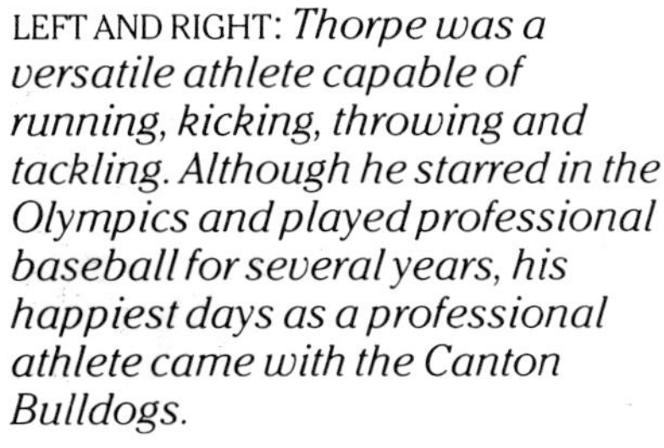

LEFT AND RIGHT: *Thorpe was a versatile athlete capable of running, kicking, throwing and tackling. Although he starred in the Olympics and played professional baseball for several years, his happiest days as a professional athlete came with the Canton Bulldogs.*

Thorpe came back up the field and chided, 'Nice going, Rock. You sure let old Jim run.'

The second game was marred by the owners' inability to turn away the overflow crowd of 8000. Spectators were given standing room only space in the end zones. Late in the game when a Massillon end caught a touchdown pass that would have given the Tigers a 6-6 tie and the championship, the crowd stripped him of the ball.

The officials initially ruled the play a fumble, then hesitated and debated their decision as the crowd's impatience increased. Finally the spectators spilled onto the field, and when the referee was unable to restore order, the game was called. The Massillon players and spectators, however, demanded a final decision on the play. The officials agreed to provide it in writing, so long as the two teams agreed not to open the envelope containing the decision until after midnight, giving the officials time to get out of town. The teams agreed and later that night learned that the original decision stood. With the Canton victory, the two teams tied for the championship.

With Thorpe leading, the Bulldogs would have few close calls the next season, 1916, as they stormed most of their opponents to claim the 'Championship of the World.' The Canton cast was studded with stars, including Greasy Neale, the end who coached at several colleges; Indian Joe Guyon, the halfback who played with Thorpe at Carlisle; Howard 'Cub' Buck, the Wisconsin lineman who went on to play for the Green Bay Packers; and Ernie Soucy of Harvard.

Even though Thorpe missed the first two games while playing professional baseball, the Bulldogs powered past their opponents. They were unscored upon through the first six games (the Cleveland Indians blocked a punt for a meaningless touchdown in the seventh

ABOVE: *Ernie Soucy of Harvard (left) and Howard 'Cub' Buck of Wisconsin were a big part of Canton's success in 1916.*

RIGHT: *Knute Rockne, the legendary Notre Dame coach and star, played for numerous professional teams. He sometimes played for several clubs in the same season.*

game) and undefeated going into the final two-game series with Massillon.

The Tigers, led by their quarterback, Gus Dorais, and Stanley Cofall, both Notre Dame grads, held the Bulldogs to a scoreless tie in the first game.

Both teams added extra players for the second game, but it was the Canton stalwart, Jim Thorpe with his power running, and the passing of quarterback Milton Ghee that propelled the Bulldogs to a 24-0 win and their 'world championship.'

The draw of players to fight World War I significantly weakened the quality of play for the 1917 season. 'Besides the drafting of manpower which made the building of teams difficult,' Cusack once recalled, 'attendance at games fell off drastically as more and more men were called to the colors.'

Again the Bulldogs ran through their schedule to a season-ending

RIGHT: *In addition to playing pro football and baseball, Thorpe – also an avid golfer – served briefly as president of the first pro football league and later formed his own team.*

BELOW: *Quarterback Milton Ghee, a Dartmouth product, was another important cog in the Canton championship machinery of 1916.*

showdown with Massillon. The championship was already the Bulldogs' because the Tigers had lost several games. Things went as expected the first game of the series, as Thorpe powered Canton to two long drives and a 14-3 win. But in the final game the Tigers, led again by Stan Cofall, upset Canton, 6-0, and took the pleasure out of the Bulldogs' second championship

The war sent pro football into hibernation until after the November 1918 Armistice. But the groundwork had been laid, and the young industry sprang back to life after the war. During the layoff, Cusack had gone to Oklahoma to work in the oil business, and Ralph Hay took over the Canton franchise. Records aren't available for 1919, but the 1920 roster showed much of the championship Canton team intact, including Thorpe, Buck and Calac.

Thorpe went on to a varied professional career, playing football and baseball with several teams, even serving as commissioner briefly of the first pro league and later organizing his own team, a storied tenure that would lead to his being named to the Professional Football Hall of Fame. Yet for the most part, those experiences proved unsatisfactory to him. Before his death in 1953, he had no problems identifying his happiest professional years: the championship teams in Canton. 'That was the best time of my life,' he said. 'I'll never forget it.'

As for professional football, it had reached a tenuous plateau in its effort to become an established industry. Teams were sprouting up in Illinois and Wisconsin. But the atmosphere was chaotic. The conditions called for the organization of a league. To the good fortune of the game, there was a group of capable young men waiting to provide the needed leadership. Football had taken hold in the heartland and was on its way.

THE 1920s: A LEAGUE IS FORMED

The National Football League marks its beginnings in 1920, but the movement toward organization actually came in 1919, amidst the new touring cars in the showroom of Ralph Hay's auto dealership in Canton.

Hay, of course, was the manager of the Bulldogs. His star, Jim Thorpe, was at the meeting, lounging on the running board of one of the touring cars. By the next year, Thorpe would be commissioner of the new league, which would be called the American Professional Football Association. Also present were many of the men who had organized teams and then held on fiercely over the previous few years to keep them alive, including Leo Lyons of the Rochester Jeffersons, Joe Carr of the Columbus Panhandles, Carl Storck of the Dayton Triangles and Frank Neid of the Akron Indians.

The terms for the five teams were light, $25 per franchise, and the rules simple. Essentially, the clubs agreed not to tamper with college athletes.

The proceedings were marked by much turbulence, particularly that caused by players jumping teams. (The Columbus Panhandles faced Knute Rockne six times one season in the uniform of six different teams.) The one consistency remained in that Canton again won the championship, again over Massillon, by a 3-0 score, with Thorpe kicking the winning field goal.

The second year of the league, 1920, the official date recognized today by the NFL, several more teams applied for franchises and were accepted. Among them were teams from Hammond, Indiana and Rock Island, Illinois, and the Decatur Staleys, headed by a young George Halas, and the Racine Cardinals. The franchise cost had risen to $100, although none of the teams ever paid it.

Again the teams met in Hay's showroom, first in August, then in September. Thorpe was chosen league president with Stan Cofall of Cleveland named vice president. The season highlight was a 95-yard punt by Canton's Joe Guyon, who would later be named to the Hall of Fame. Akron claimed the championship with an undefeated record that included scoreless ties against Decatur and Buffalo. Both Decatur and Buffalo also claimed the championship.

The following April the league reorganized in a meeting at Canton's Cortland Hotel. Joe Carr, the Columbus Panhandles' executive, was named president with a salary of $1000. His first action as new president was to declare Akron the champion of the previous season.

Carr would preside over the National Football League (the association would adopt that name for the 1922 season) until his death in 1939. If Jack Cusack was pro football's Renaissance Man, Joe Carr was its Moses, leading it to the Promised Land.

ABOVE: *George Halas left professional baseball and played a major role in the development of the Decatur Staleys, which would later become the Chicago Bears.*

LEFT: *Carl Storck and his Dayton Triangles were among the determined pro franchises that joined the American Professional Football Association (the forerunner of the NFL) in 1920.*

ABOVE: *For years, Leo Lyons was the driving force behind the Rochester Jeffersons, a neighborhood team that evolved into one of pro football's early franchises.*

LEFT: *Joe Carr ascended from the management of the Columbus Panhandles in 1920 to become the chief executive of the infant NFL, a position he would hold until his death in 1939.*

HALAS, FROM THE STALEYS TO THE BEARS

Pro football's franchises needed ramrods in those early years, and George Halas was certainly one of them. He built the Chicago Bears from an athletic program for the Staley Starch Company into one of the National Football League's stalwart clubs. It took all the toughness and cunning one man could muster. But then George Halas had plenty of both.

Although he weighed only 140 pounds, he had starred at football, baseball and basketball at the University of Illinois from 1915 to 1918. With the outbreak of World War I, he joined the navy and wound up on the Great Lakes Naval Training Station team of 1918, which featured Halas, Paddy Driscoll and Jimmy Conzelman as its stars. They went on to win the Rose Bowl on New Year's Day 1919, over the favored Mare Island Marines, and Halas caught two touchdown passes.

But baseball was his calling after the war, and he found a place in the New York Yankees' lineup. If a hip injury hadn't shoved him aside, he might never have played his role in pro football.

By 1920 he was busy establishing the Decatur (Illinois) Staleys football team for the Staley Starch Company, with talent such as Ed 'Dutch' Sternaman, Guy Chamberlain, George Trafton and Charley Dressen. Halas' efforts led to immediate success in the young APFL, with the Staleys narrowly missing the championship with a scoreless tie with Akron. As the early pros knew, winning usually was accompanied by money, and Halas was able to pay each of his players $1900 after the season.

Still, A E Staley, the company owner, was worried about sinking profits into football. He and Halas worked out an agreement in which Halas would move the team to Chicago with a $5000 check from Staley to help with expenses. In return, Halas would agree to keep the name Staleys for one more year.

In 1921 the Chicago Staleys compiled a 10-1-1 record and edged out the Buffalo All-Americans with a 9-1-2 record, a development that was protested for years in Buffalo.

The next year, Halas took Dutch Sternaman as his partner and negotiated a lease for Wrigley Field with William Veeck, Sr, the Chicago Cubs' president. Sharing a field with the Cubs, Halas decided in early 1922 to change his name to the Bears. With the name change, the championship luck slipped a little. For each of the next three years, the Bears finished second in the league standings, as the Canton Bulldogs enjoyed a championship resurgence in 1922 and 1923.

Yet, at age 26, Halas had grasped firm control of the club he would guide for the next half century. Today there is little doubt, football was all the better for it.

LEFT: *George Trafton, the great lineman, was a stalwart of the Staleys and Halas' Chicago Bears.*

ABOVE: *Ed 'Dutch' Sternaman was another star with the Decatur Staleys and Chicago Bears.*

LEFT: *Halas is shown here with his 1920 Decatur Staleys, the franchise he eventually molded into the powerhouse known as the Chicago Bears.*

RIGHT: *Over the years Halas evolved from player-coach into coach-executive and eagerly took on the challenge of dual roles.*

EARL 'CURLY' LAMBEAU AND THE GREEN BAY PACKERS

The comedy and chance of early pro football has no better illustration than the fact that one of the game's great franchises got its start because of a case of tonsillitis. That minor event tripped up the college football career of Earl 'Curly' Lambeau and sent him home to Green Bay to start the Packers.

Lambeau earned his reputation as a passer at Green Bay's East High and later played at Notre Dame for the 1918 season, Knute Rockne's first as Irish head coach. Only a freshman, Lambeau played a fullback and halfback and was one of the team's 13 lettermen. The fateful tonsillitis struck him after the season. He went home to recuperate and stayed, taking a clerk's job at the Indian Packing Company.

The next fall, Lambeau talked the company's owner, Frank Peck, into putting up $500 to start a football team, which Lambeau reasoned would be good for the company and the city. Little did anyone realize, Lambeau was beginning perhaps pro football's greatest organization, which he would rule over for more than 30 years, watching it win 236 games while losing 111 and tying 23. His impatient, demanding style would bring him the name 'the Bellicose Belgian.'

He brought good things to Green Bay almost immediately. His 1919 team, which featured him in the backfield, dominated the competition in Wisconsin. The Packers beat 10 teams by amassing

LEFT: *Curly Lambeau throws a pass in the snow. Illness forced Lambeau to leave Notre Dame after his freshman year in 1918. He returned home to Green Bay, Wisconsin, where he formed the Packers.*

TOP: *Lambeau and the 1919 Packers beat 10 teams but lost a controversial game to the Beloit Fairlies for the Wisconsin professional championship.*

LEFT: *Knute Rockne, shown here with the Notre Dame mascot, coached Lambeau in 1918 when the Packer founder started as a freshman for the Irish.*

ABOVE: *The Packers and their opponents between plays in a 1927 game.*

565 points and allowing only 6, bringing them to a season-ending showdown with the Beloit Fairlies on Beloit's home field. The crowd of more than 2000 intruded onto the field much of the game, and the Beloit referee called back two touchdowns by Lambeau, which allowed Beloit to squeak away with a controversial 6-0 win.

The 1920 season brought more success, particularly over other pro teams, but the franchise nearly folded. For the 1921 season, Lambeau turned to John Clair of the Acme Packing Company and secured financial support. But the Packers were caught using ineligible college players, and NFL president Joe Carr revoked the franchise.

With the help of friends, Lambeau raised the money to re-enter the team in the league's 1922 competition. But the Green Bay weather was their toughest opponent, pouring down a chilling rain weekend after weekend. More than $1600 behind in wages to his players, Lambeau faced the rain and the Duluth Eskimos one weekend late in the season and decided to call it quits. Andy Turnbull, publisher of the *Press-Gazette*, talked him out of it. The Packers played in the rain and lost another $2200. But the next week, Green Bay civic leaders raised $2500 to help pay the bills.

The Packers began the 1923 season with $5000 in the bank. Born of persistence, small-town football had survived in the NFL. The Packers would go on to greatness.

PART II

The Young Game Matures

1925-1945

HIKE

To the public, to many very moral newspaper editors, professional football players in the early 1920s were little more than a gin-soaked lot of thugs struggling to hold onto lost boyhoods. Viewed no better, the game's promoters were seen as low-rent rogues, fast-buck artists intent on slaking the common man's thirst for blood and violence.

There was some reality in that image. But for the most part, the players and promoters alike were men seized by the powerful attraction of an intriguing albeit rough game, much as the Ivy League dandies and English schoolboys before them had been seized. The major difference with the pros was that they attempted to make a business of it, to earn a living from their infatuation. Most of them could have done better on the assembly line, or in the mill. Regardless, they endured discouraging conditions, an absurd world of bounced checks, mud-caked uniforms, broken-down cars, lingering injuries and unpaid hospital bills. It was a world where every away game held the anxiety of doubt about money for the train ticket home.

Each week, Leo Lyons, manager of the Rochester Jeffersons, would bring his linemen four copies of the *Saturday Evening Post*, not for recreational reading, but for taping to their shins for protection in the trenches.

It was a fight for survival. In 1920 the Chicago Cards and Chicago Tigers knew the turf was too small for both. So they agreed to a playoff, with the loser shutting down operations. Paddy Driscoll scored for the Cards, enough for a 6-3 victory, and the Tigers were history. The sport was that fragile.

Through these conditions, the game and the players themselves underwent a steady refinement. The practice of smashing an opposing lineman with the open hand was still accepted, but football had achieved an order that separated it from the game played just a few decades earlier. The players now lined up across a no man's land from each other, poised in stillness until the quarterback finished barking his signals and the action erupted.

As with the jazz of the age, the game used this structured base to gather some razzle-dazzle about it. The old-fashioned T-formation spawned the new-fangled single wing. There were crisscrosses and fake handoffs, and end-around, even tackle-around, plays. And by 1920 passing had gained its footing and acceptance. The rules allowing an opposing team to recover an incomplete or out-of-bounds pass had been discarded. The ball was still fat and blunt-ended, but the quarterbacks had somehow perfected a spiral by holding the ball loosely and slinging it side-armed.

The ball's fatness kept it a plump item for kicking. This was the era of the drop kicker, and several prominent players – Jim Thorpe, Frank Nesser, Paddy Driscoll and Charlie Brickley – were accurate from 45 to 50 yards out. The point after was anything but a gimme in those days, because a player scoring a touchdown had to kick the ball out of the end zone to his teammates. Where they caught it was the spot of placement for the point after. The situation created very difficult angles.

Substitution rules still enforced a factor of toughness. If a player left the game, he could not return during that half. The players went both ways and relished it.

The weather was more of a factor. As Mac McEver, a college coach in Virginia recalled, it seemed to rain more then. The contests became mired in mud, turning uniforms into armor of goo, reducing the fourth quarters to little more than tired matches of pushing and shoving. The games in those days were played with a single ball, which was deadened by the weight of water, making kicking and throwing all the more difficult. It wasn't until the college season of 1925, when Ohio State played Iowa, that the concept of using fresh, dry balls occurred to footballers. Even then, the pros continued with one ball because of the costs. It was obvious that the pro game was second rate.

College football, meanwhile, was experiencing its 'Golden Age,' flowering as a lavish entertainment industry, with the allure of The Four Horsemen of Notre Dame and Red Grange, the Galloping Ghost. The crowds in university stadiums bulged to 50,000, even 80,000, and millions more listened on radio. On the campuses of the Big 10 and Ivy League it was a roaring time of marching bands and raccoon coats and coeds and nattily dressed fraternity boys. To tell the world about it, there were the legendary sportswriters, Grantland Rice and Damon Runyon and Lawrence Stallings and Westbrook

LEFT: *The 1920 Chicago Cardinals, forerunners of the St Louis Cardinals, played the Chicago Tigers with the agreement that the losing team would cease operations. The Cardinals, of course, won, 6-3.*

ABOVE: *Paddy Driscoll, the multi-talented star of the Cardinals, scored the only touchdown against the Tigers, thus ensuring his team would survive.*

LEFT AND BELOW: *Notre Dame's Four Horsemen – Don Miller, Elmer Layden, Jim Crowley and Harry Stuhldreher – were a sensational factor in the popularity of college football in the 1920s.*

Pegler and Heywood Broun. They turned out a colorful, overstuffed prose that projected the game many times larger than life.

After Notre Dame's 13-7 win over Army on 18 October 1924, Rice, a reporter for the *New York Herald-Tribune*, composed the most famous passage in football history:

> *Outlined against a blue, gray October sky the Four Horsemen rode again.*
>
> *In dramatic lore, they are known as famine, pestilence, destruction and death. These are only aliases. The real names are Stuhldreher, Miller, Crowley and Layden. They formed the crest of the South Bend cyclone before which another fighting Army team was swept over the precipice at the Polo Grounds this afternoon as 55,000 spectators peered down upon the bewildering panorama spread out upon the green plain below.*

Time after time, writers portrayed the college action in similar Homeric proportions. And the public responded in Homeric numbers. When Notre Dame played Southern Cal in Chicago, the gate netted $500,000. A Yale-Harvard matchup brought an easy $300,000. Yes, college football was big time, while the pros were lucky to attract 5000.

Rather than discourage them, the success of the college game did little more than stoke the dreams of men like George Halas and Leo Lyons. They knew the popularizing of the college sport would eventually stir interest in their games as well. The college stars today would be their drawing cards tomorrow.

If anything, the college success intensified the pros' talent search. Leo Lyons, who had been nursing the Rochester Jeffersons along since 1910, boosted his roster with Ben Lee Boynton from Williams College and Elmer Oliphant of West Point.

ABOVE: *Most pro teams, such as the Rochester Jeffersons, struggled against financial odds, while college football and pro baseball flourished.*

LEFT: *Jimmy Conzelman took over as player-coach of the Milwaukee Badgers in 1923, then moved to Detroit to start a team the next year.*

For 1923 Jimmy Conzelman took over as player-coach of the Milwaukee Badgers and made one of his first steps the cutting of Paul Robeson, the black player and former Rutgers star who went on to fame in the theater, from the roster. Conzelman kept two other black players, Duke Slater from Iowa and Fritz Pollard from Brown.

The next year, Conzelman started an NFL franchise in Detroit, the Panthers, and attempted to increase interest by signing the Four Horsemen from Notre Dame as a touring vaudeville act. The pros, it

seemed, were clutching at anything, so long as it reeked of the old college spirit.

From 1922 to 1925, there were 18 to 22 teams playing in the NFL, the number of clubs rising and falling with the barometer. The Canton Bulldogs, led by the great tackle and placekicker, Wilbur 'Pete' Henry, remained the dominant power in 1922 and 1923, then won the title again in 1924 after moving their franchise to Cleveland. Henry set legendary records during the stretch: a 94-yard punt against Akron in 1923 and a 50-yard drop-kick field goal against Toledo in 1922.

'Tackles will come and go,' the Canton newspaper said of the 6-foot, 250-pound Henry in 1922, 'but never will pro football enthusiasts see the peer of Wilbur Henry.'

The aging Jim Thorpe, meanwhile, had formed his own team, the Oorang Indians, only to watch it fail dismally. Against Oorang on 4 November 1923, George Halas recovered a fumble and ran 98 yards for a touchdown, then a record. When Oorang collapsed after the 1923 season, Thorpe caught on with Rock Island. For years, he had been a major pro drawing card. But time and rumor had worn him down. He was said to wear steel shoulder pads and to gamble on his games. Jack Cusack, his friend and agent, later denied both rumors, saying Thorpe wore hard leather shoulder pads with metal rivets.

Regardless, the rumors bolstered the same old pro image. The NFL needed new blood, a new superstar, a new gate draw. The college ranks were filled with hyped stars, but George Halas had his eyes on one in particular, a former ice boy from Wheaton, Illinois, a player with the power, speed and charisma to draw thousands. George Halas knew he had to sign Red Grange.

TOP: *The 1923 Canton Bulldogs again displayed the franchise's prowess by winning another championship. Link Lyman, their Hall of Fame tackle, is pictured sixth from the left in the middle row.*

ABOVE: *The Bulldogs' star tackle and kicker was Wilbur 'Pete' Henry.*

LEFT: *Jim Thorpe's team, the Oorang Indians, struggled through the 1922 season and later folded.*

THE PLAYER WHO MADE PRO FOOTBALL

If Red Grange's on-the-field exploits weren't enough to lift him to super stardom, then *New York Herald-Tribune* sportswriter Grantland Rice completed the job with his poetic newsleads:

There are two shapes now moving,
Two ghosts that drift and glide
And which of them to tackle
Each rival must decide;
They shift with spectral swiftness
Across the swarded range,
And one of them's a shadow,
And one of them is Grange.

Then the newsreels seized on that image, capturing Grange's long, gliding runs and projecting them onto the screens in movie houses across America. Quite suddenly, the country had its first media hero, a ghostly figure, in flickering black and white – the Galloping Ghost, the Wheaton Iceman.

Soon pro football, George Halas to be exact, would snatch this prize player from the college game, a move that outraged the promoters of the amateur game. It was a scandalous move, for certain. Scandalous, but gate-busting. And brilliant.

The appearance of Red Grange in a Chicago Bears uniform during a barnstorming tour of America in late 1925 and early 1926 was the singular act that thrust pro football into the public's fancy. Grange drew scores of thousands to the ballparks of the East and Midwest in a whirlwind 17-day tour, making a fortune for himself while filling the coffers of the league's struggling franchises.

The professional game had never felt such adulation. In an instant, Red Grange had shown the sport its future. Certainly, it had more difficult times, more struggles ahead. But no more would men question whether they could make money from pro football.

Grange had gained his strength as a youth toting ice blocks in his hometown of Wheaton, Illinois (thus the name the Wheaton Iceman), but it was Grange's speed, shiftiness and grace that stirred sportswriters and fans. He built his reputation as the University of Illinois with long, elusive runs. Michigan had won 20 straight games until Grange destroyed the Wolverines in the first 12 minutes of their October 1924 match with the Illini. Grange sculpted scoring runs of 95, 56, 67 and 45 yards, moving Rice to write:

A streak of fire, a breath of flame
Eluding all who reach and clutch;
A gray ghost thrown into the game
That rival hands may rarely touch.

Grange scored 31 touchdowns in his 20-game collegiate career and was a three-time Walter Camp All American. By his last season, he was no less than a young god in Illinois, which served to intensify the public's dismay when midway through the season rumors began circulating that he had signed a professional contact with C C Pyle, an agent. Pyle was immediately dubbed 'Cash and Carry' by the

LEFT: *Harold 'Red' Grange turned in performances of epic proportions at the University of Illinois, leading to his nickname, 'The Galloping Ghost.'*

RIGHT: *Grange with Illinois coach Bob Zuppke. Grange astounded the sports world by turning professional after his final college game in November 1925.*

infuriated Chicago newspapers. Newspaper stories said Grange would play with the Bears on Thanksgiving after his last college game and that he would appear in a movie, *The College Widow*.

'I have never signed even a scrap of paper,' Grange said in denial.

Illinois coach Bob Zuppke hinted that Grange would have to turn in his uniform if he had signed. 'I'm all mixed up,' Grange told reporters. 'And I'm worried. But I don't intend to sign anything until I play my last game for Illinois.'

Despite the distractions, Grange played the last game of the season against Ohio State before what was then a record crowd of 85,500, and led Illinois to a 14-9 victory.

Still weaving the legend, Grantland Rice was on hand and wrote that the record crowd had come 'to hear for the last time the thudding hoofbeats of the redhead's march. . . .' The atmosphere, Rice said, was 'like a tremendous circus, multiplied ten or twenty times. And every tongue was spinning but one name – Grange.'

Two days later he confirmed the rumors by signing a contract to begin play immediately for the Chicago Bears. Across the country, editorialists expressed outrage that the pros had lured Grange away before he earned his college degree.

The next day, Sunday, a crowd of 7500 watched as Grange sat on the Bears' bench in a raccoon coat as Chicago beat the Packers. That Monday morning of Thanksgiving week, tickets went on sale for Grange's first game in uniform. Halas had printed 20,000 tickets, but they were sold in three hours. By game time Thursday, 36,000 people jammed Wrigley Field (then known as Cubs Park) to see the Galloping Ghost lead the Bears against the crosstown rival, Chicago Cardinals.

Despite the hype, the game was disappointing. The Cardinals' Paddy Driscoll wisely directed his punts away from Grange. The mud and snow turned the Ghost's galloping to sloshing. He gained only 36 yards from scrimmage, but took home a $12,000 paycheck from his share of the gate. The game ended in a scoreless tie.

Yet there was no time for dismay. Halas had prepared a barnstorming cross-country tour, nine games in 17 days, to showcase his

LEFT: *In one of the most memorable performances in college football history, Grange scored four touchdowns to lead Illinois over undefeated Michigan in 1924.*

FAR LEFT BELOW: *George Halas of the Chicago Bears (left), Grange, and Grange's agent, C C Pyle, as Grange signs a professional contract in November 1925.*

BELOW: *The Chicago Cardinals were Grange's first pro opponents, as he joined the Bears just days after signing a contract.*

newly acquired legend.

Over the next two and a half weeks, the trains carrying the Bears rolled across the countryside, drawing throngs in each city. The name 'Grange' seemed to mesmerize the public. Despite a downpour, 40,000 fans came out in Philadelphia to see the Galloping Ghost. In New York at the Polo Grounds, 73,000 paid to see the Bears run past the Giants, 19-7. Despite the score, the day was one of New York's winningest, as the $130,000 in gate receipts floated the franchise away from financial disaster. Grange's share was $30,000. He endorsed sportswear, soft drinks, even a Red Grange doll.

The breakneck pace made him a rich man – his earnings were figured roughly at $300 an hour by a Chicago newspaper. But it also left him with a torn muscle and a blood clot in his left arm. He missed a game in Detroit, sending 20,000 fans back to the ticket booth to demand refunds.

After eight days of rest, the team embarked on a second tour, beginning in Miami on Christmas day and winding its way through the South and West. In Los Angeles, 75,000 paid to see the Grange show. After running through 19 games in 17 cities in 66 days, the Bears finished in Seattle 31 January.

Pro football would never be the same. Grange had revealed its grand potential. The next season, Pyle demanded that Halas give Grange a share of the franchise. Halas refused, and Pyle attempted to start a new league with Grange as the drawing card with a New York franchise. Both player and agent lost heavily, and by the 1927 season, Grange had made peace with the NFL. His New York team, the Yankees, joined the league. But in the third game of the season, against the Bears, Grange sustained a severe knee injury when tackled by Chicago's George Trafton. He came back in 1929 to play for seven more seasons, but the magic was gone. 'After it happened, I was just another halfback,' Grange once remarked.

For all the hoopla around him, Grange remained genuinely modest. 'Ten years from now,' he said during his playing days, 'no one will know or care what Red Grange did or who he was.'

His appraisal was off just a bit. In reality, he was the player who made pro football.

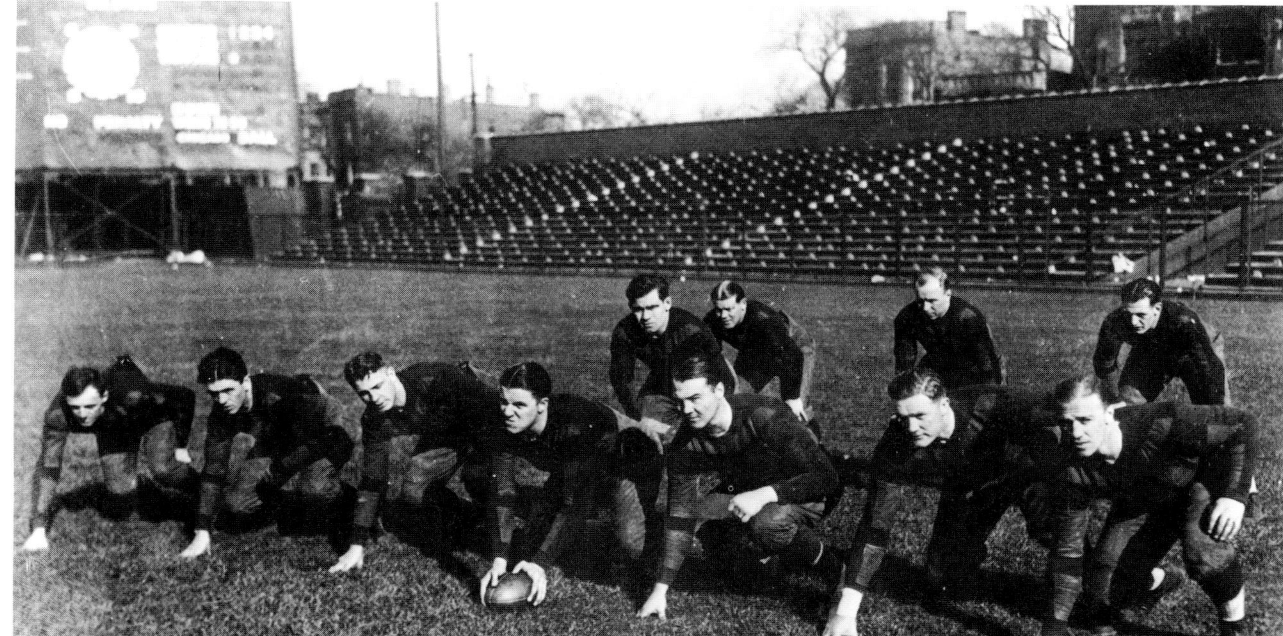

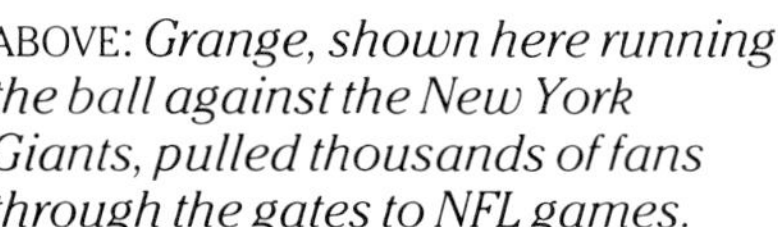

ABOVE: *Grange, shown here running the ball against the New York Giants, pulled thousands of fans through the gates to NFL games.*

TOP RIGHT: *The 1925 Bears quickly assimilated Grange (far right in backfield) into their backfield.*

RIGHT: *Grange quickly became the center of attention in the Bears' barnstorming schedule across the country in the late fall of 1925.*

MARA AND THE GIANTS, REACTION AND THE GRANGE

Joe Carr needed a promoter to start a New York franchise for the National Football League. In August 1925, he found one in Tim Mara, a successful bookmaker who knew little about football but plenty about business.

He had risen through the numbers world on New York's lower East Side to become a wealthy man. Beginning as a 13-year-old runner in the numbers games, Mara had negotiated his way to the top on two very important strengths: a mind that worked like a calculator and an unimpeachable integrity.

Accounts vary as to whether Mara paid $500 or $2500 for the New York football rights, but he did so based on the idea that the franchise of anything in New York was worth at least something. There were certainly times over the next four months when Mara had his doubts.

He signed an agreement to play games at the Polo Grounds, where the baseball New York Giants played. Mara decided he would call his football team the Giants, too.

Joining the Giants as newcomers to the NFL were Jimmy Conzelman's Detroit Panthers, the Pottsville, Pennsylvania Maroons, and the Providence Steam Rollers. All four began a scramble for talent.

Because Mara knew little about the game, he brought in Billy Gibson as president and Dr Harry March, a Canton football en-

LEFT: *Tim Mara, a successful bookmaker and businessman, bought the NFL's New York franchise in 1925 and started the Giants.*

ABOVE: *Grange (left) and his agent C C Pyle quickly moved into the business of football and in 1926 started their own league.*

ABOVE: *Mara's 1925 New York Giants featured a familiar face in the backfield, Jim Thorpe (second from left).*

RIGHT: *Stanford fullback Ernie Nevers signed with a Jacksonville, Florida team in 1925.*

thusiast, as secretary. March, in turn, hired Bob Folwell, the former Navy coach, to run the new team. The management brought in several big-name players, including halfback Hinkey Haines from Penn State and veteran tackle Century Milstead.

To promote the first game, Mara advertised broadly and gave away thousands of free tickets. With that, 25,000 curious fans came out to the Polo Grounds (few of them had paid) to see the Giants take on the Frankford Yellowjackets (who would later become the Philadelphia Eagles).

But with each game, the take at the gate shrank, until Mara announced he was $45,000 in debt. Desperate for an answer, Mara suddenly realized he could cure his problems by signing Red Grange, the Illinois star. He went to Chicago, where he learned George Halas had beaten him to the dotted line. Rather than waste the trip, Mara hastily arranged a game with the Bears and Grange at the Polo Grounds, a move that saved the New York franchise.

When Grange and the Bears came to town on 6 December, an estimated 73,000 fans packed the Polo Grounds. The gate receipts, estimated between $130,000 and $140,000, made Grange and Mara rich men.

Such numbers only increased the swirl of professional teams attempting to buy college talent. Pop Warner's great fullback at Stanford, Ernie Nevers, was paid a hefty sum, rumored to be between $20,000 and $50,000, to play an exhibition season in Jacksonville, Florida in January 1926. That next fall, Nevers would shift to the Duluth Eskimos, a 13-man team known as the 'Iron Men of the North,' for playing 28 exhibition games, 26 of them on the road.

Nevers' opponents in the 1925 Rose Bowl, Notre Dame's Four Horsemen, signed with the Hartford Blues. College coaches and administrators cried loud and long about professional teams moving in on amateur talent. To placate them, NFL Commissioner Joe Carr installed a rule for the 1926 season forbidding pro teams from signing a college player before his class graduated.

Almost immediately, a Florida exhibition game had been arranged between Nevers' Jacksonville team and the Bears, featuring Grange and the great blocker, Ed Healey. Grange's face was drawn and wearied from suffering through the earlier leg of the barnstorming tour. His performances at some of the stops, particularly in the later stages, when he was injured and tired, had left fans jeering and fuming. With the announcement of the Jacksonville game, many sportswriters promptly began predicting that Nevers would outplay him.

Although neither rookie was spectacular, the Bears won, 19-7, and Grange played competently, completing several passes, including one for a touchdown. He had no loping runs, but he played solid defense and saved a touchdown by catching a Jacksonville player from behind at the Bears' one-yard line.

If nothing else, the hype shifted the attention from the college to

LEFT: *Veteran player-coach Guy Chamberlin won his fourth NFL title in five years with the Frankford Yellowjackets in 1926. His previous titles came with Canton, then Cleveland.*

ABOVE: *Chamberlin's Frankford Yellowjackets, named after a Philadelphia suburb, were the forerunners of the Philadelphia Eagles.*

the pro game that next season, 1926, which began with 31 professional teams. That number included nine teams in the American Football League, which Grange and agent C C Pyle founded after Halas refused to give Grange a share of the Bears.

The AFL opened teams in Philadelphia, New York (Grange's team, the Yankees), Cleveland, Los Angeles, Chicago, Boston, Rock Island, Brooklyn and Newark. In an effort to showcase Grange, the Yankees played 36 games. 'We played every other day for 10 days during one period,' Mike Michalske, a Yankee lineman, once recalled. 'And we had only 15 men – seven backs, seven linemen, and our coach, Ralph Scott, who played whenever he had to.' The effort would be for naught, as the Yankees suffered financially throughout the season.

The Chicago Cardinals and Paddy Driscoll had won the 1925 NFL title, but the Frankford (a Philadelphia suburb) Yellowjackets, led by veteran player-coach Guy Chamberlin, ran off 14 victories to win in 1926. The season came to a showdown between the Chicago Cards and the Yellowjackets. The Jackets won, 7-6, when Chamberlin broke through and blocked Driscoll's extra point kick.

The championship marked an amazing record for Chamberlin, who had coached the Canton Bulldogs to two championships, then added a third when the team moved to Cleveland. The Frankford title was his fourth championship in five years.

Years later, at Chamberlin's Hall of Fame induction ceremony, Earl Blaik, the great Army coach, said Guy 'never learned how to lose.'

The Philadelphia Quakers won the 1926 AFL title and played the New York Giants in the first-ever inter-league playoff. The Giants won the 13 December game, 31-0, and the AFL went off to anonymity.

The Quakers, however, weren't the only big losers of the 1926 season. Grange had saved Tim Mara in 1925, but the AFL New York Yankees franchise and the Giants split a tentative market in 1926. As a result, Mara lost $60,000. Even worse, Pyle and Grange lost more than $100,000 and watched their new league fold. Between 1926 and 1927, 19 pro football teams met their financial deaths.

Mara, however, had gotten football in his blood. He held on and watched his team become one of the league's strongest franchises. By the 1927 season, the league was down to 12 teams, from which the Giants won the championship with an 11-1-1 record, including five consecutive shutouts. Their leader was 240-pound lineman, Steve Owen, who went on to coach the Giants for 22 years. 'We were a smash-and-shove gang,' Owen said of the 1927 Giants. The next year they would slip to 4-7-2.

The Detroit Panthers' Jimmy Conzelman switched to the Providence Steamrollers for 1928 and led them to the championship, but it wasn't a great year for pro football. Grange, sitting out with a knee injury, turned his attention to making movies. Nevers also left the NFL that season to coach at Stanford and play pro baseball.

Both players, however, would come back to the game. Professional football had gained a new momentum in the 1920s. It would weather the coming turmoil of the Great Depression headed toward a bright future.

THE PACKER RESURGENCE

Just a few days after the economy of the United States suffered the first black quake of its economic collapse, the Chicago Cardinals' Ernie Nevers ran to greatness at Comiskey Park. There, against the crosstown rival Bears on 28 November 1929, Nevers scored six touchdowns and booted four conversions to rack up 40 points, a single-game scoring record that has repelled the tests of nearly six decades.

The day belonged to 'The Blond Bull,' as Nevers was known, and Walt Kiesling, the 265-pound guard who battered down the defenders in Nevers' path.

But the 1929 season, as well as the next two or three, belonged to Curly Lambeau's Green Bay Packers. Lambeau had finished his playing days and turned his attention to picking through the league's leftover talent for a championship combination. Lambeau's findings were Johnny 'Blood' McNally, the zany halfback better known to the sports world as simply 'Johnny Blood'; August 'Mike' Michalske, the league's first great blitzing linebacker and guard; and Cal Hubbard, the 6 foot 5 inch, 250-pound tackle, all future Hall of Famers, all championship bound. In 1930 Lambeau added rookie quarterback Arnie Herber to the recipe and the Packers kept cooking.

As much as the 1929 season marked the beginning of the Packers' greatness, it also signalled the end of an era. Dayton, the last surviving team from pro football's cradle in Ohio, ceased operations. There was a coming home of sorts as well in 1929, as Red Grange, having run his course of endorsements, rejoined Halas and the Bears.

A muscled speedster at 6 feet, 200 pounds, Johnny Blood had a wild and gregarious nature. On the field, he was the master of improvisation, always creating extra yardage, always producing in the clutch. The 1929 season was marked by a dramatic showdown with the equally powerful New York Giants, led by quarterback Benny Friedman. Blood recovered a fumble leading to the Packers' first score. Then, later in the game, he caught a pass from Red Dunn and turned it into a 55-yard touchdown to kill the Giants, 20-7. The Packers finished the season 12-0-1, the league's first undefeated champion since the Canton Bulldogs of 1922 and 1923.

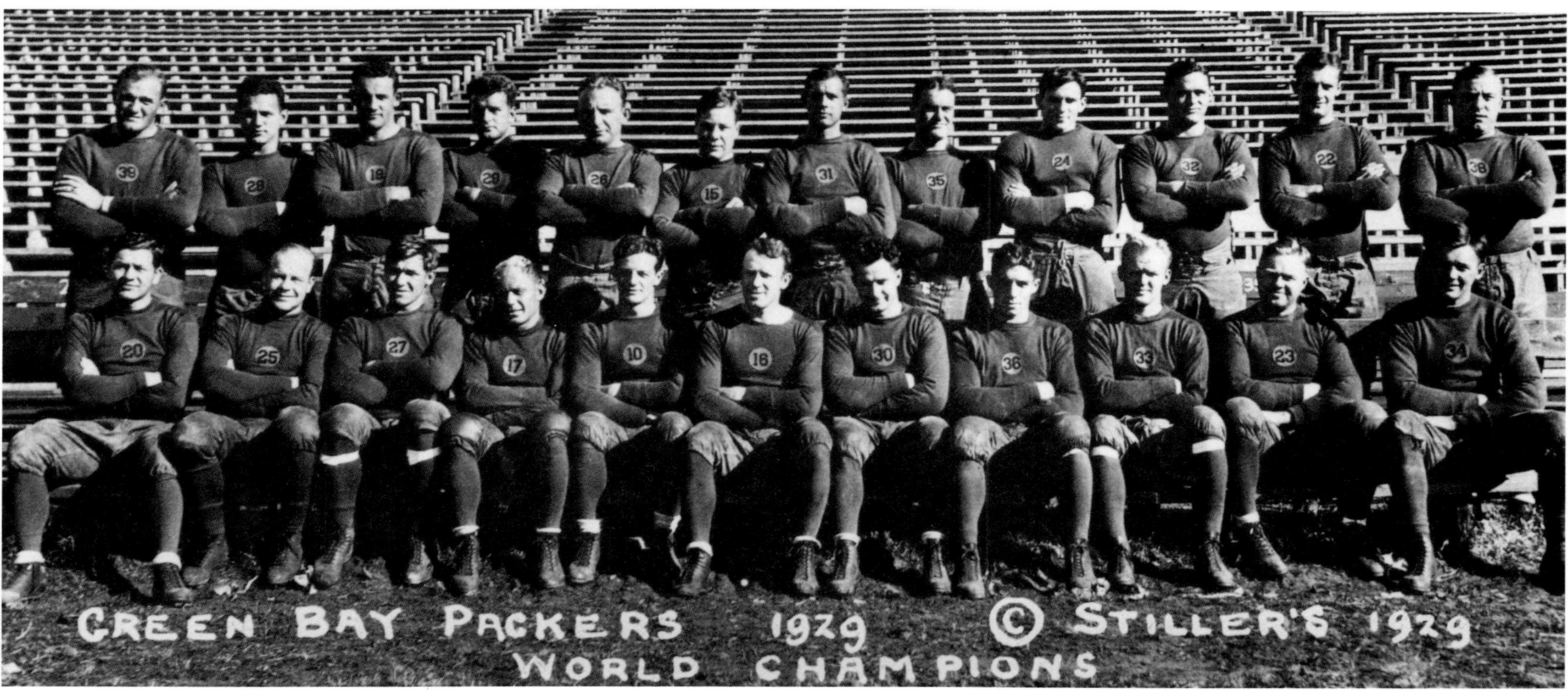

ABOVE: *The 1929 Green Bay Packers started a resurgence in Wisconsin football by winning the first of three NFL championships.*

TOP: *Ernie Nevers set an NFL single-game scoring record 28 November 1929 by scoring six touchdowns and kicking four conversions for the Chicago Cardinals.*

The acquisition of Herber, the game's early strong-armed, deep thrower, the next season assured that the Green Bay dominance would continue. A local boy from Green Bay's West High and the University of Wisconsin, Herber made his appearance against the Chicago Cards that season and threw a touchdown pass to Lavern Dilweg for a 7-0 Green Bay victory. It was hard for Lambeau to keep him out of the lineup after that.

The heart of that great early Packer defense was Michalske, a Penn State man who had broken in with Red Grange's AFL New York Yankees. Iron Mike made All-Pro six times. His weapons were the stunt and the blitz. His currency was opposing quarterbacks. 'It was legal then to rough the passer, even after he had gotten rid of the ball,' he once recalled. 'Sometimes we worked him over pretty good.'

Cal Hubbard, the Packers' enforcer at 255 pounds, had come to Green Bay from the New York Giants. Working under Lambeau, he was named all-league three times. The Packers finished 10-3-1 in 1930, edging out the 14-3 Giants.

But the big point of the season was a showdown between the college and professional games. Notre Dame's Knute Rockne was vocal in his opinion that the best of his Irish squads could easily whip any good pro team. The New York Giants took him up on the bet in a game played at the Polo Grounds on 14 December. The proceeds went to an unemployment relief fund.

Rockne called in the pride of the Irish, every former great he could muster, including the Four Horsemen. The game was a success for the unemployed, with a $115,000 purse going to the needy. But it was a disaster for Rockne and company, as the Giants, led by Benny Friedman, won, 22-0. Pro football had knocked the Four Horsemen right out of the saddle and college football's reputation with them.

The Grange effect had brought more money into the league, and over the previous five years, pro football had ceased being a part-

LEFT: *John 'Blood' McNally was the heart of the Packers' backfield from 1929 to 1931. He was inducted into the Hall of Fame in 1963.*

BELOW: *The 1929 New York Giants lost a showdown with the Packers for the league title.*

RIGHT: *The Packers acquired quarterback Arnie Herber in 1930, thus assuring they would continue to win championships. Herber was inducted into the Hall of Fame in 1966.*

38

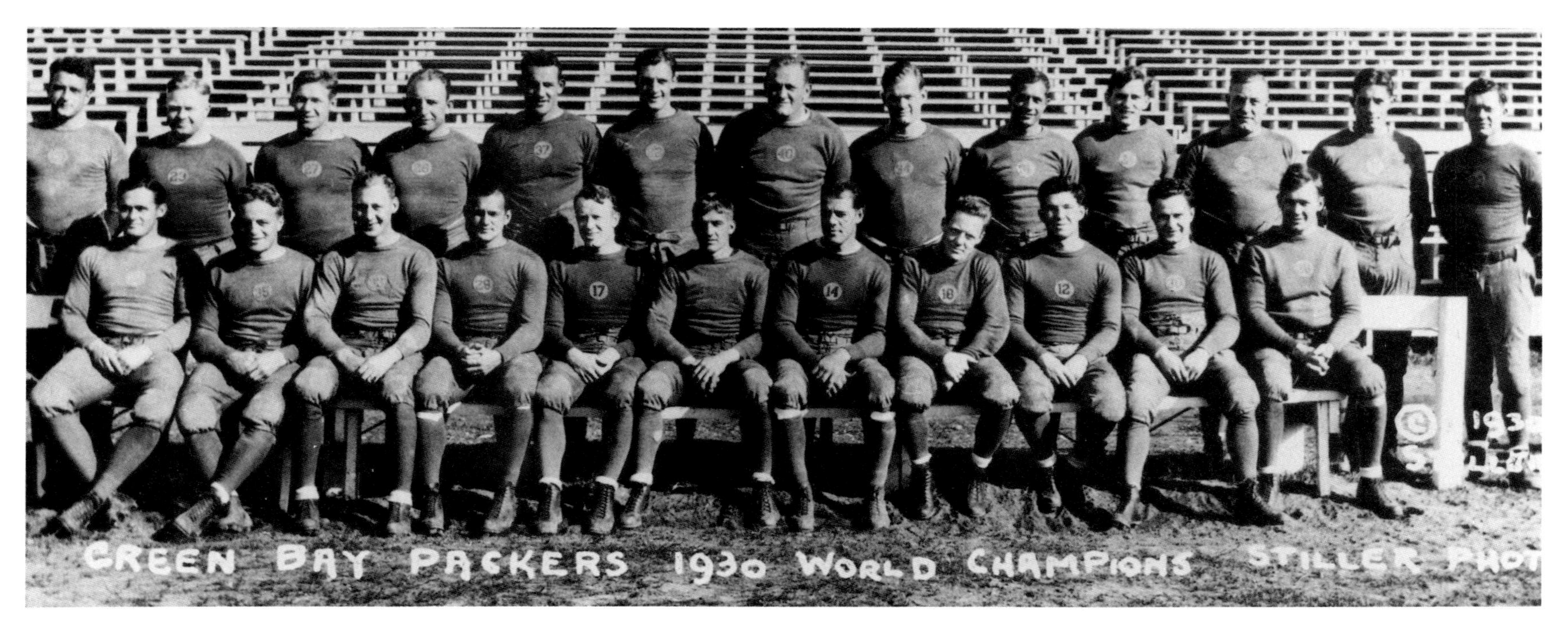

ABOVE: *The 1930 Green Bay Packers, led by McNally and Herbert, won another NFL championship.*

LEFT: *Iron Mike Michalske, a blitzing linebacker for the Packers, was named All Pro six times. He was elected to the Hall of Fame in 1964.*

RIGHT: *By 1932 Curly Lambeau had matured into a successful executive and took his Packer team on a tour of Hawaii.*

time sport. In that period, it gained the upper hand, as professionals were able to devote their full efforts to the game. As a result, pro football became the lab for football innovation. It was an unabashed entertainment industry, and its offenses reflected a razzle-dazzle unseen in the college game.

That didn't stop the Packers from bulling their way to the 1932 title with a 12-2-0 record. It was their third straight championship, a feat not equalled until Vince Lombardi repeated with the Packers in 1965/67.

Only problem was, the Packers felt they were robbed of a fourth title in 1934. They finished 10-3-1, including a victory and a tie over the Chicago Bears. But the Bears finished an odd 7-1-6 and claimed the title because ties didn't figure in the standings. 'We really won four in a row,' Cal Hubbard complained years later, 'but they didn't give it to us.'

The season marked the first year that complete statistics were kept. Earl 'Dutch' Clark of the Portsmouth, Ohio Spartans scored a measly 55 points in 12 games to lead the league. Cliff Battles of the Boston Braves was the top rusher with 576 yards; Herber the passing leader with 639 yards. Ray Flaherty of the Giants caught 21 passes for 350 yards to lead all receivers.

Feeling the crunch the Great Depression, the NFL dropped to eight teams in 1932. It might have been smaller if Commissioner Joe Carr hadn't talked a group of businessmen, headed by Washington, DC laundry chain owner George Preston Marshall, into opening the Boston Braves franchise.

The Bears had to earn their championship in a playoff game, the league's first, with the Portsmouth Spartans. A blizzard struck just before the 18 December championship, and the game had to be moved indoors to Chicago Stadium. Played on an 80-yard field, the playoff had a bizarre quality. The Bears won, 9-0, when Bronko Nagurski threw a jump pass to Red Grange.

The Spartans complained that Nagurski was less than five yards behind the line of scrimmage when he threw the pass, which violated the existing rule. If nothing else, the controversy pushed the league toward unleashing the passing game. In fact, the owners looked at other ways of making the game more attractive. Times were hard, and the public was looking to the sports world for escape.

Pro football was moving closer to the spotlight.

LEFT: *Cal Hubbard weighed 255 pounds and was the heart of the Packers' line. He made All Pro three times and was a 1963 Hall of Fame inductee.*

BELOW: *Although they had a 7-1-6 record, the Chicago Bears won their first NFL Championship by beating the Portsmouth Spartans in a playoff game played indoors.*

THE EARLY THIRTIES
LIONS, GIANTS AND BEARS

Professional football discovered much of its identity in the years before World War II. Its weak franchises died off, and the survivors established their roots. Joining the Bears, Packers, Cardinals and Giants in 1933 were the Philadelphia Eagles (formed by Bert Bell and Ludlow Wray from the Frankford franchise) and Art Rooney's Pittsburgh franchise, then called the Pirates. Before the decade was out, the Redskins would leave Boston, where they were ignored, to find their home in Washington. The Portsmouth, Ohio Spartans would move to Detroit in 1934 to become the Lions. During this period, the team roster size was gradually increased, from 18 in 1925 to 24 in 1935.

Most important of all, at the suggestion of new Boston owner George Preston Marshall, the league organized itself in 1933 into two divisions, Eastern and Western, and began offering the public a championship game. The very first one, between the New York Giants and Chicago Bears at Wrigley Field, attracted 26,000 fans.

The Chicago Bears had taken the NFL title in 1932 amid a swirl of controversy with a 7-1-6 record. Fans and opponents alike took issue with the standings, and the Portsmouth Spartans took issue with the officiating in the playoff game.

No doubt about it, the Bears set out to prove something in 1933. Their efforts that year would start them on a run toward championships and a new identity. Eventually they would become the Monsters of the Midway.

George Halas had stepped aside in 1930 to let Ralph Jones take over as coach. But in 1933 Halas bought out his partner, Ed Sternaman, and reinstated himself as coach.

The era was known for a blossoming of offensive style. The Bears' winning touchdown pass against the Spartans the year before was an item of debate because Bronko Nagurski wasn't five yards behind the line of scrimmage when he threw it, as the rules required. So the league threw the shackles off the pass for 1933, making it legal to throw one from anywhere behind the line of scrimmage. The 1932 indoors championship had other effects, most notably the moving of the goal post to the goal line.

But the biggest change came from a man with little football background, George Preston Marshall, a Washington, DC laundry magnate who had been talked into investing in the Boston Redskins. Marshall had a flair for promotion and business.

When he entered the league in 1932, he found a loosely organized affiliation where each team made its own schedule and championships were disputed. A persuasive communicator, Marshall urged the league toward organizing into Eastern and Western Divisions and adopting a playoff for the 'world championship.' He also promoted the loosening of the passing rules. Marshall predicted that a wide open game would stir fan interest. He was right. George Halas knew it and backed him.

There is a tinge of irony in the fact that as the National Football League embarked on the great offensive experiment, the Bears forged their way to the fore with a chilling defense. The great George Trafton had retired after the 1932 season, but the Bears still had the game's best defensive lineman, Roy 'Link' Lyman. A veteran, Lyman was the game's early master at reading plays. Red Grange had matured into an excellent defensive player and anchored the Chicago backfield.

The offense was led quietly by quarterback Carl Brumbaugh. It featured the T-formation with a man in motion, which was structured to maximize the considerable talents of Bronko Nagurski, the

ABOVE: *Roy 'Link' Lyman of the Chicago Bears was considered the best defensive lineman in pro football in 1932.*
ABOVE RIGHT: *George Preston Marshall, owner of a chain of laundries in Washington, DC, founded the Boston Redskins in 1932. The new owner suggested that the NFL hold a championship game between its divisional winners.*
RIGHT: *Bronko Nagurski, the bruising runner of the Chicago Bears, was inducted into the Hall of Fame in 1963.*

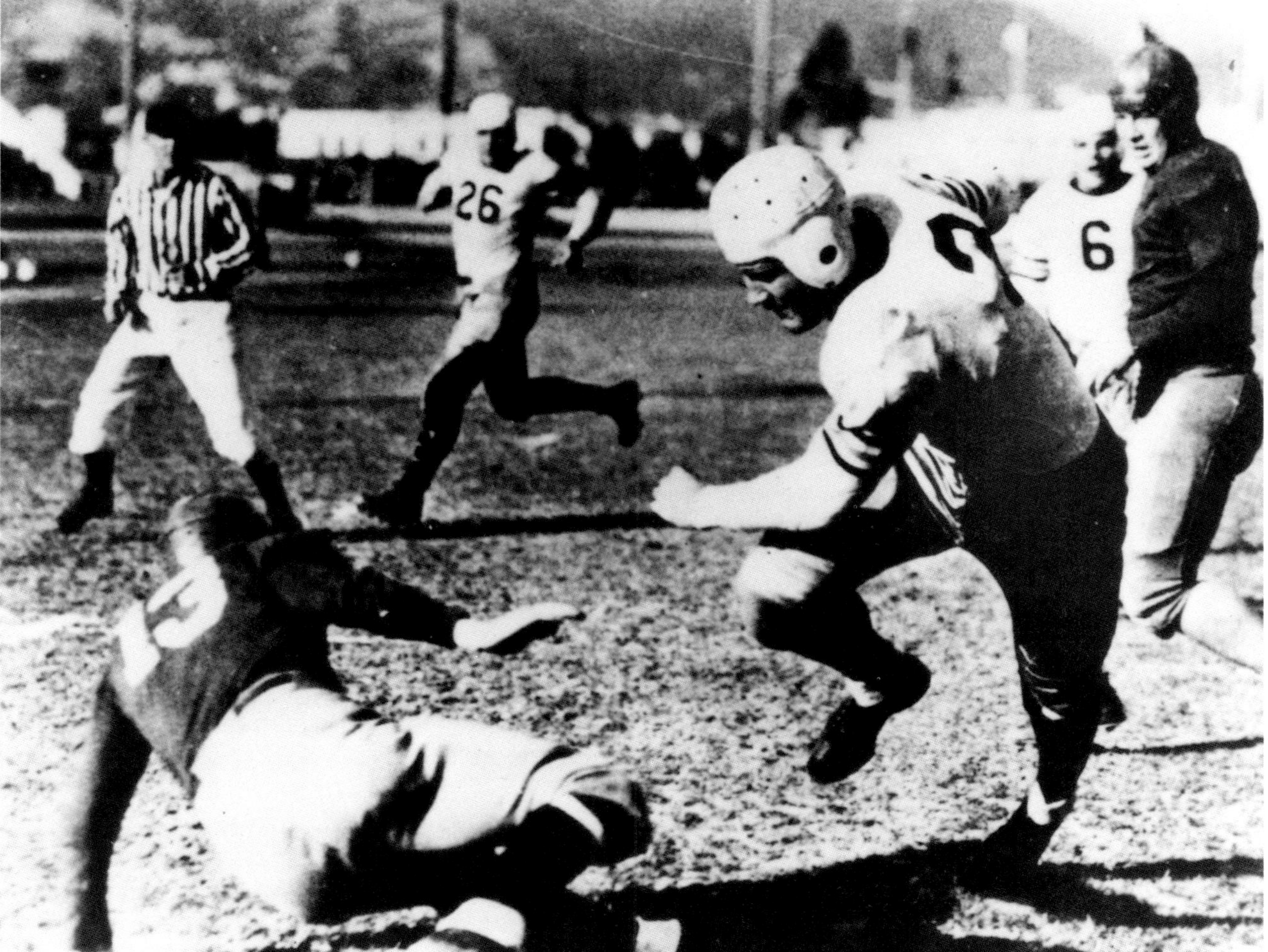

FAR LEFT: *Art Rooney entered pro football in 1933 with the founding of his Pittsburgh franchise.*
ABOVE LEFT: *Bronko Nagurski threw the winning touchdown pass in the Bears' 1932 championship victory over the Portsmouth Spartans.*

incredibly strong 235-pound fullback. An All America selection out of the University of Minnesota in 1929, Nagurski was a ball of intense power, an accurate passer and brutal runner. He was the kind of player who generated legends. He was said to have been forced out of bounds once where he collided with a policeman's horse and knocked it cold. On another such out-of-bounds excursion, he reportedly knocked a fender off a parked car.

He signed a two-year contract worth $5000 for each of the 1930 and 1931 seasons. By 1933 he was the heart of the Bears and led them to a 10-2-1 regular season record. In a crucial game with the Portsmouth Spartans, Nagurski was called for holding, leading to the Spartans taking a late 14-10 lead.

Angered at himself, Nagurski ran the kickoff back to the Chicago 45, then in the huddle on the first play he begged to be given the chance to atone. His answer was a 55-yard outburst of power, speed and emotion that sent tacklers sprawling. Unable to brake his momentum at the end zone, Nagurski slammed into the Cubs' dugout in Wrigley Field with tremendous force.

The New York Giants, on the other hand, were traveling on the fine passing of rookie quarterback Harry Newman, an All America out of the University of Michigan. The Giants' running game had been boosted with the acquisition of Ken Strong, a former All America at NYU and Yankee baseball player. He could run, throw and kick.

The brutal work went to center Mel Hein, a precise, powerful

LEFT: *Chicago's Wrigley Field was the setting for the 1933 NFL Championship game between the Bears and Giants. The Bears won, 23-21.*

ABOVE: *Center Mel Hein was the strength of the New York Giants' line in 1933, on offense and defense. He was a charter inductee of the Hall of Fame.*

BELOW: *The Giants' running game was powered by Ken Strong, a former baseball player with the New York Yankees. He was named to the Hall of Fame in 1967.*

tackler, also an All America out of Washington State who played 15 years for the Giants, making All Pro eight of them.

The Giants' defense had been tested briefly. Boston running back Cliff Battles had gained 215 yards against them on only 16 carries in October. But they had finished the season 11-3 and took plenty of confidence into the league's first championship.

Played at Wrigley Field before 23,000 fans, the match was a seesaw affair that confirmed everything George Preston Marshall had said about a playoff.

Nagurski moved the Bears along with his running and throwing, and 'Automatic' Jack Manders kicked three Chicago field goals. That was barely enough to counter a sterling effort by Harry Newman,

LEFT: *Boston running back Cliff Battles gained 215 yards on 16 carries against the vaunted New York defense in 1934.*

ABOVE: *New York's stars of 1934 (counterclockwise beginning with number 12) Harry Newman, Red Badgro, Ed Danowski, Mel Hein, Ken Strong, unidentified, Harrison Stafford and Ike Franklin.*

RIGHT: *Feathers, a rookie for the Bears in 1934, became the league's first 1000-yard rusher, gaining 1004 yards on only 101 carries.*

who completed 12 of 20 passes for 201 yards and two touchdowns.

Late in the fourth quarter, it appeared New York would win, 21-16, until Chicago got the ball back at the Giant 47 after a bad punt. The Bears moved to the 32, then Nagurski threw short to Bill Hewitt. As Hewitt was about to be tackled, he lateralled to end Billy Karr who streaked 25 yards for the touchdown and a 23-21 lead.

In the closing seconds, Newman threw to Dale Burnett, who broke into the open with Mel Hein running beside him, setting up a perfect lateral play for the winning score. Only Grange stood in their way. But Grange tackled Burnett high and hard, pinning his arms from lateralling and saving the game.

If the Bears' pride waxed with the title, it waned before the 1934 season when they played to a scoreless tie against a team of college all-stars in Chicago's first All-Star game, played at Soldier Field before 79,000 fans.

Halas brought in veteran lineman Walt Kiesling and rookie half-back Beattie Feathers to bolster the team for 1934. Then he turned

18

RIGHT: *The Bears' Bronko Nagurski bulled for eight yards as Chicago took an early lead over New York in the 1934 championship game.*

FAR RIGHT BELOW: *The Giants donned basketball shoes to negotiate the slick field and won a come-from-behind victory over the Bears in 1934. In this photo, several Giants close in on the Bears' Bronko Nagurski.*

BELOW: *NFL Commissioner Joe Carr presents the 1934 championship trophy to New York Giants owner Tim Mara.*

the Monsters of the Midway loose, and they growled to 13 straight victories and the Western championship. On the way, Feathers became the NFL's first 1000-yard rusher, gaining 1004 on only 101 rushes for an amazing 9.9-yard average carry.

The Giants had been one of the Monsters' regular-season victims, but they survived to win the Eastern Division. The championship game seemed a foregone conclusion, especially in the early going as 35,000 fans at the Polo Grounds watched Chicago methodically bull to a 13-3 lead through the third quarter.

The frozen field had left the New York ground game with spinning wheels until the Giants' running backs donned rubber-soled basketball shoes at halftime. Finding their traction as the third period closed, the Giants turned the game into a track meet, scoring 27 points to win 30-13. The stunned Bears seemed helpless spectators.

For all the hype about basketball shoes, much of the credit really belonged to the Giants' inspired offensive line, led by tackle Bill Morgan. First, New York pulled to 13-10 on a 35-yard scoring pass from Ed Danowski to Ike Frankian. Then Ken Strong gave the Giants the lead with a 42-yard scoring run. With Nagurski hampered by injuries, the Bears' response was ineffective. They threw an interception, the Giants scored again and the league had its first 'instant rout' – four touchdowns in less than 15 minutes!

After playing an exhibition game in January, Red Grange retired from football, and the Monsters receded into mediocrity, finishing

the 1935 season with a 6-4-2 record.

The Giants, however, kept their appointment for the championship game, winning the East with a 9-3 record as Ed Danowski led the league in passing with 794 yards.

Regardless, it was the year of the Lions. G A 'Dick' Richards had bought the Portsmouth Spartans, moved them to Detroit for the 1934 season and was determined to make them the flashiest in the league. He outfitted them in silver and blue and set up radio broadcasts of the games.

Fortunately, the team was worthy of such attention. The Lions' leader was the heady All-Pro quarterback, Dutch Clark, a former All America out of little Colorado College. Teamed with him in the backfield were fullback Leroy Gutowsky and halfbacks Ernie Caddel and Frank Christiansen. In 1934 their defense ran seven straight shutouts, as they went 10-3, losing twice to the Bears.

The tables turned in 1935 as the Lions went to the championship with a 7-3-2 record. Few people believed they had a chance. But in the title game at the University of Detroit Stadium, they whipped the Giants, 26-7, with a power ground game, giving Detroit its second trophy to celebrate (the Tigers had won the World Series a few months earlier).

Bert Bell of Philadelphia proposed a college draft, which the league approved in 1935. The team with the worst record would pick first. The first day of the draft was 19 May 1936. The Eagles, who finished the 1935 season 2-9, selected University of Chicago back Jay Berwanger first. Later, they traded his rights to the Bears, but Berwanger never played pro ball.

A rival, another American Football League, mustered six franchises and survived the 1936 season with the Boston Shamrocks winning its championship.

For the NFL, stability was the word. No teams died, and none was added. Better yet, they all played the same number of games. Pro football, it seemed, was finding itself.

THE AGE OF THE PASSERS

GREEN BAY AND HERBER; WASHINGTON AND BAUGH

The 1936 season marks the dawning of the NFL's great age of passers. Arnie Herber of Green Bay initiated it with the league's first 1000-yard performance. In 12 games he completed 77 of 173 attempts for 1239 yards.

That paved the way in 1937 for Samuel 'Slingin' Sammy' Baugh, the Washington Redskin rookie out of TCU who threw for 1127 yards. Parker Hall, the Cleveland Rams' rookie, would continue that tradition in 1939, nearly breaking Herber's record with 1227 yards.

By 1938 the league would awaken to its passing phenomenon and realize it better begin protecting its richest resource, the quarterback. A rule against roughing the passer was adopted with a 15-yard penalty.

Throwing quarterbacks begat record-setting receivers. Green Bay's Don Hutson, 'the Alabama Antelope,' caught 34 passes for 536 yards in 1936. His and Herber's performances sent Curly Lambeau's Packers into the NFL title game with a 10-1-1 record. Their opponents were George Marshall's Boston Redskins. The game had been scheduled for Boston, but when only 4500 fans paid to see the Redskins' final home game, Marshall decided he'd had enough of trying to please the Boston market.

LEFT: *In his rookie year Parker Hall, the Cleveland Rams' quarterback from 1939 to 1942, won the Joe Carr trophy, awarded to the NFL's most valuable player.*

RIGHT: *Don Hutson, 'the Alabama Antelope,' was quarterback Arnie Herber's primary receiving target. The Green Bay end led the league in receptions in 1936 and carried the Packers into the championship game against the Boston Redskins.*

'They don't deserve to see this championship game,' Marshall told reporters. 'They don't deserve the team, either. We will never play another game in Boston.'

The site was shifted to the Polo Grounds where 29,545 saw the Herber-Hutson combination dispatch the Redskins, 21-6. In addition to showing Marshall that he needed to move, the game proved he needed a passer.

He had his eye on one. TCU's Baugh was taking the Southwest Conference by storm. But the pro scouts were lukewarm about him. He was tall and skinny, and they figured he wouldn't last. Marshall disagreed and made Baugh the second player selected in the draft, signing him to the then outrageous sum of nearly $20,000 per season. For good measure, Baugh also signed a baseball contract with the St Louis Cardinals.

The young quarterback wasted little time in proving Marshall correct, as he led the College All Stars to a 6-0 victory over the world champion Packers that summer of 1937. The public would soon learn that Baugh was only getting started. He would go on to play 16

LEFT: *The Redskins moved to Washington in 1937 and were led to the NFL Championship by rookie quarterback Sammy Baugh, from Texas Christian.*

BELOW: *Baugh practices throwing before the 1937 championship game with Chicago. He passed for more than 22,000 yards during his career.*

RIGHT: *The Redskins posed for this publicity photo before their crucial late-season game against New York in 1937. The Redskins won and went on to the championship.*

seasons of pro ball, most of it going two ways for 60 minutes a game, and would pass for more than 22,000 yards, a little better than 13 miles.

Marshall moved his team to Washington and then did his best to make a show for the hometown. 'Football is a game of pageantry,' he once said. 'It derives its spectacle from the gladiator shows of the Romans in the pages of history. It is strictly amphitheater. Its great success is due to the color surrounding it. It needs music and bands. Football without a band is like music without an orchestra.'

He lived up to that credo by outfitting a 110-member band in $25,000 worth of uniforms. His wife did her part by helping to write the team fight song, 'Hail to the Redskins.' Washington fans responded in droves. In his first game, Baugh completed 11 of 16 passes, which opened up the defense for running backs Cliff Battles and Riley Smith as the Redskins won.

After some initial struggles, Baugh and the Redskins found their stride and went into a crucial late game with New York with a 7-3 record. More than 10,000 Washington fans went to the Polo Grounds to see the game, as the Redskins routed New York, 49-14, on their way to the title game.

The Western Division had been won by Halas' Bears with an impressive 9-1-1 record. Beyond that they had the home advantage at cold, cold Wrigley Field on 12 December.

Like Red Grange before him, Baugh showed the league its future that day. He hurled an all-star passing performance into the face of the wind and sent the favored Bears to defeat, 28-21. Despite the weather, he turned in numbers typical of the pro game of the 1980s – 17 of 34 passes completed for 352 yards and three touchdowns.

The 1937 championship game developed as a classic struggle, with the Bears and Redskins trading touchdowns and the lead

LEFT: *Green Bay receiver Don Hutson and quarterback Cecil Isbell watch coach Curly Lambeau diagram plays.*

RIGHT: *Redskins owner George Preston Marshall (left) and his entourage saw the Giants whip Washington, 36-0, at the Polo Grounds in 1938.*

through the first half. The decisive offensive moments came in the third quarter, as Baugh shook off a leg injury and guided the Skins to three touchdowns.

The first strike was a 55-yard shot to Wayne Millner. Then a series later, Baugh hit Millner again, this time for 78 yards. That was followed by the decisive toss to Charlie 'Choo-Choo' Justice for 35 yards and the winning margin. For the period, Baugh had completed seven of nine passes for 220 yards.

The Washington defense still needed to deflect three serious Bear drives in the fourth quarter. The battering ram at the heart of the Bears' offense, aging fullback Bronko Nagurski, was slowed by injuries, and the Redskins held on for the win. That effort and the third quarter scoring outburst earned each of the Redskins their $234.36 championship payoff.

The day was ample proof to league owners that it was time to put their money on a passer. If they failed to see it, the next two seasons hammered it home, as the Packers and Giants turned the championship into their exclusive party.

ABOVE: *Johnny Blood, Byron 'Whizzer' White and Art Rooney at White's signing in 1938. White, who later was named to the US Supreme Court, led the league in rushing as a rookie with Pittsburgh.*

Byron 'Whizzer' White, who went on to a career as a United States Supreme Court Justice, led the league in rushing (567 yards) as a rookie with Pittsburgh. But it was the Herber-and-Hudson act that again led Green Bay to the title game. New York had the leading passer in Ed Danowski, and a pack of All Pros in center Mel Hein,

ABOVE: *The Redskins' Cliff Battles runs the ball against Chicago in the 1937 championship, won by Washington, 28-21.*

LEFT: *Chicago Bears end Dick Plasman catches a pass in the 1937 championship game.*

RIGHT: *The 1938 New York Giants powered past the Green Bay Packers to win the NFL Championship.*

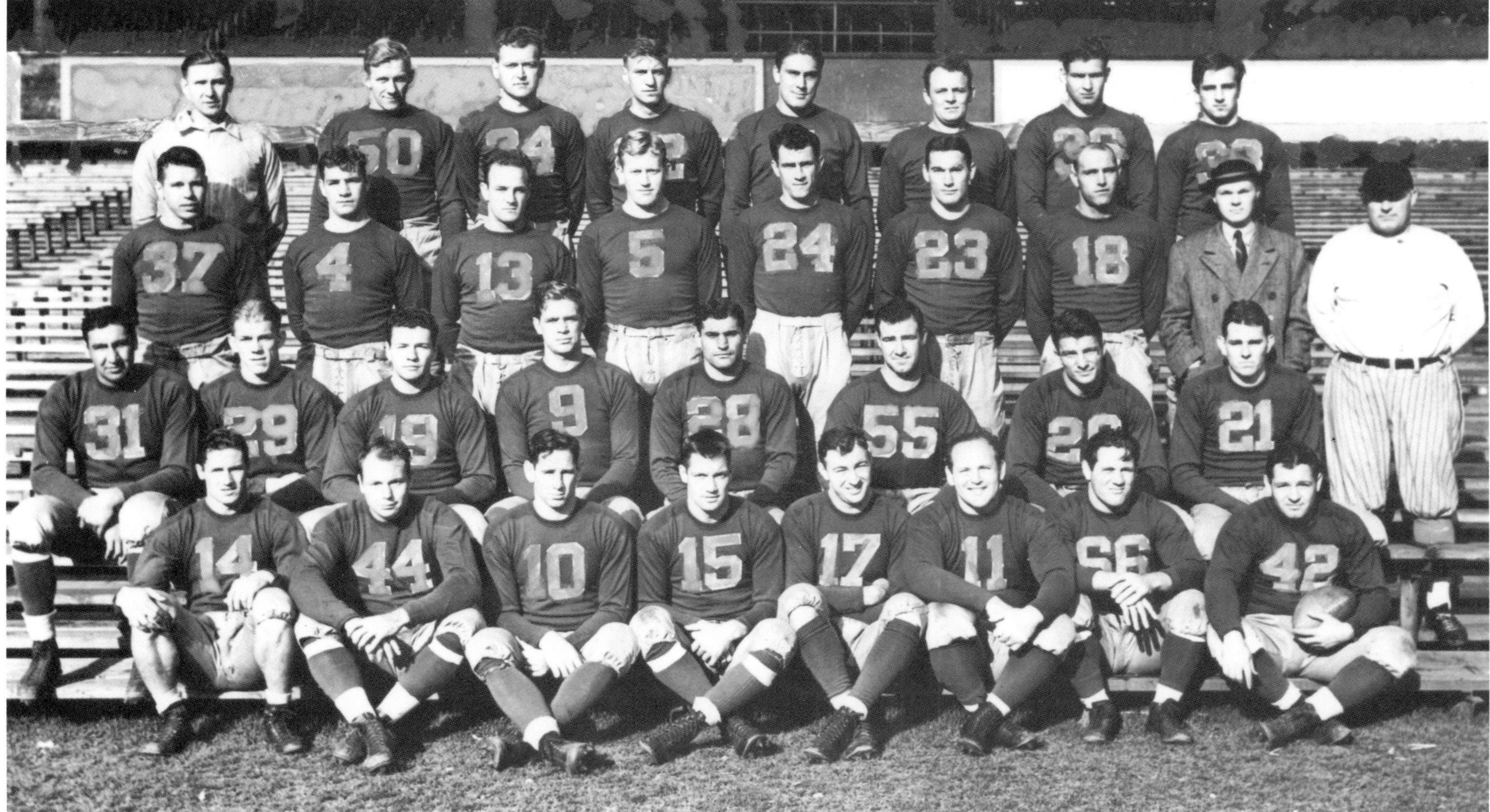

ABOVE: *The Packers kick a conversion in their 27-0 rout of the Giants for the 1939 championship.*

RIGHT: *Green Bay's Cecil Isbell carries the ball against New York in the 1939 championship game at Milwaukee.*

BELOW RIGHT: *Ed Jankowski of the Packers powers his way to extra yardage against the Giants in the 1939 championship.*

guard Hohn Dell Isola, end Jim Lee Howell and halfback Ward Cuff. Both teams had good defenses, and neither cared much for the other.

More than 48,000 crammed the Polo Grounds, and the Giants kept them on their feet throughout the nasty slugfest. A 29-yard pass from Danowski to Hank Soar won it, 23-17, for the Giants. Soar leaped between two defenders at the Green Bay six, caught the ball, then dragged a tackler into the end zone.

For 1939 Herber gave a portion of his playing time to Cecil Isbell, and the Packers renewed their rivalry with New York in the championship, played this time in a rickety stadium at the State Fair Grounds in Milwaukee. The Giants had gone 9-1-1 in the East but were hammered 27-0 by a Packer team intent on revenge. The Milwaukee crowd taunted the losers throughout the game, then pelted their bus with rocks and bottles afterward.

'For a day, at least,' wrote Stanley Woodward, 'professional football slipped back into its unsavory past and did itself incalculable harm.'

The past, however, proved to be the least of the league's concerns. The future, and all that it held, was fast upon it in 1939. Particularly a newfangled invention, television. Not everyone knew it then, but the two, pro football and the tube, were made for each other.

LEFT: *Ed Danowski, New York Giants quarterback and former Fordham star, poses for a publicity shot during practice in the late 1930s.*

AN ERA ENDS, AN ERA BEGINS

Sometimes history moves in a neat manner, sometimes in a catastrophic mess. It offered both to pro football heading into the twentieth century's fifth decade.

In retrospect, there was an almost eerie tidiness to the affairs of the National Football League in 1939. One era ended in mourning, another began as a quiet infant.

Joe Carr, heart and soul of the NFL since becoming its president in 1921, died 20 May 1939. His successor, Carl Storck, was named five days later.

That fall, the National Broadcasting Company placed a camera at a Brooklyn Dodgers-Philadelphia Eagles game at Ebbets Field and sent a hopeful broadcast out to the small number of sets scattered across New York City. The bluish image that flickered and rolled across the screen provided those few viewers with a glimpse of the game's bountiful future. The realization of that bounty, however, wouldn't come for another two decades.

As for Joe Carr, he bequeathed the sports world a much better NFL than he had inherited. It's newest competitor, the six-team American Football League, had died after the 1937 season. Three years later, yet another AFL appeared, again with six teams, gasped through 1940 and 1941, and also expired.

The NFL had expanded a bit in 1937, when Homer Marshman established the Rams in Cleveland. By 1946 the team would grow weary of fighting the weather and move to Los Angeles, making the NFL truly national, or at least bi-coastal.

Washington Redskins owner George Preston Marshall contributed another dash of promotional genius to the league in 1939, when he and several Los Angeles executives established the Pro Bowl, pitting the league's All-Stars against its championship team.

ABOVE: *Redskins owner George Preston Marshall poses with his players during spring practice, 1940.*

LEFT: *Joe Carr, president of the NFL since 1921, died in May of 1939 after guiding the league to stability.*

BELOW: *The Chicago Bears humiliated the Washington Redskins, 73-0, in the 1940 championship in Washington.*

The Giants defeated the All-Stars, 13-10, in the game played at Los Angeles' Wrigley Field.

The 1940 season saw Art Rooney sell his Pittsburgh stock to pick up a portion of the Eagles. It also saw one of the biggest routs in league history. The size and scope of Chicago's 73-0 victory over Washington in the NFL Championship bout on 8 December 1940 make it one of the most astounding pro games ever played. If anything, the outcome emphasized the power of the T-formation

1940 Championship Playoff
Chicago Bears (73) vs. Washington Redskins (0)
at Washington, D.C., Dec. 8
Attendance 36,034

RIGHT: *The Chicago Bears' Bill Osmanski is tackled by Redskin Willie Wilkin during the 1940 championship.*

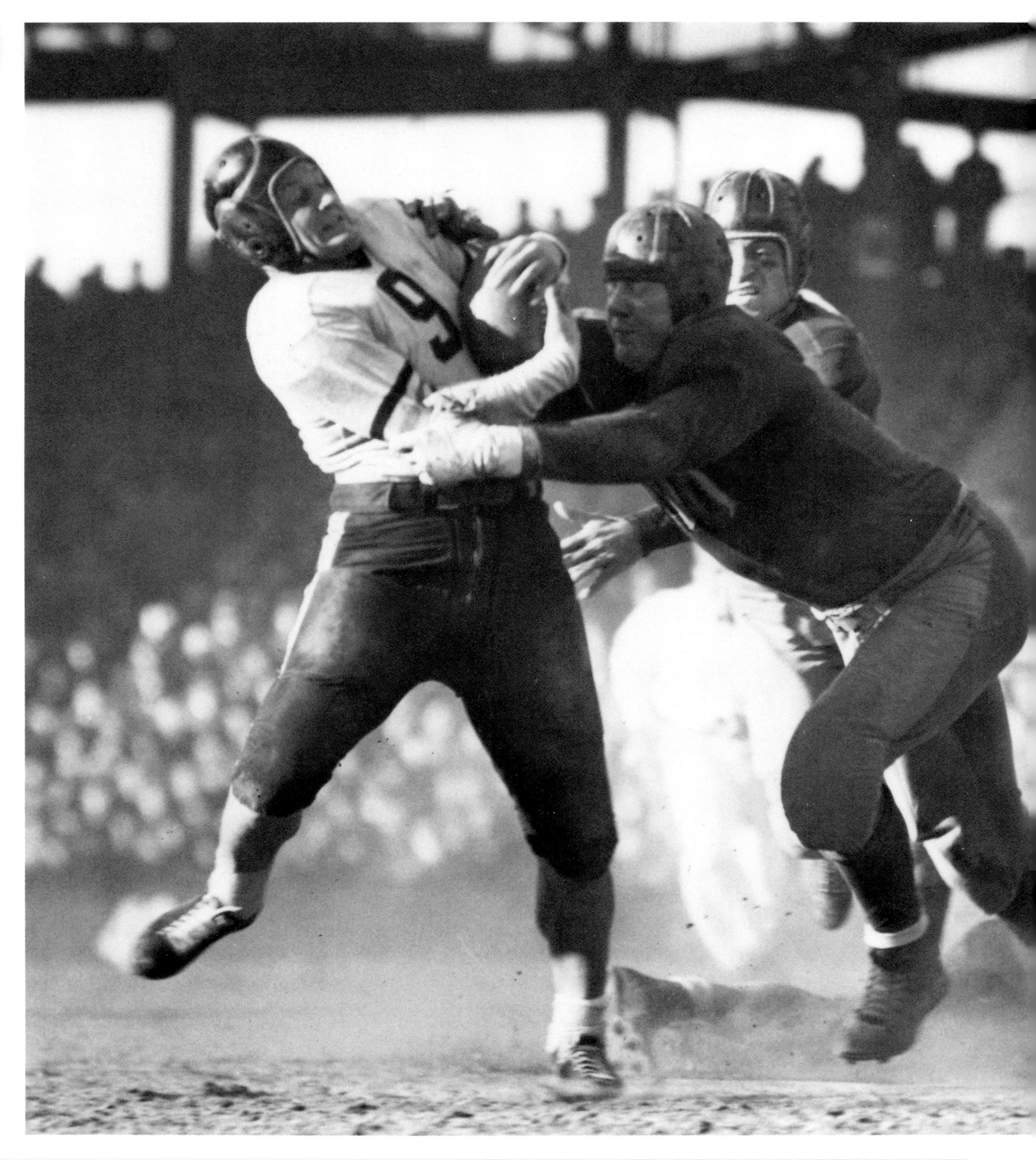

BELOW: *Chicago's George McAfee runs to the outside in the 1940 championship win over the Redskins.*

BELOW: *Bear quarterback Sid Luckman and coach George Halas share a smile on the bench during their 73-0 victory over the Redskins.*

offense. It also said a little something about the importance of coaching preparation and studying game films.

The results were almost unfathomable, considering that Washington, the divisional winner in the East with a 9-2 record, was a 7-5 favorite playing at home. Just three weeks earlier the Redskins had beaten the Bears, 7-3. That earlier victory, in fact, was the rub. With less than a minute to play, the Bears had moved to the Washington one-yard line, only to see time expire without their scoring. They complained bitterly of interference on a final pass play.

When the Washington papers described them as 'crybabies' and George Preston Marshall called them a 'first-half ball club,' George Halas and his Bears were bent on vengeance.

Halas posted Washington newspaper clippings in the team's locker room and sought the help of Stanford coach Clark Shaughnessy, who had a hand in devising the T-formation. Upon dissecting films of their earlier loss, the Bears' coaches realized the Redskins were particularly vulnerable to the counter play. So Chicago packed its offensive game plan with counters.

The Bears received the opening kickoff and on their second offensive play, big Bill 'Bull' Osmanski, their mammoth fullback, took a counter step to his right, then reversed and took the handoff for the left. He found the hole closed inside and slipped outside headed for the sideline. His size and speed turned the play into a nice gain, but it appeared two Skins safeties would drop him on the Washington 35. Just then Chicago end George Wilson came from across the field and threw a withering block on both backs, clearing

ABOVE: *George Halas and his Chicago Bears celebrate their 1940 championship in the locker room afterward.*

LEFT: *Pro football finally began to attract the attention of radio broadcasters in the late thirties and early forties, a sign that the game was finally receiving some long-deserved respect.*

Osmanski's way for a 77-yard scoring run. Speaking with reporters afterward, Halas called it the 'greatest, most vicious block I ever saw.'

Shortly thereafter, the Bears sustained another scoring drive and the rout was on. The first half ended 28-0, and the Bears might have been satisfied to let up the second half, if they hadn't been angered by Marshall's calling them a 'first-half team.' So they added 45 points in the second stanza, piling up the largest total in NFL Championship history.

Unfortunately for Washington and Marshall, the game was the first ever carried by network radio nationwide. With Red Barber giving the gruesome details, the Mutual Radio Network broadcast the game through its 120 stations. The rights fee was $2500.

Perhaps Marshall and his Redskins hoped the nation was too preoccupied with the thunder of the war in Europe and Asia to listen closely. As America moved closer to involvement, football games suddenly weren't so important anymore.

And with that, history would play its catastrophic card, wrecking lives and families. It also played havoc with football schedules. But, then again, that was the least of worries.

THE WAR YEARS

Their 73-0 win over the Washington Redskins in the 1940 championship was only the beginning for the Chicago Bears. With their T-formation, man-in-motion offense, they would dominate the NFL during World War II, powering their way to five title game appearances and four championships for 1940 to 1946.

The defenses of the era, which featured seven or eight down linemen, needed time to adjust to the man in motion, an offense that Chicago coach George Halas was said to have discovered in practice one day when an offensive back erred and went in motion ahead of the snap. Seeing his defense's uncertainty in countering the motion, Halas realized he had found an advantage. To cover the man in motion, a linebacker or defensive back would have to leave formation, thus opening and weakening the defense inside. If the defense ignored the motion man, he was open for a quick pass and a gain. Eventually, the defenses would learn to shift to four- and five-man fronts, which left more defenders in upright position to read offenses and adjust to their shifts and formations.

RIGHT: *Quarterback Sid Luckman was just the player to run the Chicago Bears' man-in-motion T-formation offense.*

LEFT: *George McAfee was an excellent power runner in the Bears' T-formation. He was inducted into the Hall of Fame in 1966.*

The T meant that the quarterback moved up under the center to call signals, placing him in the position to control the play. One at a time, opposing pro teams shelved the shotgun center of the single wing to adopt the T. But the new variation of old formation required an excellent athlete at quarterback, for all the pivoting and faking and flashy ball handling. If you had that player, the offense worked brilliantly. If you didn't, it was a newfangled disappointment.

Chicago had that player. Led by strong-armed quarterback Sid Luckman, the Bears' offense racked up a record 396 points in 1941 against an 11-game schedule. Their power backfield featured three excellent runners – Norm Standlee, George McAfee and Hugh Gallerneau. Their line was studded by center-linebacker Clyde 'Bulldog' Turner, utility man Danny Fortmann, tackle George Musso and tackle Joe Stydahar, all future Hall of Famers along with McAfee and Luckman. They beat Green Bay in a playoff game (the league had adopted the use of playoff games earlier that year) and faced New York in the league title game at Wrigley Field. Tougher than expected, the Giants trailed only 9-6 at the half, but the Bears

33

FAR LEFT: *Washington's Sammy Baugh was one of the all-time versatile players. Not only a great passer, Baugh led the league in interceptions (with 11) as a defensive back going both ways in 1942. He also led the league in punting from 1940 to 1944.*

LEFT: *Chicago's Sid Luckman was inducted into the Hall of Fame in 1965.*

BELOW: *Green Bay's Don Hutson became the NFL's first 1000-yard receiver with an incredible 1211 yards on 74 receptions in 1942.*

erupted for four second-half touchdowns (Standlee, the 230-pound rookie out of Stanford, scored twice) to win their second consecutive championship, 38-9.

History holds the 1941 Bears as a great, great team. But football championships were the least of the country's worries in December of 1941. Two weeks before the title game, the Japanese had bombed Pearl Harbor. Shortly after the season, George Halas dropped his coaching duties to become a lieutenant commander in the Navy, and several of his championship players, including McAfee, Turner, Luckman and Stydahar, eventually took their turns at military duty. By the war's end, 638 NFL players had served in the armed forces. Twenty-one of them lost their lives.

At home, the war left the NFL struggling along with the rest of society. Elmer Layden, the great Notre Dame coach, had become the league's first commissioner in 1941 (Carl Storck resigned as president shortly thereafter), and ran the NFL firmly during the war. As the fighting drained off more manpower, team rosters were reduced and franchises were combined briefly to compensate. Despite the handicaps, the spirit of competition was strong, and the individual accomplishments were notable:

*Green Bay's Don Hutson became the league's first 1000-yard receiver, by gaining 1211 yards on 74 receptions in 1942. He led the league in touchdowns from 1940 to 1944, and was tops in that category for a total of eight seasons.

*Washington quarterback Sammy Baugh was a top defensive player in 1943 with 11 pass interceptions. Baugh also led the league in punting from 1940 to 1944, averaging 51 yards per kick in 1940 and better than 45 yards per kick the remaining seasons. Baugh also holds a record for leading the league in passing – six seasons.

*Chicago's Sid Luckman turned in the NFL's first 400-yard passing game when he hit 21 of 32 for 433 yards and a record seven touchdowns against the New York Giants 14 November 1943 at the Polo Grounds. The game had been billed as 'Sid Luckman Day' to honor the Brooklyn boy who had gone to greatness with the Bears. In the emotion of that setting, Luckman responded with the greatest performance by a quarterback to that date. His seven touchdown passes have since been equalled but never bettered.

*The Giants' Bill Paschal led the league in rushing two consecutive seasons, 1943 and 1944.

*In 1942 Green Bay's Cecil Isbell became the league's first 2000-yard passer with 2021 yards on 146 completions. That led to another record, 24 touchdown passes, making him the first passer to break the 20-touchdown barrier.

*'Bullet Bill' Dudley, out of the University of Virginia, broke into the league with Pittsburgh in 1942 and immediately took the NFL rushing title with 696 yards.

The Bears, coached by Hunk Anderson and Luke Johnson, appeared headed toward a third consecutive title after they finished the regular season 11-0 in 1942. Their date in the title game was the Redskins, who had finished 10-1 and were still smarting from the 73-0 whipping in 1940.

As expected, the Bears were heavily favored to win their third consecutive championship. They took an early 6-0 lead, but then the Skins gathered their pride and toughed out a 14-6 victory on their single-wing attack featuring Sammy Baugh's throwing and the running of Andy Farkas. The winners' checks were $965 each, the largest ever.

The next year, the teams kept their date with a rematch, but this time Chicago's Sid Luckman took control. He closed out a fantastic season (including the earlier seven-touchdown performance over New York) by throwing five touchdown passes to destroy the Redskins, 41-21.

The war had so decimated the Bears' roster that Bronko Nagurski ended a five-year retirement to rejoin the team. After the 1943 season, Luckman joined the Merchant Marines, and the Bears got a look at their future without him. They were nosed out of the championship game by the Packers. The Giants did the same to the Redskins, and the 1944 championship game had a new look, the Giants vs. the Packers.

Another wrinkle came when former Packer great, quarterback Arnie Herber, came out of retirement to play for the Giants. Ken Strong, at age 40, was needed too badly by the Giants to retire. The Packers won, 14-7, on the second quarter passing combination of Irv Comp to Don Hutson.

The influence of the war remained heavy on the league. The Cleveland Rams suspended operations for the 1943 season, while the Pittsburgh and Philadelphia franchises merged for a year. The next season, Pittsburgh merged with the Chicago Cardinals for a year. The war years also brought expansion as owner Ted Collins opened the Boston Yanks franchise in 1944. There was substantial

LEFT: *Quarterback Frank Filchock helped guide the Washington Redskins to the championship game in 1945, where they lost 15-14 to the Cleveland Rams.*

RIGHT: *Bronko Nagurski ignored his injuries and came out of retirement to play during World War II when pro football's ranks were thinned by players entering the armed forces.*

BELOW: *End Wayne Millner was an important factor in the offense of the Redskins during the 1940s.*

rule change, as well, with 1943 bringing a mandatory helmet rule and free substitution. In 1944 the league allowed coaching from the bench, which had been prohibited. For 1945 the league required all players to wear long stockings.

The big rule, however, was a little noticed change that made a safety of any forward pass striking the goal posts and going out of bounds. That year in the championship game, one of Sammy Baugh's early passes would follow such a route, giving the Cleveland Rams a two-point score and ultimately enough margin for the championship. In the snow of Cleveland Stadium, they beat the favored Redskins, 15-14. The Redskins were led by Frank Filchock and end Wayne Millner.

The Rams were powered by the passing and kicking of rookie Bob Waterfield. Despite the championship, Rams owner Dan Reeves was fed up with the small crowd, 32,178, and the cold weather. He petitioned the other league owners to allow him to move the franchise to Los Angeles. Worried about increased travel costs, they refused. When Reeves threatened to leave the league, they relented. After all, they were worried. A new league had begun forming in 1944. The All-America Football Conference would begin play in 1946, bringing a storm of football brilliance with it.

That storm, of course, would be centered in Cleveland. At its eye was the incomparable Paul Brown.

PART III

The Golden Age of Pro Football

Peering back through the maze of Super Bowls and instant replays and colorful hype of the high tech professional game, it's understandable that the average fan of the 1980s and 1990s finds the 1950s brand of football a bit drab and pedestrian. Yet, hidden in those days of high-top black shoes and black-and-white television was the nugget, the adolescent essence of a great sports entertainment, that, given the advancement of technology, would explode into a sunburst, a motherlode.

The embodiment of this essence came in a succession of postwar stars, the Otto Grahams and Marion Motleys and Bill Dudleys and Bob Waterfields and Steve Van Burens and Norm Van Brocklins and Bobby Laynes and Doak Walkers and Jim Browns and Johnny Unitases and Y A Tittles. The league courted its fans on the strength of their offensive flash. But it also chiseled its foundation from the ruggedness and hard, mean edge of men like Chuck Bednarik.

Without the benefit of color broadcasts and instant replay, the players of the 1950s created an excitement that stirred the public. Often this excitement is traced to the 1958 sudden-death championship game between the New York Giants and Baltimore Colts. Certainly the coming of age of Johnny Unitas before a nationwide television audience was a major factor. But more than a game, it was a decade that booted pro football into its gaudy, high-dollar future. The players of the 1950s achieved the appreciation of pro football's currency. They played the game well. They did it with grit. They brought it greatness. And they made relatively little money doing it. 'There's no tougher way to make easy money than pro football,' Van Brocklin once said. Because the athletes of the 1950s played for thousands, their counterparts in the 1980s can play for millions. ('No player is worth a million dollars,' Red Grange said recently. 'I can understand why a player would have an agent. I couldn't keep from laughing if I went in and demanded a million dollars from an owner.')

An NFL franchise in 1940 was worth approximately $50,000, an iota of its value two decades later. The men who persisted in fomenting this odd entertainment – George Halas, Tim Mara, Art Rooney and a score of others – made substantial wealth for themselves and their families. Certainly they contributed greatly and were rewarded.

But the game was also built on the backs of hundreds of anonymous players, or on the mind of Hugh 'Shorty' Ray, the diminutive statistician who tinkered with pro football's rules through the forties and fifties, learning the warp and rhythm of the passing game, streamlining its features toward a sleek modern vehicle, suited for the spectator, prime for modern television production. This group of men was the last to profit little from the game. For the most part, they gave to it more than they took away. They were the essence of pro football's golden age.

THE BROWN REVOLUTION
THE ALL-AMERICA FOOTBALL CONFERENCE

In the first quarter century of the NFL, rival leagues were born and died with amazing frequency. Once or twice a decade, these leagues would appear, threatening the NFL by competing for players and fans, driving up costs and shaking what little stability organized football had mustered. Thus, it was no surprise that Commissioner Elmer Layden responded with irritation when the All-America Football Conference began stirring in 1944 and 1945.

'Let them get a football,' Layden had retorted when the new league announced its intentions to begin play with eight teams in 1946. Little did Layden, who resigned in January of 1946, or anyone else forsee that this new organization would contribute to the fabric of pro football in such a quick, powerful manner.

The AAFC offered teams in four established NFL markets – the Los Angeles Dons, the Chicago Rockets, the New York Yankees and the Brooklyn Dodgers – and filled the vacancy left in Cleveland when the Rams moved to Los Angeles. In addition, the new league moved into Baltimore, Miami and San Francisco.

The competition would bring a vicious bloodletting in pro football, as franchises in both leagues began bidding for players and suffering financially soon after. The New York Yankees registered a coup in luring star quarterback Clarence 'Ace' Parker away from the Boston Yanks of the NFL. The Yankees also picked up veteran NFL coach Ray Flaherty, whose Redskin teams had played in four NFL championship games and won two of them. The new league would also introduce players such as Joe Perry and Arnie Weinmeister on their way to football greatness.

But the AAFC's major contribution was the discovering and promotion of gridiron genius. Overwhelming genius. Mickey McBride, owner of the league's new Cleveland franchise, went looking for the best coach in football. When McBride found that coach, he not only gave him a five-year contract and a percentage of franchise ownership, he named the team after the man. Paul Brown

RIGHT: *Coach Paul Brown was a precise, disciplined man who brought greatness to the Cleveland Browns of the infant All-America Football Conference in 1946. He continued that greatness when the Browns joined the NFL in 1950.*

LEFT: *Quarterback Otto Graham was the central figure in the Cleveland Browns' powerful precision offense.*

was 36 years old at the time and still in the service when he took over as head of what would become the Cleveland Browns. He had been the head coach at a Massillon high school, then moved on to Ohio State, where he guided the Buckeyes to a national championship.

His first act as Browns coach was to seek out the services of Otto Graham, another serviceman who had been a utility tailback of sorts at Northwestern University. Although Graham ran and blocked, Brown had seen him throw a pass and instantly recognized his ability. An accomplished player of the cornet, violin and French horn (he was the child of music teachers), Graham was tall, strong and fast. Plus, he had the peripheral vision that made him a great quarterback and an incredibly accurate thrower.

Around him, Brown built an awesomely efficient, powerful team, with Dante Lavelli and Mac Speedie as lightning receivers. Looking in remote places for talent, Brown added Marion Motley, a great black running back from the University of Nevada, and Ray Renfro from North Texas State. Brown was a slender, cultured man, balding and unassuming. Yet he encased this talent he had collected in a

regimen unknown to the brawling, rowdy sport. His players were required to keep notebooks, which they religiously stuffed with the football knowledge Brown fed them. Conditioning and diet were carefully controlled.

Brown believed heartily in the passing game and directed his attention to perfecting a great one. His major innovation was the shifting of the offense to a complicated attack with multiple receivers. In Graham, Speedie, Lavelli and Motley, he had the ideal ingredients.The results were terrifying, nearly fatal, to the rest of the AAFC. In the four years of the league's existence, the Browns won all four championships, compiling a record of 52 wins, four losses and two ties. In each of the 1947, 1948 and 1949 seasons, Graham passed for more than 2700 yards, far more than any other quarterback had totalled in a three-year period.

The Browns' first game drew more than 60,000 fans, but it quickly became apparent that they dominated the league. They ran up enormous leads that killed fan interest. When reporters and rival owners complained, Brown responded that he'd rather win in front of 10,000 than lose in front of 50,000.

The financial competition was too much for both leagues, and in 1949 NFL Commissioner Bert Bell announced the merger of the two into the National-American Football League for the 1950 season. From the eight AAFC teams, only three – the Browns, the Baltimore Colts and the San Francisco 49ers – survived to the NFL. Yet their competitive effect would be felt almost immediately, particularly that of Paul Brown. He proved to the pro football world that genius has a way of creating its own elbow room.

LEFT: *NFL Commissioner Bert Bell announced that the NFL would merge with the All-America Football Conference in 1950.*

TOP: *The Cleveland Browns' gifted backfield included (left to right) Bob Brown, Otto Graham, Marion Motley and Edgar Jones.*

REGROUPING
THE NFL 1946-1947

Price 15 Cents

NEW YORK GIANTS

vs.

PHILADELPHIA EAGLES

MERLE HAPES

POLO GROUNDS

Sunday October 11, 1942

Although Commissioner Elmer Layden resigned in early 1946 and was replaced by Bert Bell, co-owner of the Pittsburgh Steelers, the NFL regained its footing on familiar turf in the aftermath of World War II. Specifically, the Chicago Bears and George Halas won another championship with Sid Luckman at quarterback.

The league experimented for a year with free substitution, and it added the West Coast look with the Rams moving to Los Angeles. But any upbeat developments were dampened by a gambling investigation of two New York Giant players – Frank Filchock and Merle Hapes – just before the Giants met the Bears for the title game. Hapes reported he had been offered money to throw the title game, and for his honesty, he was suspended. Filchock denied he had been offered anything (he later admitted he had) and was allowed to play. Despite a strong effort by Filchock, the Giants' quarterback, the Bears won, 24-14.

The league immediately strengthened its gambling penalties in early 1947, and Bell, who had moved the league offices from the Chicago suburbs to the Philadelphia suburbs, was given a contract extension.

The NFL teams were feeling the pressure of competition from the AAFC, and it's no coincidence that the team owners decided to initiate a 'bonus' draft, giving them an extra early pick of college players. The league also brought back sudden-death playoff rules and added a fifth game official, the back judge.

On the field, the elder league saw substantial development in 1947. Washington's Sammy Baugh passed for an incredible 2938

LEFT: *New York's Merle Hapes was the center of a gambling investigation just before the 1946 NFL Championship, when he reported he had been offered money to throw the game.*

BELOW: *The Bears and the Giants scramble for a loose ball and the trophy in the 1946 title game at the Polo Grounds. The Bears won, 24-14.*

ABOVE: *The Chicago Bears were all smiles in the Polo Grounds locker room after their 1946 championship victory.*

RIGHT: *Fullback Pat Harder was one of the reasons the Chicago Cardinals claimed the 1947 NFL Championship.*

yards. Frank Gehrke of the Los Angeles Rams added some color when he painted horns on the team's helmets, giving pro football its first helmet insignias.

But the big story of the league was the first championship of the Chicago Cardinals, who had struggled for years in the shadow of Halas and his Bears. Owner Charles Bidwell had sunk much effort into making the Cards a success, the misfortune of that being that he died in 1947 before the title game. The aces in the Cards were fullback Pat Harder, quarterback Paul Christman, and halfbacks Marshall Goldberg, Elmer Angsman and Charley Trippi. The Cards' title game opponents were another league surprise, the Philadelphia Eagles, who had blanked Pittsburgh to win the Eastern Division playoff. The Eagles were powered by emerging star running back Steve Van Buren and quarterback Tommy Thompson.

Thompson played magnificently in the title game, completing 27 of 44 passes for 297 yards, but the Cards broke a series of long runs to edge Philly, 28-21. Van Buren had gained 1008 yards during the 1947 season, making him the second runner to do so (Beattie Feathers of the Chicago Bears was the first), but the Cards' defense held him to 26 yards in the championship game.

Meanwhile, Angsman (with two 70-yard touchdown runs) and Trippi (with a 75-yard punt return) ran wild. The crowd of 30,000 at Comiskey Park, most of them loyal Cardinal fans, had plenty to cheer about. As for the Eagles, their appearance in the championship game was no fluke. They served notice to the rest of the league that they would be back.

LEFT: *Running back Charley Trippi scored a touchdown off a 75-yard punt return for the Chicago Cardinals in the 1947 championship game. He was inducted into the Hall of Fame in 1968.*

BELOW: *The Eagles complete a pass during the 1947 title game played at Chicago's Comiskey Park before a crowd of 30,000.*

Chicago Cardinals Charley Trippi is tackled during a first-quarter punt return in the 1947 championship game.

68
77
79

PHILADELPHIA AND THE FLYING DUTCHMAN

In its three decades of existence, the NFL had seen its brand of fortune settle on a select few. The Chicago Bears, the Green Bay Packers, the Washington Redskins, even the New York Giants occasionally, all had their share of the championship spotlight. The menu for the league's other clubs was mostly leftovers.

That all changed with the winds that swept in after World War II. The Chicago Cardinals and Philadelphia Eagles had met in the 1947 title game and liked it so much, they decided on a rematch for 1948. It was there, in their first championship, that Earle 'Greasy' Neale's players attained the status of a powerhouse.

The Eagles' great power back, Steve Van Buren, continued to dominate the league's rushing statistics with his blend of strength and speed. A 6 foot 1 inch 210-pounder out of LSU, Van Buren had been the Eagles' top draft choice in 1944, and after a rookie year hampered by injuries, he rushed to the top in 1945, taking the league's rushing and scoring titles. His 18 touchdowns would stand as a record until Green Bay's Jim Taylor scored 19 in 1962. By 1948 Van Buren would set a new league seasonal rushing record, 1146 yards, fueled by 205-yard performance on 27 carries against Pittsburgh

ABOVE: *Philadelphia Eagle guard Bucko Kilroy played a big role in his team's powerful running game of the late 1940s.*

TOP RIGHT: *Philadelphia quarterback Tommy Thompson threw for 1965 yards in 1948 and led his team to the league championship.*

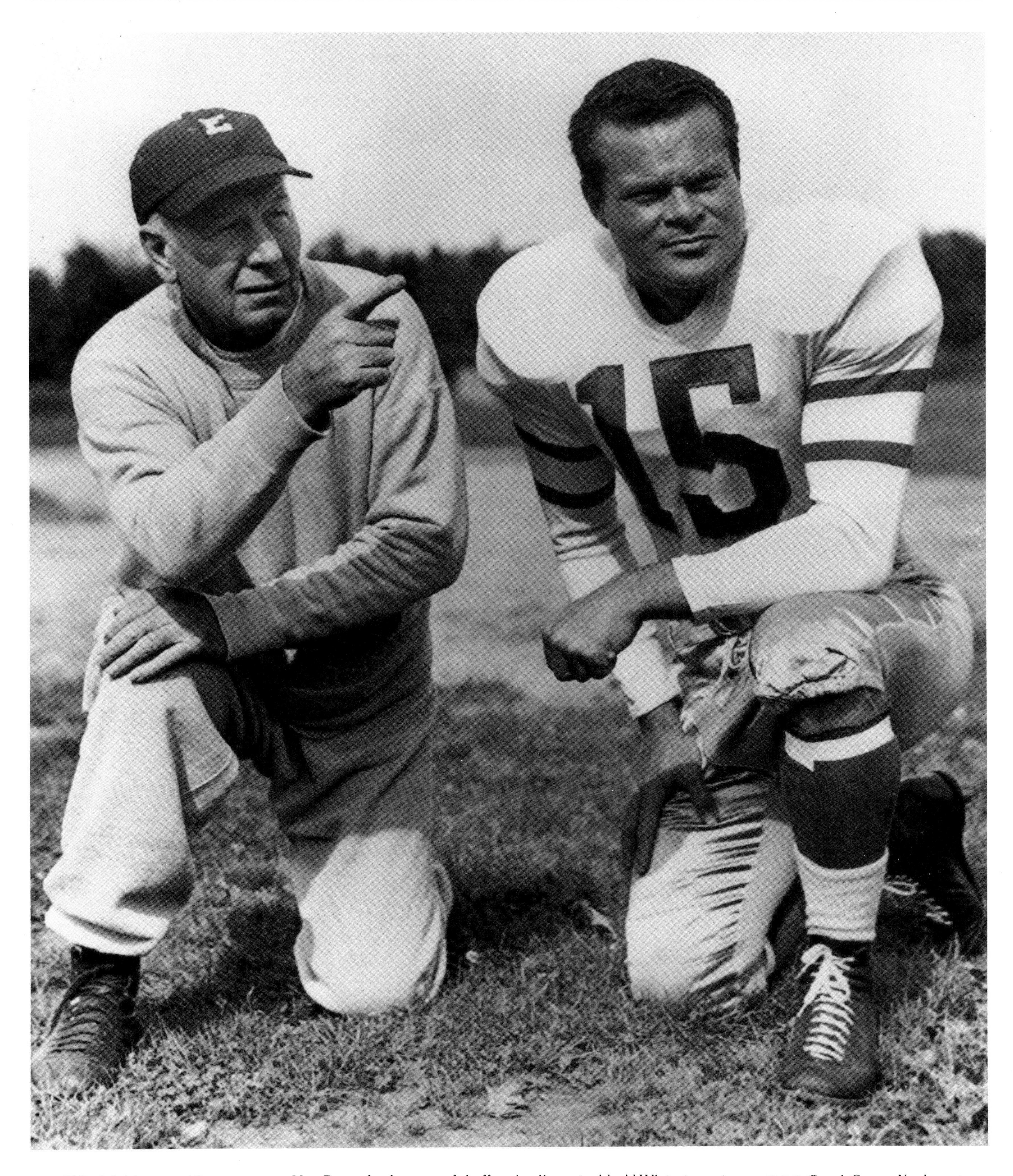

LEFT: *Philadelphia center Vic Lindskog was the core of a powerful Eagle offensive line that opened the way for running back Steve Van Buren.*

Van Buren had a powerful offensive line – tackle Al Wistert, center Vic Lindskog, and guards Cliff Patton and Bucko Kilroy. He loved to display his power running over right tackle.

But Neale's Eagles were by no means one dimensional. Quarterback Tommy Thompson threw for 1965 yards in 1948. Another feature was Neale's fabled 7-4 defense, led by 240-pound linebacker, Alex Wojchiechowicz, whose playing style was described by Eagle assistant Allie Sherman as 'hands and feet and arms and maybe even fingernails, plus some conversation.'

ABOVE: *Coach Greasy Neale and running back Steve Van Buren were respectively the brains and the brawn of the 1948 Philadelphia Eagles.*

That combination helped the Eagles back to the title game in 1948, which was played in a blizzard at Philadelphia's Shibe Field. There was little offensive movement in the snow that day, save for the 98 yards Van Buren hammered out in 26 carries, which was good enough for a 7-0 victory.

The weather served Philadelphia no better in the 1949 championship, played against the Los Angeles Rams at their Memorial Coliseum. This time the deterrent was torrential rain. Ram officials considered postponing the game, but NFL Commissioner Bert Bell had arranged a radio broadcast and a $30,000 deal with the Dumont Network to televise the game coast to coast.

Thus, the championship became the slosh-and-slide bowl. Luckily for the Eagles, Van Buren was up to the weather. His 1146 yards rushing during the season had helped them to an 11-1 record. That was only a prelude to his 196 yards on 31 carries against the Rams. On down after down, he moved through the ankle-deep mud, punching the Eagles to a 14-0 win and their second championship.

But if fans in Philadelphia were thinking dynasty, it didn't last long. Just days before the title game, Commissioner Bell had announced the NFL and the AAFC would merge for the 1950 season. Suddenly, the Eagles had another powerhouse to confront, the Cleveland Browns.

Although the AAFC was considered an inferior league, the football world was curious about Paul Brown's juggernaut. Just how good were they? It didn't take much of the 1950 season to find out. They were very good.

BELOW: *Steve Van Buren, Philadelphia's 'Flying Dutchman,' carries for extra yardage in a 1948 game against the Chicago Cardinals.*

ABOVE: *Philadelphia running back Clyde Scott runs into the Los Angeles defense during the 1949 championship game in the mud at Los Angeles' Memorial Coliseum.*

LEFT: *Eagle tackle Al Wistert (left) holds a trophy presented to the team at a chamber of commerce dinner following the 1948 championship.*

MERGER

The 1950 season brought a classic pro football confrontation. The AAFC was merged with the NFL. First, the teams had to straighten out their league name. They began the season calling themselves 'The National-American Football League,' but three months into 1950, they wisely reverted to the good old NFL.

It was a big year for pro ball. The Los Angeles Rams arranged a deal to have all their games televised, making them the first team to do so. George Preston Marshall also arranged substantial television coverage for his Washington Redskins, although they struggled, due in part to Marshall's insistence on not using black players.

The league also passed a free substitution rule, which opened the way for two-platoon football and played into the hands of the very innovative Paul Brown. He used the rule to run players in and out of the game with plays from the bench, which brought all his craft and experience to bear on the contest. This practice, for some reason, annoyed newspapermen and opposing coaches. Otto Graham, the Browns' great quarterback, wasn't exactly pleased either. But he kept quiet. Brown, after all, was a master. And his Browns were a masterpiece.

The NFL found that out on the first game of the season, when the Browns met the defending NFL Champions, the Eagles. In all fairness, Philadelphia was hurting, with back Steve Van Buren out with a foot injury. Halfback Bosh Pritchard was also out, and Captain Al Wistert, a tackle, was playing hurt.

Graham completed 21 of 38 passes for 310 yards and three touchdowns. For good measure, he sneaked over a score in the fourth period, as Cleveland won, 35-10. Commissioner Bell conceded the issue in Cleveland's locker room afterward. 'You have as fine a football team as I've ever seen,' he told Brown.

The remainder of the season bore that out as the Browns won the American Conference with a 10-2 record and blew past the New York Giants, 8-3, to face Los Angeles for the crown on Christmas Eve.

The Rams had come into their own, having come back to the title game for a second year after winning the National Conference with a 9-3 record. They had thumped the Bears, 24-14, in the playoffs. Alternating quarterbacks Bob Waterfield and Norm Van Brocklin,

LEFT: *Quarterback Otto Graham was more than ready for the Cleveland Browns' move into NFL competition in 1950.*

RIGHT: The two fine quarterbacks for the Los Angeles Rams – Bob Waterfield and Norm Van Brocklin – confer with backfield coach Hamp Pool in November 1950.

PAGES 102-103: *Cleveland quarterback Otto Graham picks up 12 yards against the Los Angeles Rams in the 1950 championship game, a thriller won by the Browns, 30-28.*

BROWNS WERE 1300
EAST OHIO GAS
CLEVELAND

BALL AT BAT VISITORS
STRIKE OUT INN CLEVELAND

they had averaged nearly 40 points a contest over 12 regular season games. Van Brocklin and Waterfield combined for 3709 yards passing, more than 300 per game. They had scored 10 touchdowns against Baltimore and nine against Green Bay. Receiver Tom Fears had caught 84 passes, extending his league receiving crown to a third straight season.

The Rams also had a good stable of running backs in Glenn Davis, Verda Smith, Tom Kalminir, Paul Younger, Dan Towler and Dan Pasquariello. LA's single liability came when Van Brocklin injured his ribs in the playoffs with Chicago.

Some, including Commissioner Bell, have argued that the 1950 NFL Championship was the greatest ever played. In all, six records would be set and three others tied. On the first offensive play, Davis hesitated as the action went right, then released from the backfield and caught a pass from Waterfield and ran 82 yards for the score. Graham answered with a scoring pass for Cleveland and the race was on. LA led at the half, 14-13.

When Marion Motley fumbled on the Browns' six in the second half, Larry Brink picked up the ball and ran it in for a 28-20 Rams' lead. Graham threw a TD pass to bring the score to 28-27. Then he guided a late drive to the LA 10, where Lou Groza kicked a field goal with 20 seconds left for a 30-28 win and the championship.

If the Browns' championship wasn't enough insult for the NFL, the American Conference added to it that January by defeating the National Conference 28-27 in the Pro Bowl, which had been revived for the first time since 1942.

There were other changes for 1951. Owner Abraham Watner decided to give up on the Baltimore Colts' franchise and returned it to the league. On the field, the league decided to make interior linemen ineligible for the forward pass.

LEFT: *Cleveland's Lou Groza kicks the winning field goal in the Browns' 30-28 win over Los Angeles for the 1950 NFL Championship.*

ABOVE: *The Los Angeles Rams' backfield was dubbed the 'Bull Elephants' by the press because its players averaged well over 200 pounds. Left to right are Dan Towler, Dick Hoerner, Tank Younger, and Bob Waterfield.*

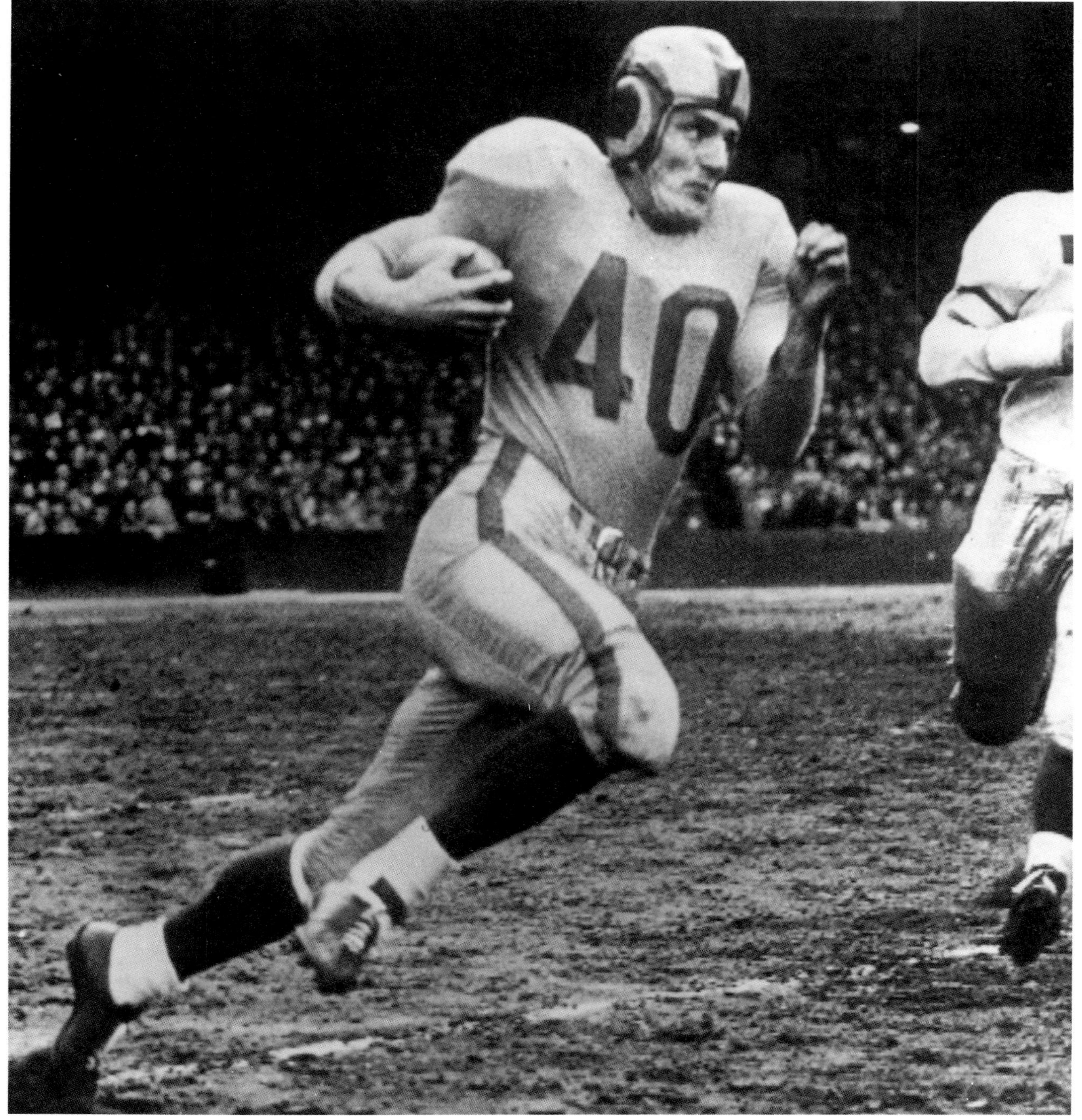

LEFT: *Rams receiver Elroy 'Crazy Legs' Hirsch broke Don Hutson's receiving record in 1951 with 1495 yards. He also scored 17 touchdowns. Hirsch was named to the Hall of Fame in 1968.*

ABOVE: *The Rams gained vengeance over the Browns in the 1951 championship, winning 24-17. Here Los Angeles threatens the Cleveland goal.*

However, there were no changes in the championship match-up. The fiesty Browns with an 11-1 record went to Memorial Coliseum to play the Rams, who had mustered only an 8-4 season. The DuMont Network again bought the broadcast rights, this time for $75,000.

The Rams worked a magnificent upset to return some respect to the NFL, with Van Brocklin throwing to Fears and Elroy 'Crazy Legs' Hirsch. During the season, Hirsch had shattered Don Hutson's receiving record with 1495 yards and 17 touchdowns. Hirsch and Fears combined for 212 yards on eight receptions against the Browns.

But it was the LA defense, led by Larry Brink and Andy Robustelli, that sacked Graham for 47 yards in losses and held Marion Motley to only 23 yards rushing.

In the fourth quarter, Van Brocklin threw 73 yards to Fears for the winning touchdown in a 24-17 victory.

TOP RIGHT: *Rams coach Joe Stydahar gets a victory ride after the 1951 championship.*

RIGHT: *The rowdy Rams celebrate their title in the locker room after the 1951 championship.*

11

REVOLVING CHAMPIONS, 1952-1955
DETROIT – LA – CLEVELAND

The 1952 season held a sad mix of new and old. A new franchise, the Dallas Texans, finished the year 1-11 and folded. And the Pittsburgh Steelers finally gave up the single wing for the T-formation, becoming the last pro team to do so.

Meanwhile, Cleveland continued its mastery of the American Division. But the focus of the championship shifted. Across Lake Erie, the Detroit Lions had assembled a nifty little offense around two Texas boys, quarterback Bobby Layne and halfback Doak Walker, who had played on the same high school team. They had gone to separate colleges, Walker to SMU, Layne to the University of Texas. But they reunited to lead Detroit to a 17-7 victory over the Browns in the 1952 championship game.

Still, the experts noted that the Browns had mostly fumbled the game away, and the Lions seemed to have something to prove all over again as the 1953 season began.

It was a red-letter year for several reasons. Carroll Rosenbloom organized a group in Baltimore, and the Colts were reborn. On a sad note, Jim Thorpe died that March. And in a court battle, the league ascertained its right to black out television broadcasts of home games to which all tickets weren't sold.

On the field, the Battle of Lake Erie continued. From the outset of the season, the Browns, fired by Paul Brown's desire, seemed primed to smash their way right to the championship. They won their first 11 games, including a 62-14 humiliation of the rival New York Giants, and claimed the divisional title handily. Cleveland seemed invincible in taking a 21-0 lead over Philadelphia in the last regular-season game. Suddenly the Eagles came alive and buried the Browns, 42-27, in one of the most startling comebacks in NFL history.

The game, however, is merely a footnote, for the Browns had already claimed the division and were headed for the title game with Detroit. The real impact of the loss to the Eagles was that it left a cloud of doubt in Cleveland's confidence.

For their part, the Lions had dallied a bit before winning their division with a 10-2 record. But they had finished strong and carried their momentum into the championship on their home field,

LEFT: Bobby Layne came out of the University of Texas and led the Detroit Lions to the NFL Championship in 1952. Detroit beat Cleveland 17-7 for the title.

RIGHT: Doak Walker, an SMU product, provided the ground game for the Detroit Lions' powerhouses of the 1950s. He's shown here in a 1950 game against the New York Yankees.

Detroit's Briggs Stadium.

All in all, the 1953 game was marked by tremendous defense. But as always seems the case, the golden moments fell to the quarterbacks and receivers, and like any great NFL quarterback, Bobby Layne was eager for the gold.

On the down side, either quarterback – Layne or Cleveland's Otto Graham – could have worn the goat's horns that day. Both contributed their share of turnovers leading to opponent's scores. The game opened with Lions rookie linebacker Joe Schmidt nailing Graham and forcing a fumble inside the Browns' 20. The Lions battered the ball in after several plays, with Walker scoring on a one-yard dive, then kicking the conversion.

The Browns got a similar opportunity in the second quarter when they recovered a fumble at the Detroit six. But the defense held, and Cleveland was resigned to a Lou Groza field goal.

RIGHT: *Cleveland kicker Lou Groza, shown here with holder Tom James, was the talented toe in coach Paul Brown's scoring machine.*

LEFT: *Detroit end Jim Doran catches a Bobby Layne pass to set up the winning field goal in the Lions' 17-16 victory over the Cleveland Browns for the 1953 championship.*

RIGHT: *The Lions (top row, left to right) Sherwin Candee, Thurman McGraw, Jim David, John Prchlik, Les Bingaman, and (bottom row) Yale Lary, Jack Christiansen and assistant coach Gerrard Ramsey celebrate their 1953 championship.*

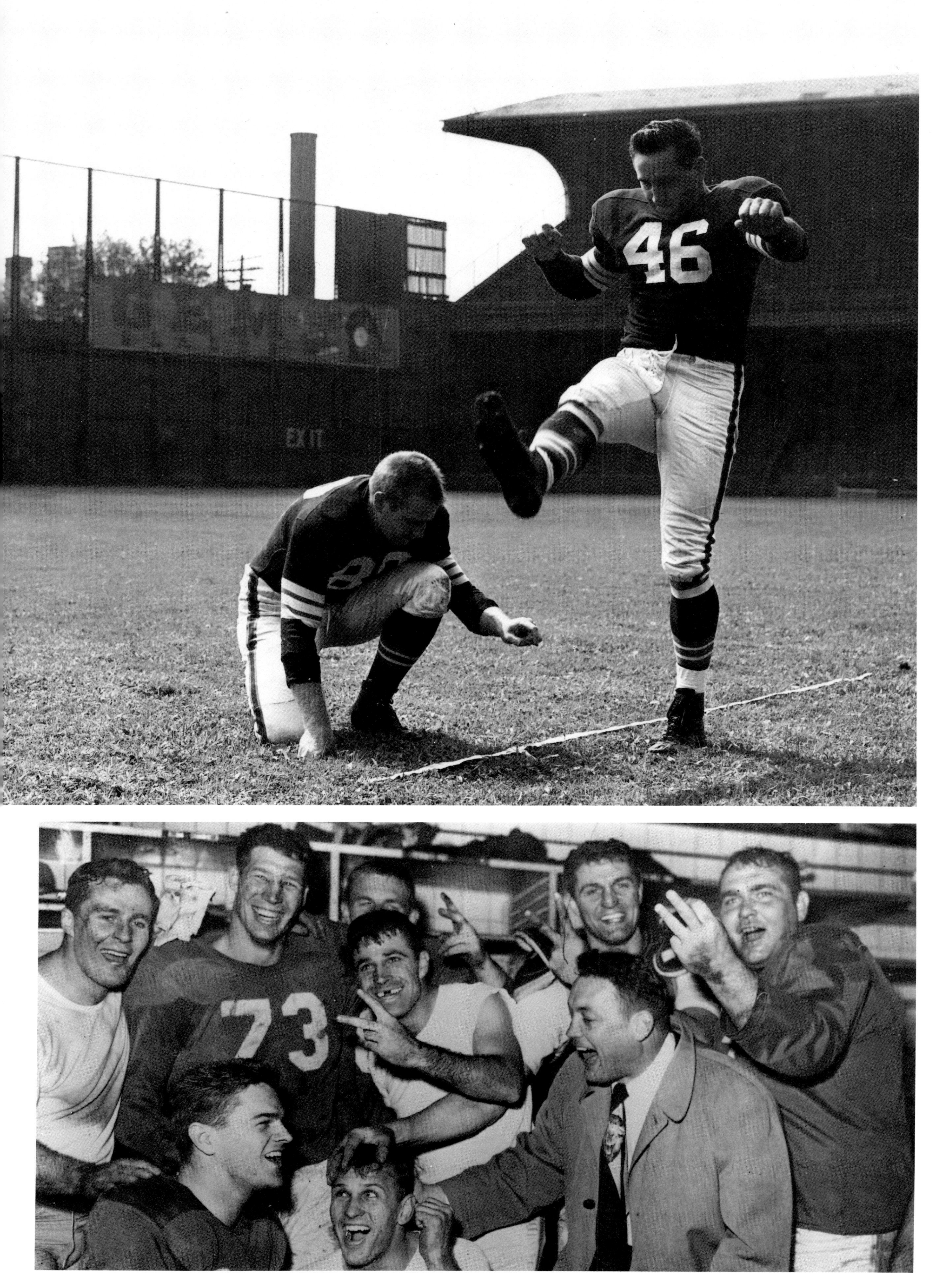
EXIT

It was a miserable day for Graham, the league's leading passer who had completed better than 62 percent of his passes during the regular season. His performance changed completely in the championship. The Lions sacked and befuddled the normally unshakeable Graham into connecting on only 2 of 15 attempts for 31 yards. While he struggled, Detroit forged ahead, as Walker added a field goal, giving Detroit a 10-3 halftime lead.

The Cleveland players were steamed in a scathing talk from Brown at intermission, which was enough to reverse the tide in the third quarter. Layne contributed two turnovers to the Browns' effort. First, he threw an interception, which led to Cleveland's drive to tie the score. Then at the end of the quarter, Layne fumbled, the Browns recovered and Groza kicked a field goal for a 13-10 lead.

With 4:10 to play, Groza added another field goal for a 16-10 lead that seemed solid on a day dominated by defenses. It was the type of challenge Layne thrived on.

Detroit's hopes for an offensive resurgence were dimmed by the loss of all-star end Leon Hart in the first half. His substitute was Jim Doran, a converted defensive back who had been the team's MVP the year before but had played little during the last half of the 1953 season. Doran and Browns defensive back Warren Lahr had tussled through the second half, a confrontation that would become the focus of Detroit's last-ditch drive.

Starting at his own 20, Layne drove the Lions with a series of passes to Doran. Quickly, the Lions found themselves at the Cleveland 33 with a first down, a perfect setting for surprise. Lions' coach Buddy Parker wanted a screen pass, but Doran came to the huddle pleading for a chance to beat Lahr long. Layne listened.

On the snap, Doran headed at Lahr as if to block him, then bolted long with a yard lead on the Browns' defender. The pass was there for a 33-yard touchdown, just one of the many completions that nailed down Layne's reputation as the original comeback quarterback. It also helped reserve him a place in the Hall of Fame. The home crowd roared that day as Walker came on the field to kick the extra point, for a 17-16 Detroit championship. Carl Karilivacz intercepted Graham's last pass and killed Cleveland's drive.

The Browns salved any hurt they might have felt the next year, when the teams met for a third consecutive championship bout.

LEFT: *Doak Walker calmly kicks the conversion point to give the Lions their 17-16 victory for the 1953 championship.*

LEFT: *Cleveland quarterback Otto Graham was all smiles after the Browns' championship drive of 1955. He retired at the close of the season after having led the Browns to consecutive championships in 1954 and 1955.*

RIGHT: *San Francisco running back Joe Perry (no. 34) became the first NFL runner to produce back-to-back 1000-yard seasons, in 1954 and 1955. He was inducted into the Hall of Fame in 1969.*

Cleveland settled the rubber match by soundly thumping the favored Lions, 56-10, for the 1954 championship. Layne suffered through a terrible day, throwing six interceptions.

Graham, who had passed for more than 2700 yards during the season, had announced his retirement before the game. But after he passed for 163 yards and ran for three touchdowns, he changed his mind.

It was a good decision. He shared the spotlight that season with San Francisco running back Joe Perry, who became the first man to have back-to-back 1000-yard rushing seasons. But in the end, it was all Graham.

The Browns returned to the championship in 1955 to meet the Rams, who had been led there by Van Brocklin's 2637 yards passing. A crowd of 85,693 crammed into Los Angeles Coliseum, a sign that pro football had arrived. They saw Graham complete 14 of 25 passes for 202 yards and two touchdowns. He ran two other scores across. With a 38-14 win and another championship, it was finally time to retire.

FULL STRIDE

The networks made their move in the mid-1950s. NBC paid $100,000 to replace the DuMont Network for the broadcast rights to the 1955 championship. That next fall, CBS began limited broadcasts of regular-season games.

For an instant, the old hands made their appearance on center stage. George Halas turned over the coaching of the Bears to Paddy Driscoll, who promptly took them to the 1956 title game where they were humiliated by another old-timer, the New York Giants, 47-7. Chicago's Rick Casares had led the league in rushing and Ed Brown had done the same in passing. But the day belonged to the Giants, with young names like Gifford and Webster.

The 1957 season would bring the league good fortune, particularly in another record crowd at Los Angeles Coliseum, as 102,368 fans turned out for an October Rams game with the 49ers.

Yet 1957 is best remembered for its resumption of the Battle of Lake Erie, although an appearance by Detroit in the title game didn't seem possible at the start of the season. At least coach Buddy Parker thought not. 'I can't handle a losing season,' he told reporters. 'This team of ours is the worst I've ever seen in training. I'm leaving Detroit . . . tonight.'

Assistant coach George Wilson took over, and somehow Detroit moved along, staying in contention for the title. Then, with two games remaining, the Lions faced another setback – the loss of quarterback Bobby Layne to a leg injury.

With substitute Tobin Rote at quarterback, Detroit tied San Francisco for the Western Conference regular season title (both

ABOVE: *New York Giants Bill Svoboda, Em Tunnell and Alex Webster celebrate the team's first championship in 18 years, a 47-7 triumph over the Chicago Bears, in the 1956 title game.*

RIGHT: *New York fullback Mel Triplett scored on an 18-yard run in the first quarter of the 1956 championship. The sequence shows Triplett powering his way over a group of Bear defenders and the referee.*

LEFT: *The Giants' Dick Modzelewski (no. 77) moves in to tackle Bears running back Rick Casares in the first quarter of the 1956 championship.*

1
2
3

LEFT: *New York's Alex Webster was the power in the Giants' backfield of the 1950s.*

RIGHT: *Quarterback Tobin Rote led the Detroit Lions along a storybook path to the 1957 championship. The route included an incredible come-from-behind playoff victory over Y A Tittle and the San Francisco 49ers.*

teams had 8-4 records). But San Francisco – with Y A Tittle at quarterback, Hugh McElhenny in the backfield and R C Owens at receiver – was the favorite for the playoffs. The 49ers were playing at home, in Kezar Stadium, before a crowd of nearly 60,000. Without Layne, Detroit's main offensive weapon was running back Tom 'the Bomb' Tracy. But the public sentiment was that Detroit would get bombed, rather than turn any loose.

On Tittle's passing, the 49ers moved to an early 14-0 lead before the Lions momentarily found their offensive stride. Rote threw Steve Junker a three-yard touchdown pass to pull Detroit to 14-7. The 49ers answered with Tittle's third touchdown pass for a 21-7 lead. After Gordy Soltau added a field goal right before the half, San Francisco team officials seemed comfortable enough with a 24-7 lead to announce the sale of championship game tickets over the stadium public address system. Smarting, the Lions sat in their locker room where through the walls they could hear the 49ers beginning their celebration early.

The insult immediately deepened as McElhenny took the second half kickoff and spun his way to the Lions' nine-yard line before being tackled by Detroit's great defensive halfback, Yale Lary. In that dark moment backed up against their goal line, the Lions turned tough, and allowed the 49ers only a field goal for a 27-7 lead.

BELOW: *Y A Tittle had a brilliant career as a pro quarterback with the San Francisco 49ers and the New York Giants, but was ultimately frustrated in that his teams never won a championship.*

From that point on, the San Francisco offense resembled a train stalled on a hill. On the next series, Tittle fumbled on his own 28. The Lions recovered, and nine plays later, Tracy rammed in for a score, making it 27-14. The Lion defense held, but when the offense got the ball back, it went nowhere. Then came the call of the decade. Facing fourth down on his own 20, George Wilson told Rote to pass instead of punt.

The gamble worked, with Rote throwing to Howard 'Hopalong' Cassidy for 14 yards and a first down. Moments later, Tracy exploded on a weaving, exhilarating 58-yard touchdown run. The score was 27-21, with almost three minutes left in the third quarter.

RIGHT: *Detroit's Gene Gedman scores the winning touchdown in the Lions' miraculous victory over San Francisco for the 1957 Western Conference crown.*

BELOW: *The Lions – quarterback Tobin Rote, coach George Wilson, back Tom Tracy, assistant coach Buster Ramsey and team captain Joe Schmidt – celebrate their conference championship.*

The 49ers, it seemed, had fixed their minds on the clock, as they relinquished the ball again after three downs. The quarter ended with Detroit driving for the go-ahead touchdown. That came with not quite a minute gone in the fourth period, on a two-yard run by Gene Gedman. The Lions led, 28-27, and the 49ers came apart, first with a fumble, then an interception.

Tracy also fizzled a Detroit drive with a fumble at San Francisco's three-yard line. But the Lions got yet another interception, and after the 49ers' defense held, Jim Martin kicked a field goal for a 31-27 lead.

The victory sent the Lions into the title game against their old foes, the Browns. Otto Graham, of course, was gone, but Paul Brown had a new weapon, the greatest ever, rookie running back Jim Brown. With Brown leading the league in rushing (942 yards), the rebuilt Browns had finished the regular season 9-2-1. Brown had set the single-game rushing record against the Rams that year (237 yards in 31 attempts).

The offensive spotlight, however, belonged to Rote that day. The Detroit sub threw four touchdown passes and ran for another as the Lions obliterated Cleveland, 59-14, for the NFL Championship. Each player on the championship team earned $4,295.41; the losers each received $2,750.31.

RIGHT: *Rookie running back Jim Brown made his appearance for Cleveland in 1957, leading the league in rushing with 942 yards and setting a single-game rushing record (237 yards in 31 attempts) against the Rams during the season.*

BELOW: *Tobin Rote scores for the Lions in their 59-14 demolition of the Cleveland Browns for the 1957 championship.*

A GREAT GAME, A GREAT SEASON

Jim Brown set a new single-season rushing record in 1958 with 1527 yards, as Cleveland finished tied with New York in the Eastern Division standings.

The Giants, however, quickly settled things in the playoffs by shutting down Paul Brown's fullback-oriented offense, 10-0. Folks figured the New Yorkers had the championship as good as won. What followed is history, the kind that soon made people across the country sit up and take notice of pro football.

The 1958 title game was the league's very first sudden-death overtime championship, broadcast to nail-biting football fans around the world. It revealed a new, exciting edge to this old game of thuds and thumps.

The cast involved many of the truly great ones. Tom Landry and Vince Lombardi were assistants to Giant coach Jim Lee Howell. Alex Webster and Frank Gifford were residents of the New York backfield, along with grizzled Charlie Conerly at quarterback. Pat Summerall was the place kicker. But that was merely the offensive unit. The rocks in New York's ribs were defenders: Sam Huff and Cliff Levingston at linebacker, Dick Modzelewski and Rosey Grier at tackle; Andy Robustelli at end; Jimmy Patton and Emlen Tunnell in the secondary. Landry was the mind behind the monster, aligning this talent in a 4-3 that flexed and crushed opponents, creating a resurgence in New York football that filled the throngs in Yankee Stadium with raving, noisy madness each home game. 'Defense!' the Giant crowd repeatedly roared.

Defense Landry gave them. The Giants had given up a league-low 183 points and outlasted Cleveland three times to win the Eastern Conference title.

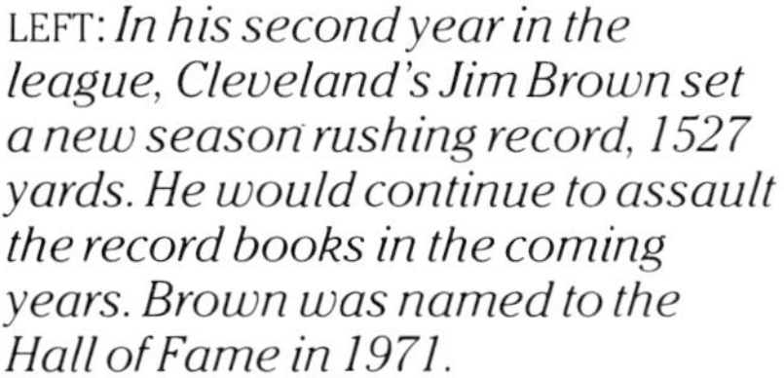

LEFT: *In his second year in the league, Cleveland's Jim Brown set a new season rushing record, 1527 yards. He would continue to assault the record books in the coming years. Brown was named to the Hall of Fame in 1971.*

ABOVE and RIGHT: *Frank Gifford was the gifted runner in the New York Giants' backfield in the 1950s. He went on to fame as an ABC television broadcaster on Monday Night Football. He was named to the Hall of Fame in 1977.*

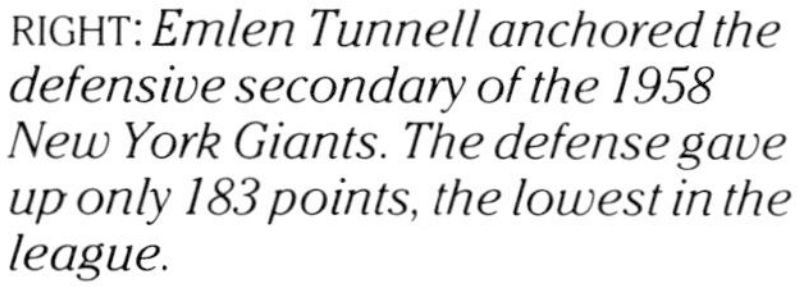

RIGHT: *Emlen Tunnell anchored the defensive secondary of the 1958 New York Giants. The defense gave up only 183 points, the lowest in the league.*

ABOVE: *Sam Huff was the big-name linebacker in the 1958 Giant defense. He was named to the Hall of Fame in 1982.*

LEFT: *Baltimore quarterback John Unitas had already begun to build his name when the 1958 championship boosted him to superstar status. He was named to the Hall of Fame in 1979.*

The Colts? They were led by a nearly anonymous supernova, John Unitas, a ninth round draft pick out of basketball country, the University of Louisville, who had been cut by the Pittsburgh Steelers and wound up playing semipro ball for the Bloomfield Rams (in Pittsburgh) for six dollars a week. Somehow the Colts dug him up when their regular, George Shaw, was injured, and watched Johnny U become the league MVP for 1957. He was still a reasonably well kept secret by the 1958 title game. Until then, no one realized he could work absolute magic.

Nevertheless, Baltimore was anything but a one-man show. Rangy and precise Raymond Berry was the split end and Unitas' main target. L G Dupre and Alan 'The Horse' Ameche were the power in the backfield. Lenny Moore was the philly, the flanker/halfback, the gamebreaker.

The Colts played a little defense, too, with Gino Marchetti at end, Gene 'Big Daddy' Lipscomb at tackle, and Don Shinnick and Bill Pellington backing the line. And nasty, naughty Johnny Sample in the secondary. Combined, they were team enough for a 9-3 record and the Western championship over Chicago.

Still, New York had won the regular-season contest between the two teams, and Baltimore hadn't beaten the Giants since 1954. Furthermore, the setting for their epic collision was Yankee Stadium, filled with 64,175 truly lucky fans lusting for the thud of the Giants' defense. A few million more tuned in on television.

The first quarter brought them the slightest taste of offense, as neither team could gain a first down in the opening 10 minutes. Finally, New York sustained a drive, only to see it gasp and die on the Colts' 36, from where Summerall kicked a field goal.

The Colts cracked their scoreboard goose egg in the second quarter, after Big Daddy Lipscomb recovered a Gifford fumble (he was to lose the ball three times in the quarter) inside the New York 20-yard line. Baltimore hammered into the end zone on a series of drives, with Ameche going the final two yards for a 7-3 lead.

Toward the close of the half, the Giants again threatened, but Gifford lost a second fumble, this time inside the Baltimore 15-yard line. The Colts recovered and began another grinding march. Using

45
Best to a swell Boss; "Bob" Conrad

New York linebacker Sam Huff (no. 70) blocks a field goal attempt by the Baltimore Colts' Steve Myra in the first quarter of the 1958 championship game.

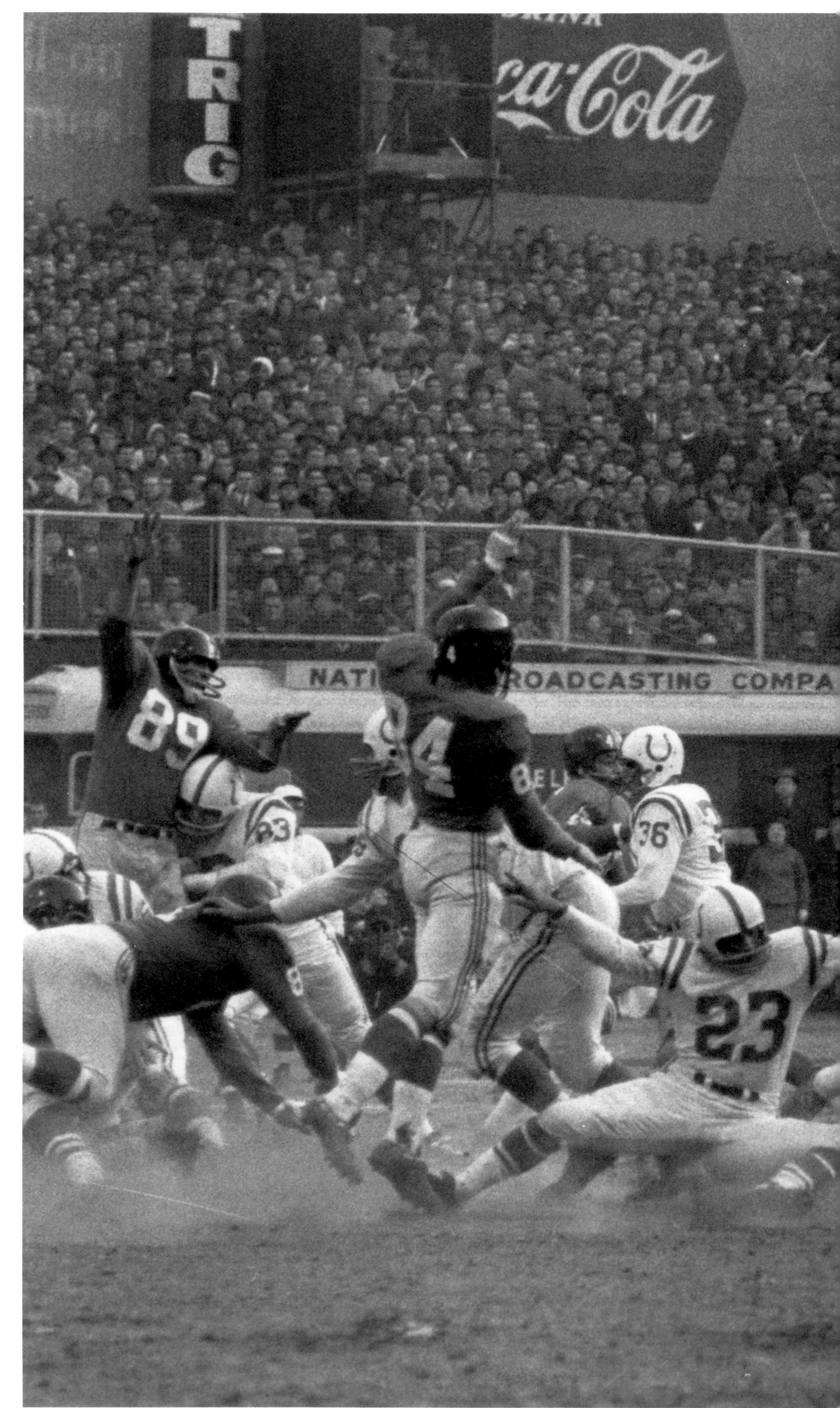

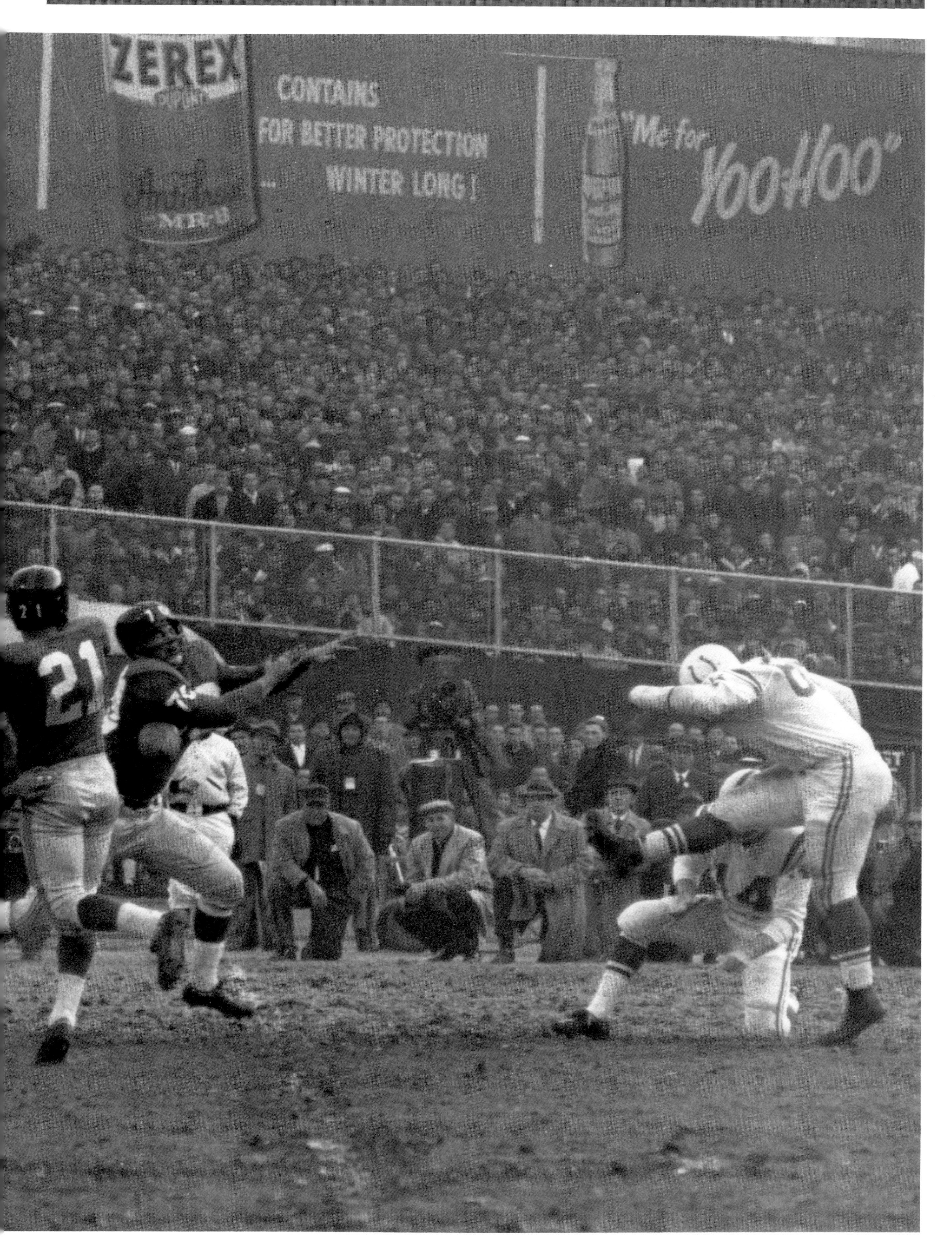
ZEREX
DUPONT
CONTAINS
FOR BETTER PROTECTION
WINTER LONG!
"Me for Yoo-Hoo"
21

mostly running plays, Unitas directed the Colts to the New York 15. There he zipped a pass to Berry in the end zone. With a 14-3 halftime advantage, the Colts were able to take some of the zeal out of the home crowd.

The numbness deepened in the third quarter as Baltimore drove to the Giants' three-yard line, where Landry's unit dug in. For three downs, the defense held. On fourth down, Colts coach Weeb Ewbank disdained a field goal and went for six points. The Giants repelled Ameche and started their comeback.

'We talked about it (a field goal),' Ewbank told reporters afterward, 'but I wanted to bury them right there with a touchdown.'

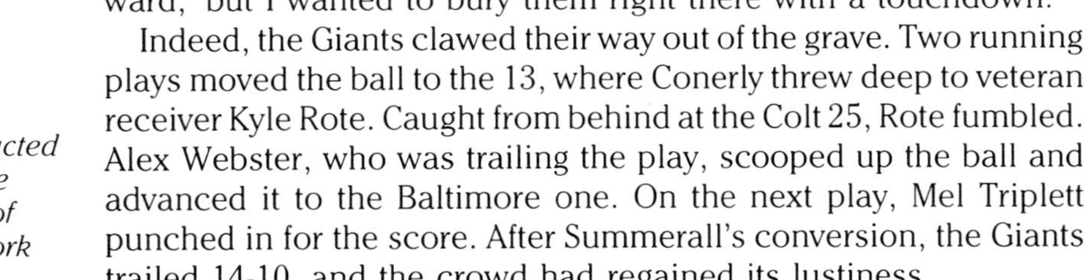

Indeed, the Giants clawed their way out of the grave. Two running plays moved the ball to the 13, where Conerly threw deep to veteran receiver Kyle Rote. Caught from behind at the Colt 25, Rote fumbled. Alex Webster, who was trailing the play, scooped up the ball and advanced it to the Baltimore one. On the next play, Mel Triplett punched in for the score. After Summerall's conversion, the Giants trailed 14-10, and the crowd had regained its lustiness.

ABOVE: *The Colts' Gino Marchetti attempts to block a pass by New York's Charlie Conerly during the 1958 title game. The pass fell incomplete.*

BELOW: *Weeb Ewbank was inducted into the Hall of Fame in 1978. He won championships as coach of the Baltimore Colts and New York Jets.*

Landry's defense did its job throughout the remainder of the period, and the fourth quarter opened with the Giants driving for the go-ahead score. With less than a minute gone in the period, Gifford caught a 15-yard touchdown pass, and New York regained the lead, 17-14. The darkness that descended on the late afternoon couldn't have been more figurative for the Colts. The stadium lights were turned on as they set up to receive the kickoff.

Again Landry's unit prevailed, dousing two Baltimore drives and giving the offense the opportunity to control the ball and the game with a late drive to eat the clock. Facing a third and four at the New York 40, Conerly called for Gifford to power off tackle.

Gifford, better known today as an ABC-TV broadcaster, still swears that he made it. Gino Marchetti and Lipscomb were the stoppers for Baltimore. Gifford seemed to nudge past the first-down marker, but veteran head linesman Charley Berry and referee Ron Gibbs assessed the forward progress and moved the ball back to where they saw Gifford downed. When the pile was untangled, Marchetti was carried from the field with a fractured leg, and New

ABOVE: *New York fullback Mel Triplett scores on a dive during the 1958 championship game. Baltimore's Art Donovan (no. 70) can be seen atop the pile.*

TOP RIGHT: *Baltimore's running back Alan 'The Horse' Ameche watches from the bench during a break.*

LEFT: *The Colts' Unitas rushes for 16 yards in the second quarter of the 1958 championship game, as Giant linebacker Sam Huff (no. 70) reaches for him.*

York was inches short of the first down. The crowd, of course, howled otherwise.

Howell had little choice but to punt, and Giant kicker Don Chandler responded with a beauty, pinning the Colts at their 14 with 1:56 left. 'I was sure then it was all over,' Lombardi said afterward.

But Unitas found a spark and turned it into a flame. On third and 10, he passed to Lenny Moore for a first down at the 25. Then came three brilliant completions to Berry, first a slant up the middle for 25 yards, followed by a diving reception at the 35 and finished by a quick hook at the 13.

With 0:07 left, kicker Steve Myhra calmly entered the game and tied the score at 17. The numbness again descended on the New York crowd. This sudden-death overtime stuff was new territory, even in the Big Apple.

'We were so damn disgusted with ourselves that when we got the ball for that last series, we struck back at the Giants in a sort of blind fury,' Unitas said afterward of the drive to tie the game.

His magic, however, drooped briefly as he made a bad call on the

coin toss for overtime. New York won and elected to receive. After three plays, the Giants still needed a yard for a first down, so Chandler again punted beautifully. The Colts took over on their 20, and Unitas started them down the field into history.

To minimize the chances of a turnover, he kept the ball on the ground. Dupre ran for 11 yards, then after two failed drives, Unitas gambled and shot a flare pass to Ameche in the flats, and The Horse bulled to another first down. The progress was halted momentarily when Modzelewski lanced through the heart of the pocket and sacked Unitas for an eight-yard loss. Looking at third and long, Unitas executed what the analysts came to savor as the game's most crucial play. First, he dropped to pass, hesitated, then broke to the left seemingly headed for the end, stopped, faked a pass, then faded farther out. Berry, shaking and darting, broke open when Giant halfback Carl Karilivacz stumbled. Still, Unitas hesitated, motioning for Berry to go farther. Finally satisfied, he zipped the ball 21 yards to Berry's wide target, No. 82, for another first down at the New York 42.

The unsung heroes of that great moment were the Colts' offensive linemen – George Preas, Buzz Nutter and company – who kept Unitas free for a leisurely scramble.

With the Giants plump for the fall, Unitas called the draw to Ameche. It went for 22 yards and another first down just inside the Giants' 20. The New York defense tightened and stopped a run for a yard gain. But Unitas threw to Berry at the eight.

BELOW: *New York defenders scramble for a fumble by Unitas. The Giants' Jim Patton (no. 20) covers the ball.*

LEFT: *Baltimore's Gene 'Big Daddy' Lipscomb poses with two youngsters and shows a bit of the strength that made him the heart of the Colt defense.*

ABOVE RIGHT: *The Colts' Alan Ameche bulls his way to extra yardage against Giants Jim Patton (no. 20) and Sam Huff (no. 70) in the 1958 NFL title game.*

BELOW RIGHT: *Later Ameche blasts into the end zone to give the Colts the 23-17 victory in sudden-death overtime, ending what many have called 'pro football's greatest game.'*

On the verge of one of football's greatest moment with nearly everyone in Yankee Stadium sensing an imminent field goal, a fan broke loose from the crowd and headed onto the field. Play was stopped for a full minute until police could entice him back into the stands. Unitas watched calmly, then crossed up the defense again when play resumed, throwing a sideline pass to tight end Jim Mutscheller, who went out of bounds at the one-yard line.

The next call was a dive to Ameche. The hole was wide, to say the least, and instead of defenders, The Horse was greeted by joyous Baltimore fans who rushed the end zone to greet him.

'When I slapped the ball into Ameche's belly and saw him take off,' Unitas told reporters, 'I knew nobody was gonna stop him.'

The fans wrested away the game ball, and several Colts chased them down to retrieve it. Lost momentarily in the celebration were the statistics. Unitas had completed 26 of 40 passes for 349 yards. Berry had caught 12 for 178 yards. The Giants had set a record with six fumbles. Soon after the roar grew to a din, the Colts retired to the locker room to savor their winners' checks – $4,718.77 apiece.

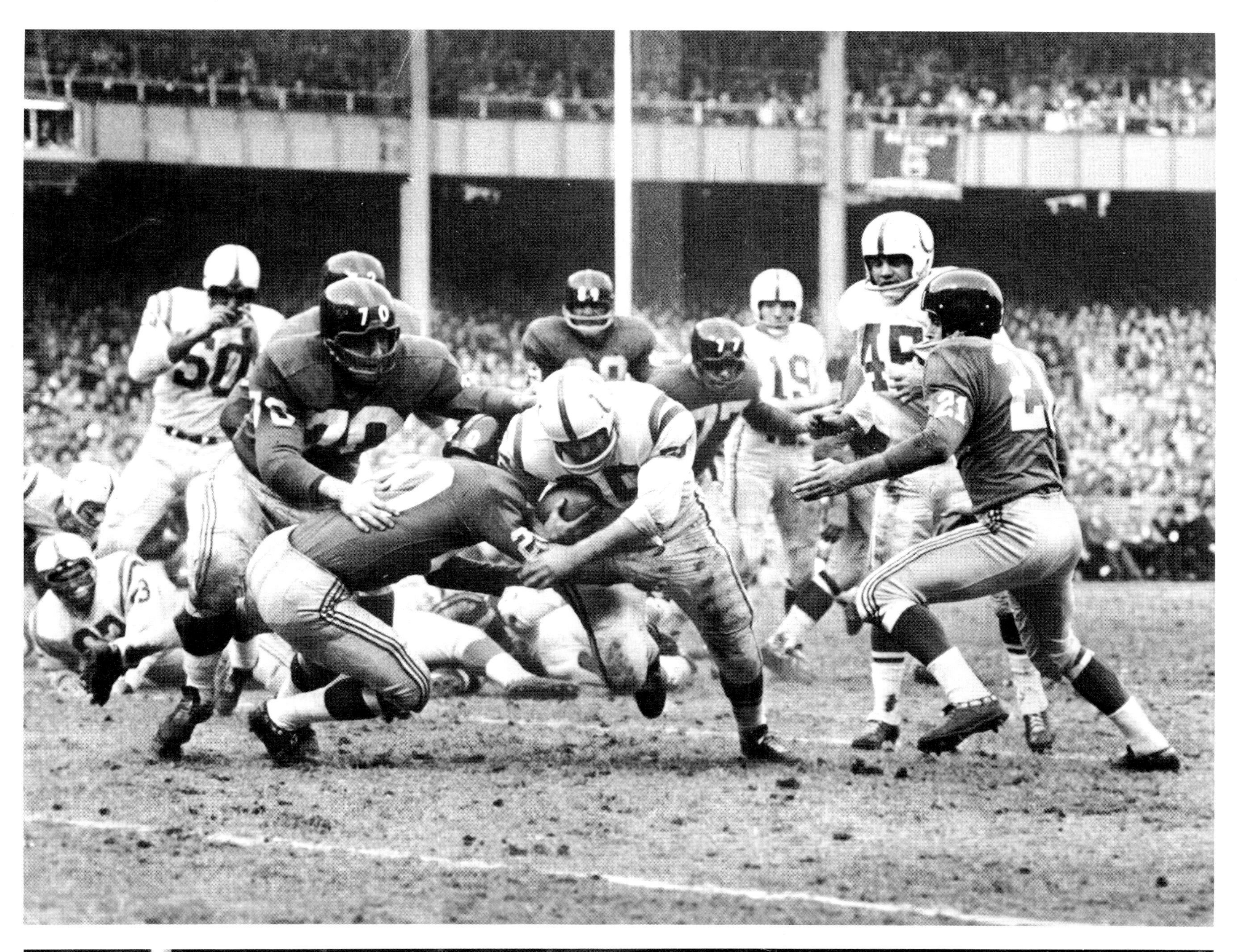

A number of people, including Commissioner Bell, declared the game the 'Greatest Ever Played.' That seemed reason enough to resume the rivalry in the 1959 championship. There were, however, some absences. Tim Mara, co-founder of the Giants, died that February. Bert Bell, the commissioner, died of a heart attack in October while watching his beloved Eagles and Steelers play.

On the field, Jim Brown added another rushing title. On 1 November, the Colts and Browns clashed in an epic battle. Brown was magnificent, piling up 176 yards and five touchdowns, 'one of the greatest performances ever,' according to Cleveland coach Paul Brown.

For his part, Unitas did nothing to hurt his own legend, passing for 397 yards and four touchdowns. It just wasn't enough to offset Brown, as Cleveland won, 38-31. As time wound down, the fans in Baltimore gave Brown a standing ovation. But the Browns were too far behind in the standings.

The Giants and Colts returned to the title game. Through three periods, their 1959 match-up seemed intent on bettering the 1958 contest. The Giants led 9-7 on three Pat Summerall field goals until the Colts erupted for three touchdowns in the fourth period.

The killer score was Johnny Sample's 42-yard return of an interception. Unitas had done it again, completing 18 of 29 passes for 265 yards and two touchdowns.

At the time, it certainly didn't seem like the beginning of a new era. But a group of Texas businessmen announced their intention to form a new pro football organization. Yes, like so many before, it would be called the American Football League. Yet this one would be different. Very different.

ABOVE: *Cleveland's Jim Brown scored a late touchdown, capping a magnificent performance and beating the world champion Baltimore Colts, 38-31, during an epic confrontation on 1 November 1959.*

RIGHT: *Colt wide receiver Raymond Berry was one of Johnny Unitas' primary targets in Baltimore's championship drives of 1958 and 1959. Named to the Hall of Fame in 1973, Berry coached the New England Patriots to the Super Bowl in 1985-86.*

LEFT: *Cleveland's Preston Carpenter (no. 40) just misses a pass thrown by quarterback Milt Plum during the Browns' 1 November 1959 victory over Baltimore.*

PART IV

Thoroughly Modern:

The NFL from 1960

Once again history and pro football neatly wrapped up their eras, ending one almost precisely as another began. Far more than any other year, 1960 marks the maturation of the modern game. That 26 January, the league representatives met to select a replacement for Bert Bell. Finally, on the twenty-third ballot, they compromised and elected Pete Rozelle, the young general manager of the Los Angeles Rams, as the NFL's new commissioner.

That same day, the upstart American Football League elected its founder, Lamar Hunt, as president. Four days later, Oakland became the eighth team to join. By June the AFL had negotiated a very healthy television contract with ABC, signaling the beginning of a transfusion of big dollars into professional football. The greatest contribution from the newcomers was their swirl of imagery and color – the black and silver of the Oakland Raiders, the lightning bolt of the Los Angeles Chargers, the early orange-red and blue of the Denver Broncos.

Seeing the threat, the NFL expanded, granting the Dallas Cowboys a franchise for 1960, and clearing the way for the Minnesota Vikings in 1961. The next piece was put into place in March when the Chicago Cardinals moved to St Louis. Despite being a bit stodgy, the NFL captured the public's imagination with Cowboys and Vikings and Redskins. Also, there was little question where the power lay in the 1960s. Vince Lombardi's Green Bay Packers were the perfect image of dominating precision.

With this colorful cast of characters, a fitting drama developed, generating metaphor after metaphor for the everyday fan. The underdog league would stage a rebellion fueled by the brash talk of a young quarterback named Super Joe playing with a high-tech franchise, the Jets. That he would succeed seemed unfathomable. That he did was pure storybook. The Jets' Super Bowl victory over the Baltimore Colts in 1969 gave Americans something to believe in at a time when they needed it most. To say the least, the public was consumed by the continuing developments, much to the glee of the marketing specialists and agents and PR men.

From that early drama, the Super Bowl would evolve as a grand sports spectacle, becoming a showcase for anything gaudy and grandiose in America.

To the delight of many, to the dismay of a few (mostly old timers who preferred high-top shoes and leather headgear), pro football had found its high place in society. It was entertainment, sometimes brutal, for the most part harmless. Week after week and season after season it was colorful and dramatic and self-sustaining. But best of all, it made money. Lots of money.

THE AMERICAN DREAM: A NEW LEAGUE, 1960-1966

The NFL might have avoided the hassle of competition if only it had been willing to expand a little faster. The AFL was started because two Texas boys – Lamar Hunt in Dallas and Kenneth S 'Bud' Adams in Houston – couldn't persuade the NFL owners to grant them franchises.

As most rival leagues had before it, the American Football League initiated play in 1960 with a mix of castoffs, tired talents and second chancers. Here and there, amid the crowd, a nugget of legitimate big-league ability would glisten.

Yet whatever the individual assessments, the young teams made a beginning that year, and from it would grow a unit of style and savvy that would eventually meld with the NFL, bringing the old league a new look, a new color, a new energy.

The first season brought a rush to get teams organized and games scheduled. For the snobs, the AFL was definitely a backlot league in 1960. Real football connoisseurs, however, knew a thrill when they felt it. If nothing else, these awkward young teams were entertaining. On occasion, they were even sophisticated.

ABC helped things tremendously by offering a five-year television contract worth nearly $9 million; it was the first trickle in a soon-to-be tide of media money aimed at promoting and developing professional football. So the bills, for the most part, were paid. And the teams, despite speculation to the contrary, survived.

BELOW LEFT: *During a Boston game in 1960. Frank Leahy (left) talks with Joe Foss, AFL commissioner and Lamar Hunt (right), AFL founder.*

BELOW RIGHT: *During the 1961 AFL Championship game, Billy Cannon of the Houston Oilers gains nine yards against the San Diego Chargers.*

As was expected, a bidding skirmish broke out immediately, the first one coming over LSU's Heisman winner, Billy Cannon, who signed contracts with both Los Angeles of the NFL and Houston of the AFL. Pete Rozelle challenged Cannon's plans to go with Houston, but the courts decided in Houston's favor.

In retrospect, NFL partisans might concede that the new league made great gains for pro football by opening markets in new places such as Dallas, Denver, Oakland, Buffalo and Houston (the infatuation would later spread to Miami, Kansas City and San Diego), or reestablishing them in Boston, or blatantly challenging the NFL in Los Angeles and New York.

It helped that the first game, played 9 September, was an upset. But that's about all you could honestly say for it. Speed, power, precise blocking and crisp tackling – all were absent. Underdog Denver came back to defeat Boston, 13-10, with no-names such as Carmichael, Tripucka, Mingo and Colclough doing the scoring.

The premiere team in the early AFL was Houston, with old NFL hand George Blanda flinging bombs. Bud Adams, the Houston president, had wanted a passing attack. Mac Speedie, the former

LEFT: *NFL Commissioner Pete Rozelle challenged the AFL with a lawsuit over the rights to Billy Cannon, the Heisman Trophy winner from Louisiana State.*

LEFT: *Al Carmichael, a fast halfback, came out of Southern California and joined the Denver Broncos in 1960, the AFL's first year of operation.*

RIGHT: *Frank Tripucka offered Denver great promise at quarterback in 1960. He is shown here throwing against Boston in September 1960.*

BELOW: *Charley Hennigan, a receiver for the Houston Oilers, set a new pro record during the 1961 AFL season, breaking the 1500-yard barrier for pass receiving in a season.*

Cleveland great who coached the Oilers' receivers, helped put one together. Charley Hennigan out of Northwest Louisiana College developed into a great receiver. Teamed with him were two other prizes, Bill Groman and Johnny Carson.

Cannon, out of the backfield, wasn't a bad target either. With that offense, Houston played its way to the championship game against Los Angeles. There, the Oilers won, 24-16, when Cannon pulled in a Blanda aerial for an 88-yard TD to secure the victory.

That offense worked its same magic the next year, again nudging out the Chargers, who had moved to San Diego, 10-3. Adams, it seemed, had developed a powerhouse.

Before play began in 1960, the leagues had reached a verbal agreement not to steal each other's players. But Chicago Bears end Willard Dewveall found an avenue to the new league by playing out his option and joining the Oilers in January 1961. The dislike between the two leagues grew, reaching a milestone of sorts in May 1962 when a federal court judge in Baltimore ruled against the antitrust suit filled by the AFL against the NFL.

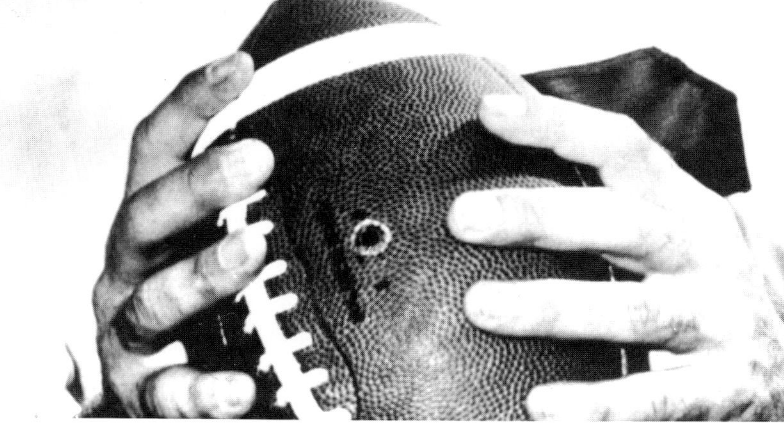

If the AFL was going to make it, it would have to do so by generating excitement on the field. Fortunately, that had been little problem. The new league had quickly established a reputation for gunslinging. In its first season, the Chargers' Jack Kemp, who went on to fame as a conservative congressman, became the first pro quarterback to break the 3000-yard mark in a season of passing. He totalled 3018 in leading Los Angeles to the title game.

Blanda quickly bettered that in 1961 with a whopping 3330 yards and 36 touchdowns. He also threw 22 interceptions. The AFL's currency was thrill. Ultimately, it would have the effect of juicing up offenses throughout pro football. By 1963 Y A Tittle of the New York Giants had thrown for over 3100 yards and equalled Blanda's 36 touchdown pass mark.

For the AFL, its thrill image was epitomized in the 1962 championship game between the Dallas Texans and Houston Oilers. As with the pivotal 1958 NFL Championship, this one was also played before a nationwide television audience. And just like the 1958 game, this one went to sudden-dêath overtime. Make that double sudden-death overtime.

Pro football's second championship tiebreaker lasted most of six periods, until Dallas rookie placekicker Tommy Brooker nailed a 25-yarder with 2:54 left in the second overtime to give the Texans the title with a 20-17 win. The 37,981 fans in Houston's Jeppesen Stadium were held captive by the outcome and dampened by a drizzle throughout the long afternoon. As much as anything, the game was a battle against the elements, as both teams were slowed by loose, muddy turf and befuddled by gusting winds.

LEFT: *George Blanda, a veteran quarterback with the NFL's Chicago Bears, became a star with the AFL's Houston Oilers. He is shown here in a 1961 photo.*

BELOW: *Cookie Gilchrist of the Buffalo Bills gains yardage against San Diego during a November 1963 game.*

RIGHT: *San Diego Chargers quarterback Jack Kemp (left) is pictured with teammate Ron Mix before an October 1961 game. Kemp later played for the Buffalo Bills, served as a congressman and sought the Republican presidential nomination.*

Regulation play was as perfectly symmetrical as any football game can be. The Dallas offense, guided by quarterback Len Dawson, racked up 17 points in the first half. Then in the second half Blanda pushed the Oilers through their paces to match that, leaving the game hinging on his 42-yard field goal attempt as time expired. Dallas linebacker Sherrill Headrick blocked it, and the damp fans settled down for the extra period.

Then Dallas' runningback Abner Haynes miscalled the coin toss, giving Houston the ball and the advantage of the wind to start the sudden death. The Oilers hooted at the mistake, but wasted their opportunity with two interceptions and failed to score in the first overtime.

The Texans opened the second overtime with the ball and the wind and used that advantage to sail downfield to the 25, where finally Brooker complied with his championship kick.

The 1963 season began with a shock for the San Diego Chargers, who placed quarterback Jack Kemp on waivers because of an office error. He was quickly claimed by Buffalo. The Chargers replaced

him with Tobin Rote, who teamed with Lance Allworth to take San Diego to the championship game. There, they bombed Boston and veteran quarterback Babe Parilli, 51-10.

The major developments of the season had taken place off the field. Lamar Hunt had moved his Dallas Texans to Kansas City and named them the Chiefs. A syndicate headed by Sonny Werblin had taken over the suffering New York Titans and renamed them the Jets. To bring more balance, the league allowed New York and Oakland to select players off other teams' rosters.

After his team won the 1962 AFL championship, Lamar Hunt, owner of the Dallas Texans, announced he was moving the franchise to Kansas City, where it became the Chiefs.

In 1964 things improved dramatically for the new league when ABC signed a five-year, $36-million television deal that would pay each franchise $900,000 per year. The all important New York market showed signs of vitality as the Jets attracted a league-record crowd of 46,665 to their opening game in Shea Stadium, a 30-6 victory over Denver.

The Chargers realized how much they regretted losing Kemp that next season when he and the Bills defeated them in the championship game, 20-7. The Bills' varied offense also featured 250-pound fullback, Cookie Gilchrist, who had won the league rushing title in 1962 and 1964.

Buffalo also gave pro football a new look on offense with placekicker Pete Gogolak out of Cornell. The first soccer-style kicker in pro football, Gogolak started a craze that spread throughout all levels of the sport. By 1965 Gogolak had set a pro football season record with 28 field goals.

That Kemp/Gilchrist/Gogolak combination doubled the Chargers' agony the next season, 1965, as the Bills again met San Diego in the championship, and again won, 23-0.

By far, the more interesting competition was off the field, where the two leagues were spending money as fast as the television networks would give it to them. The bidding for new talent made unproven college stars wealthy and happy. It also left the veterans grumbling. Both leagues faced a looming reality: merge or go under.

THE NFL's CHANGING FACES 1960-1965

GREEN BAY'S GLORY; NEW YORK'S PAIN

Faced with a challenge from the AFL in 1960, the NFL needed stability. Coach Vince Lombardi provided it in his Green Bay Packers, a team so complete, so sound in its execution that it left little question in the 1960s as to which was the better league.

The Packers, the NFL's new tomorrow, emerged with surprising quickness in 1960, making the first of their six championship appearances. They were future Hall of Famers, on the verge of their greatness: Bart Starr, Jim Taylor, Paul Hornung, Max McGee, Ray Nitschke, Forrest Gregg, Willie Davis and company.

Coming as an assistant from New York in 1959, Lombardi had taken over a 1-10-1 team. 'Gentlemen,' he told his players, 'I have never been associated with a losing team, and I do not intend to start now.' They finished 7-5 that year, and by the next season, they had played their way to the championship game.

Their equally unexpected opponents were the Philadelphia Eagles, who had wallowed in mediocrity since their championship appearances in 1948 and 1949. After winning the 1960 title, they would again disappear into the NFL pack for two more decades.

The old era of pro football was represented by the Eagles' Chuck Bednarik, the last of the two-way players, a 35-year-old center-linebacker of immense toughness. He played the full 60 minutes of the title game, and the outcome would prove that he was needed to very last second.

The Eagles were a loose collection of veterans and rookies who jelled as a team and played beyond their potential. They were led by Norm Van Brocklin at quarterback and receiver Tommy McDonald and sparked by rookie running back Ted Dean.

Despite their youth, the Packers gained most of the yardage and reaped a bushel of Philly turnovers. Only in points, only where it really mattered, did they fall short. About nine yards short, to be exact.

ABOVE: *Coach Vince Lombardi drove the Green Bay Packers to greatness in the 1960s. He later coached the Washington Redskins for a year. He was named to the Hall of Fame in 1971.*

LEFT: *Paul Hornung, the Heisman Trophy winner out of Notre Dame, was a vital part of the Green Bay Packers' success under Vince Lombardi. He is shown here scoring against the Minnesota Vikings in 1962.*

RIGHT: *The bull in the Packers' backfield was fullback Jim Taylor. He was inducted into the Hall of Fame in 1976.*

31

ABOVE: *Receiver Tommy McDonald, one of the Philadelphia Eagles' leaders, returns from the sidelines after scoring a touchdown during the second quarter of the 1960 NFL Championship game.*

LEFT: *Green Bay quarterback Bart Starr had played for the University of Alabama in college. He helped take the Packers to the 1960 championship, where the young team almost won the title.*

RIGHT: *Chuck Bednarik was a center/linebacker, the last of the NFL's great two-way players. He played the full 60 minutes of the 1960 championship. Bednarik was inducted into the Hall of Fame in 1967.*

The championship came down to the fourth quarter, where, with more than nine minutes left, Philadelphia led, 17-13. The Packers saw three comeback drives fail. Bednarik snuffed one drive with a fumble recovery. Two other Green Bay possessions died on downs.

Finally, quarterback Bart Starr was given one last opportunity, getting the ball back on his own 35 with 1:30 left. It was a masterful drive that came to its climax on the Eagles' 22 with just 17 seconds and no Green Bay timeouts left.

There, the old and new collided, the old being Bednarik, playing the last few seconds of his 60 minutes; the new being Jim Taylor, the Packers' bullish young fullback, who had just pulled in an outlet pass at the line of scrimmage after Starr had been unable to find an open receiver in the end zone.

Taylor broke through several defenders and found only Bednarik at the nine-yard line between him and the championship. The game clock favored the old, but time favored the new. Bednarik executed a masterful tackle and then lay on top Taylor, who was fussing and twisting to get up, until the last seconds ran off the clock and Philadelphia had won.

Eagle fullback Ted Dean returns a field goal that fell short during a December 1960 game with the Washington Redskins. Washington's Andy Stynchula attempts to break through the interference.

The Packers, however, were young, strong and ready. Just how much so they would display over the next two seasons.

For the 1961 season, Y A Tittle, after playing 13 seasons with Baltimore and San Francisco, was traded to the hastily rebuilt New York Giants, where his career gained a new momentum. For three seasons, he laced Eastern Conference opponents with touchdown passes. In 1962 he threw 33 scoring strikes to lead the league, and the next year he retained the crown by throwing a league-record 36.

Three times he led the Giants to the NFL Championship game, and three times Tittle was denied. It seemed that when he needed touchdown passes the most, he couldn't find the range.

The Packers stood in his path in 1961 and 1962. Kramer, Dowler, Starr, Taylor and Hornung put on a show in the 1961 title game, smashing New York, 37-0, for Green Bay's first championship since 1944. The next year the Packers worked their power again, snuffing Tittle and the Giants, 16-7, for Lombardi's second championship.

Then, in early 1963, Commissioner Rozelle lowered the boom. He suspended Golden Boy Paul Hornung and Detroit Lions defensive tackle Alex Karras indefinitely for betting on their own and other games.

Without Hornung, the Packers finished 11-2-1 in 1963 and were nudged out by George Halas' 11-1-2 Chicago Bears. The Monsters of the Midway were about to give the Old Man of Football his last league title. Again, Tittle, now the 37-year-old 'Bald Eagle,' and the Giants were the unfortunate victims.

With the championship dancing just out of his reach, Tittle fought off injury and interceptions with a memorable effort. While he didn't win in the bitter cold of Chicago's Wrigley Field on 29 December 1963, Tittle offered the sports world ample evidence of his great undefeated spirit.

ABOVE: *Green Bay Packers swarm around Joel Wells of the New York Giants during the 1961 NFL Championship game, won by the Packers, 37-0.*

TOP RIGHT: *With Jim Taylor leading the way, Paul Hornung takes a handoff in the Green Bay backfield during the 1961 championship. The New York Giants' Andy Robustelli waits on defense.*

LEFT: *Paul Hornung, who together with Detroit Lions, tackle Alex Karras, was suspended in 1963 for betting on NFL games. Hornung was inducted into the Hall of Fame in 1986.*

RIGHT: *Jim Taylor, coach Vince Lombardi, Hornung, and Bart Starr celebrate in the Packer locker room after the 1961 title game.*

The Bears' trademark was their defense, directed by assistant coach George Allen. The Giants, of course, cornered the offensive market, averaging better than 32 points a game with Tittle throwing for more than 3100 yards. He would, however, have trouble de-icing his air attack in Chicago's eight degree weather and lashing winds.

Tittle was injured in the first half but returned in the third quarter to protect a 10-7 lead. His misfortune was to throw an interception that led to the Bears' second score and a 14-10 lead, the winning margin. Twice after that the limping Tittle drove the Giants down-

LEFT: *Y A Tittle, Jerry Hillebrand, Joe Morrison and Frank Gifford share a smile in the New York Giants' locker room after a November 1963 win over the San Francisco 49ers.*

BELOW: *New York quarterback Glynn Griffing, a substitute for the injured Y A Tittle, faces the rush of the Chicago Bears during the 1963 NFL Championship game.*

RIGHT: *Chicago quarterback Bill Wade, shown here throwing in the face of the Giants' rush, scored two touchdowns and led the Bears to the 1963 title.*

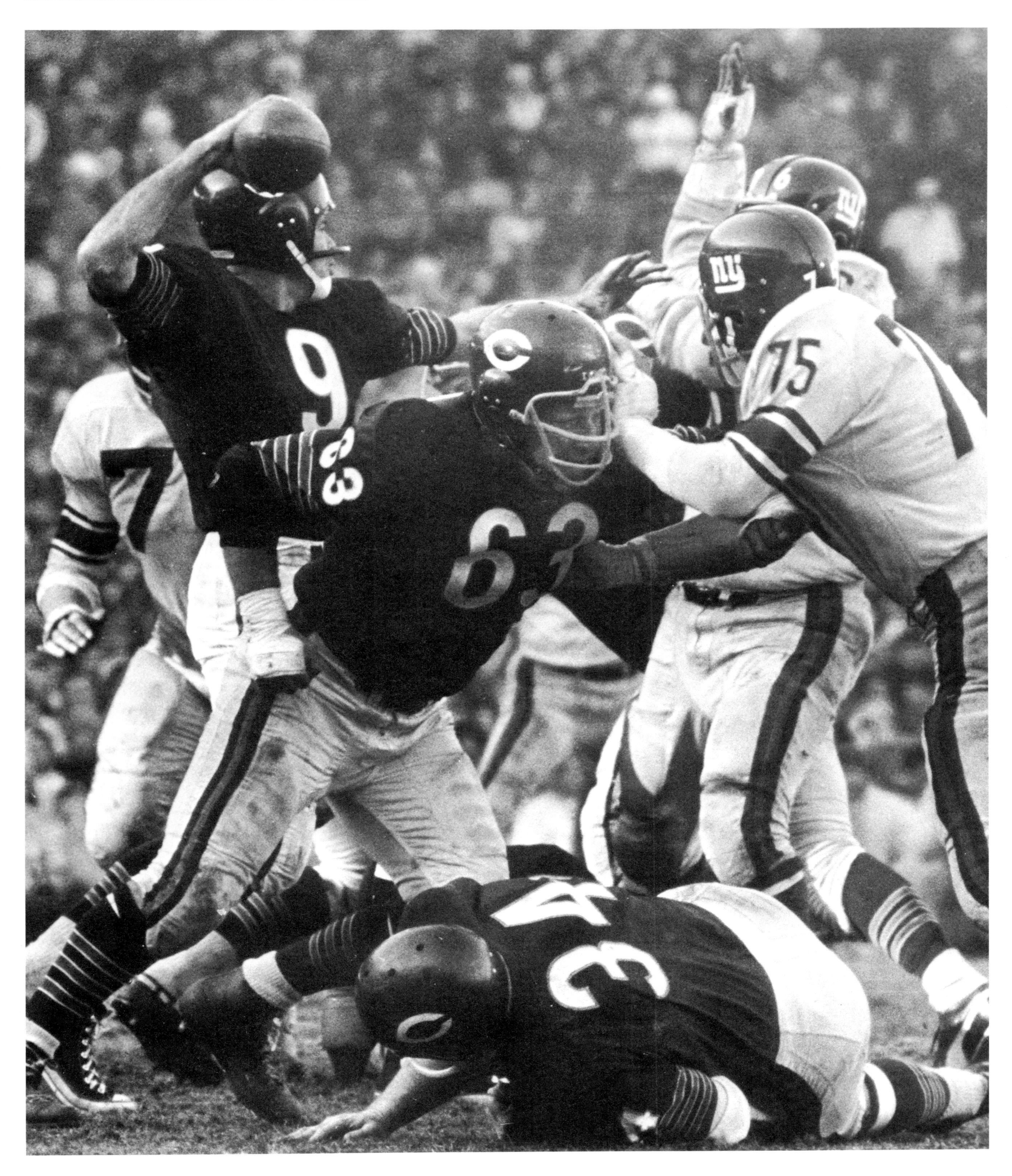

field only to be intercepted each time. The game ended with his fifth interception.

The Packers, shaken from their title grip in 1963, couldn't regain it in 1964 either. The tussle fell to the Baltimore Colts and the Cleveland Browns, who had dropped the legendary Paul Brown to name Blanton Collier their coach.

The Colts, coached by Don Shula, were considered substantial favorites to win the 1964 championship over the Cleveland Browns. In the days leading up to the title game, that forecast wore a bit thin with Collier. But he knew that emotion alone wouldn't beat the Colts. To do that, he and his assistants would have to figure out how their slow defensive secondary was going to stop Baltimore's passing whiz, Johnny Unitas.

In studying game films, Collier detected that Unitas shuffled his feet in the pocket toward his primary receiver, who was usually Raymond Berry. The defensive backfield could read that cue, then focus extra effort on momentarily cutting off Unitas from his prime target. That, Collier and his coaches figured, would allow the

ABOVE: *Frank Ryan of the Cleveland Browns throws his third touchdown pass against the Baltimore Colts during the 1964 NFL Championship game.*

RIGHT: *Cleveland coach Blanton Collier directed his underdog Browns to an astounding victory over the Colts in the 1964 NFL title game.*

Browns' pass rush an extra instant to reach the Colts' quarterback.

The home crowd of nearly 80,000 had something to cheer about that afternoon in Cleveland Municipal Stadium. With a mix of man-for-man and zone pass defense, the Browns threw a net over Unitas' options and turned the first half into a scoreless defensive testing ground. The Colts threatened once early, but from there the day belonged to the underdogs.

In the second half, Cleveland's offensive performance caught up with the defense. Browns quarterback Frank Ryan ran the Colts' secondary crazy with a 27-point outburst that included three touchdown passes to veteran receiver Gary Collins. For the day, Ryan threw for 206 yards, completing 11 of 18 passes. Collins caught five passes for 130 yards and the three scores.

Whenever the Baltimore defense focused on the air game, Jim Brown gouged them on the ground.

The Cleveland defense continued to shackle and confuse Unitas throughout the second half, holding him to just 95 yards passing for the game. When it was over, the Browns had added a 27-0 shutout to their stock of championships.

'They took it away from us,' Baltimore coach Don Shula told reporters afterward. 'They were better prepared than we were.'

TWO RUNNERS

The 1965 season crossed the stars of two very great NFL running backs, one a power player for the ages, a ground gainer for all time, the other a dancing, shifting, flashing of talent destined to a brief career.

The runners, of course, were the Cleveland Browns' great fullback, Jim Brown, who was coming to the close of his career in 1965, and the Chicago Bears' dynamic rookie, Gale Sayers.

As far as pro football careers go, Gale Sayers' was brief but bright. Very bright. And Brown's was strong and enduring. Very enduring.

Brown had entered the league out of Syracuse University in 1957 and immediately claimed the NFL's rushing title, keeping it for five seasons before relinquishing it to Green Bay's Jim Taylor in 1962. Brown resumed the lead with a vengeance in 1963, rushing for an all-time record 1863 yards (which would stand until O J Simpson broke it with the Buffalo Bills). Brown then continued to lead the league through his retirement in 1965, racking up 12,312 yards in only nine seasons. He exhibited a brutal power in his running style, one that chilled defenders and left them offering testimonials that he was the greatest to ever play the game.

Gale Sayers also won league rushing titles, in 1966 and 1969, but his brilliance and style were more fleeting. A college star from the University of Kansas, Sayers was the third player selected in the first round of the 1965 pro draft by Chicago's George Halas.

For all his elation, Halas didn't rush Sayers into the fray. Instead, the Chicago coach held back the young runner in the first two games, allowing him to adjust slowly to the NFL. But after a time, Halas realized there was no way to restrain brilliance. In the fifth game, Sayers led the Bears to a 54-37 victory over the Minnesota Vikings by shifting and feinting his way to four touchdowns. Fans knew it wouldn't be long before Sayers would be pushing the single-game touchdown record of six scores shared by Dub Jones and Ernie Nevers.

With Sayers scoring seemingly at will, the Bears ran off eight victories after having lost the season's first three games. Going into the twelfth game against San Francisco, Sayers had scored 16

RIGHT: *Gale Sayers came out of the University of Kansas in 1965 and wasted little time setting NFL rushing records. He was named to the Hall of Fame in 1977.*

BELOW: *George Halas of the Chicago Bears had been watching Gale Sayers as a college star with Kansas and was intent on drafting him.*

touchdowns, four short of the NFL season record set by Baltimore's Lenny Moore in 1964.

The 49ers had pounded the Bears, 52-24, early in the season, but this was a new Chicago team with Sayers. It didn't take long for the 49ers to find that out. Chicago's Wrigley Field was soggy that December afternoon, but Sayers seemed to glide along the loose turf, cutting and reversing with ease. He dazzled the 49ers early with an 80-yard run with a screen pass in which he broke through a crowd of defenders and then sprinted to the goal. He followed that with runs of 21, 7, 50 and 1 yards. Late in the game, he capped a perfect afternoon with an 85-yard punt return.

When it was over, the rookie had scored six touchdowns and amassed 336 all-purpose yards as the Bears returned the favor to San Francisco, 61-20.

'That was the greatest performance I've ever seen on the football field by one man,' Halas told sportswriters afterward.

Cleveland's Paul Brown had often said the same thing about his great runner. Both today are Hall of Famers.

LEFT: *By the time Cleveland's Jim Brown retired in 1965, he had rushed for more than 12,000 yards. He is shown here in a 1965 exhibition game against the 49ers.*

RIGHT: *Gale Sayers scored six touchdowns and amassed 336 all-purpose yards against the San Francisco 49ers in December 1965.*

BELOW: *Sayers scored one of his six touchdowns on this third-quarter dive against the 49ers in December 1965.*

LOMBARDI'S REIGN

Vince Lombardi brought his dynasty out of hibernaton in 1965, and it roared over the football world for three consecutive years.

Commissioner Rozelle had allowed Hornung to return from his gambling suspension in March 1964. After a season of tuning up, the Packers set out after another championship. Their competition in the Eastern Division was again John Unitas and company, the Baltimore Colts, with the great Jim Parker on the offensive line. Both teams ended the regular season 10-3-1 and readied themselves for a playoff.

Their battle for the division crown would be remembered as one of the roughest games in league history. Actually it was a rough game in a rough season. The close of the regular schedule had left the Colts decimated at quarterback. First, Unitas injured his back, then backup Gary Cuozzo separated his shoulder in the eleventh game, a loss.

They were replaced by Tom Matte, a third stringer converted from running back. He had played quarterback in Woody Hayes' run-oriented T-formation at Ohio State. Colts coach Don Shula adjusted the offense and even typed up some plays to fit inside Matte's wristband.

Despite the problems with quarterback, Baltimore almost finessed the playoffs. Matte led them to a win in the last game

ABOVE: *The face of Baltimore coach Don Shula shows anguish and disappointment after the Colts lost the 1965 playoff game with Green Bay.*

LEFT: *Green Bay coach Vince Lombardi won the third of his five NFL Championships in 1965. He later served as general manager of the team.*

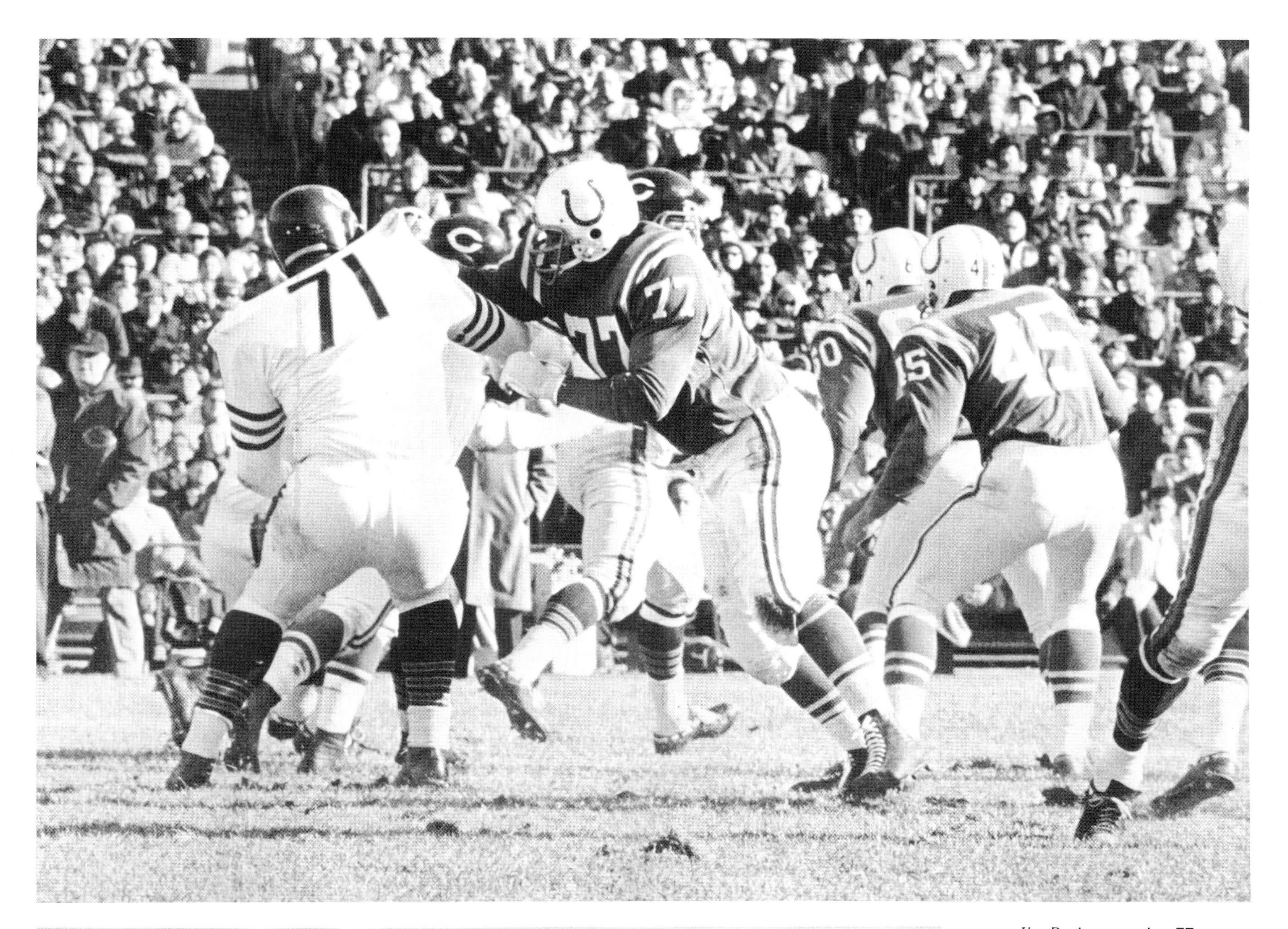

ABOVE: *Jim Parker, number 77, was the vital cog in the Baltimore offensive line. He was named to the Hall of Fame in 1973.*

LEFT: *Tom Matte, a third-string quarterback converted from running back, led the Colts in the 1965 playoffs.*

12
31
30

LEFT: *Packer quarterback Zeke Bratkowski gets off a pass just as Baltimore's Steve Stonebreaker wraps him up in the 26 December 1965 playoff game.*

RIGHT: *Paul Hornung scored a touchdown for Green Bay in the third period of the 1965 playoff game against the Colts.*

ABOVE: *Herb Adderley was the rugged factor in the Packer backfield. He was named to the Hall of Fame in 1980.*

RIGHT: *Packer Don Chandler kicks the winning field goal to give Green Bay a 13-10 playoff win over the Colts in sudden-death overtime.*

against Los Angeles. Things looked even brighter when he helped them to a 10-0 first half lead in the playoffs the next week against the Packers. But Green Bay drove for a late-game field goal to tie the score at 10, then pushed into position for the winning field goal with more than 13 minutes gone in sudden-death overtime.

The 13-10 victory had a dear price. The Packers' battered casualties included quarterback Bart Starr, runningback Paul Hornung, ends Boyd Dowler and Bill Anderson, and tackles Ron Kostelnik and Henry Jordan. 'This was the roughest game I've ever been in,' a weary Herb Adderly said in the locker room.

When Starr went out with injuries early in the first quarter, the game became a battle of backup quarterbacks. Green Bay's match for Matte was 34-year-old Zeke Bratkowski, who found his stride late in the game and directed the drives for the winning points.

Having won the West with an 11-3 record, the Cleveland Browns were waiting as the Packers' championship foe. The 2 January 1966 game at Green Bay's Lambeau Field was a contest of slush running. The electric coils under the field had turned a morning snow into a

RIGHT: *Green Bay's Henry Jordan leaps to block a pass by Cleveland quarterback Frank Ryan in the 1965 championship game.*

RIGHT BELOW: *Cleveland's Bill Glass moves in to stop Green Bay's Jim Taylor after a short gain in the 1965 championship.*

LEFT and BELOW: *Two stalwarts of the Packer defense were end Willie Davis (left) and linebacker Ray Nitschke (below). Both are Hall of Famers.*

cold soup. Both teams, however, were more than able to conduct a ground attack.

The Browns were powered by Jim Brown, Gary Collins and quarterback Frank Ryan. Bart Starr hit quickly with a 47-yard touchdown pass to Carroll Dale. Ryan answered with a 17-yard toss to Collins, but the extra point was missed. From there, the kickers, Cleveland's Lou Groza and the Packers' Chandler, took over, trading a pair of field goals each, which gave Green Bay a 13-12 halftime lead.

With end Willie Davis, linebacker Ray Nitschke, and defensive back Adderly leading the crunch, the second half belonged to the Packer defense. They shut down Cleveland and allowed only 26 yards total offense the final two quarters. After Hornung added a touchdown and Chandler a field goal, the Packers went home with the title, 23-12.

TRUCE

The 1966 season brought a whirlwind of competition, in and out of the stadium. Two new pieces were added to the board – Miami joined the AFL and Minnesota the NFL – as the leagues parried for television dollars. The ante was jumping. CBS paid $18.8 million for the right to broadcast NFL regular season games in 1966/67. That spring, the AFL and NFL handed out a total of $7 million to the top college draft choices.

The beneficiaries of the mid-sixties spending spree were a few bonus baby rookies – namely Joe Namath with a $400,000 contract, Tommy Nobis with $600,000 and Donnie Anderson with $711,000 – a development that didn't sit well with established NFL stars, most of whom were making far less than $100,000.

Then Al Davis, head coach and general manager of the Oakland Raiders, replaced Joe Foss as AFL commissioner in 1966. Swiftly, Davis dropped the agreement that the two leagues would not sign

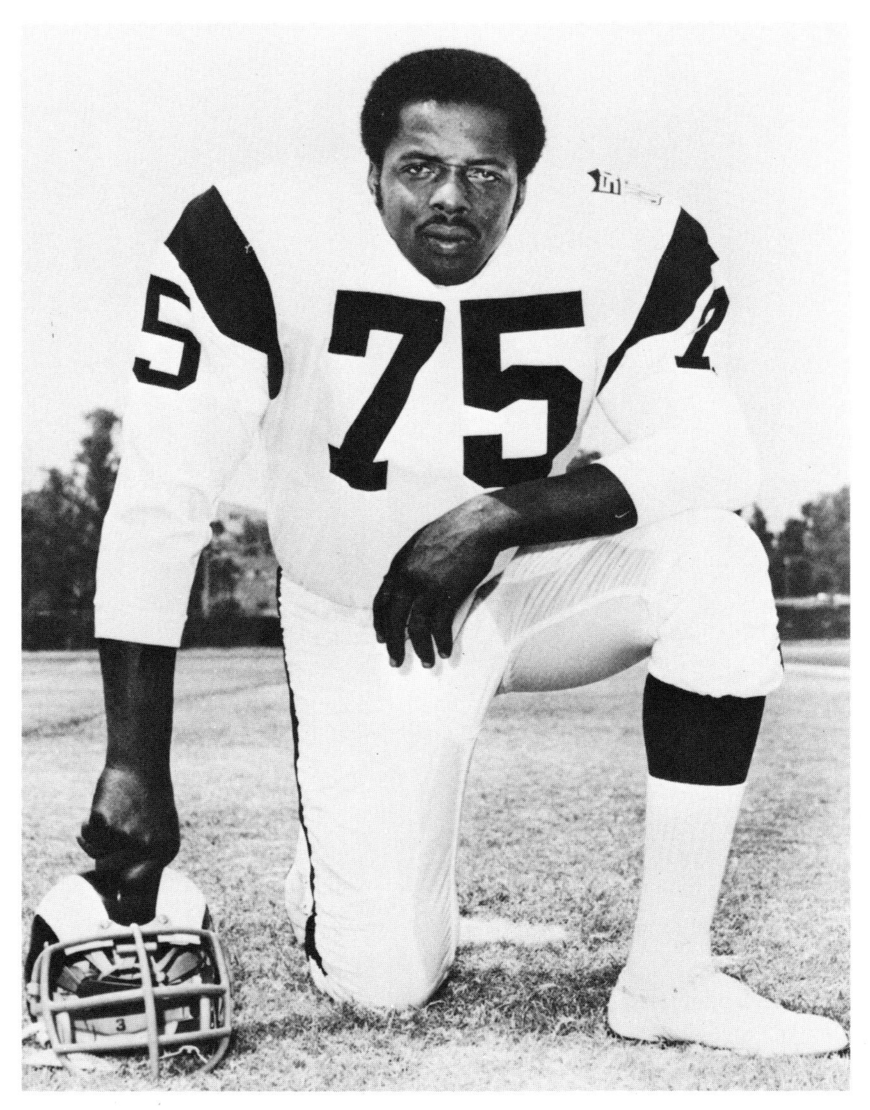

ABOVE: *Deacon Jones was a member of the Los Angeles Rams' much publicized defensive line, the Fearsome Foursome. He was named to the Hall of Fame in 1980.*

RIGHT: *Sonny Jurgensen, one of the game's all-time great passers, played for both the Eagles and the Redskins. He was named to the Hall of Fame in 1983.*

LEFT: *Dick Butkus, the great linebacker of the Chicago Bears, instilled fear in the minds of opposing ball carriers throughout his career.*

LEFT: *Al Davis, head coach and general manager of the Oakland Raiders, became commissioner of the AFL in 1966 and began dealing firmly with the NFL.*

players off each other's rosters. He targeted the NFL's low-paid veterans as the AFL's talent pool. Facing a bidding war that threatened to wreck both leagues, the NFL owners realized it was time for a merger.

As a prelude, the two leagues decided to feel each other out in a championship game, dubiously dubbed the Super Bowl. Lamar Hunt, one of the AFL founders, had come up with the name, reportedly after watching his daughter play with a Super Ball.

On the field, the competition in the NFL was getting tougher. Deacon Jones and Merlin Olsen had given the Rams a Fearsome Foursome on the defensive front that helped lift Los Angeles from the league cellar into contention. Linebacker Dick Butkus had come into the league with Chicago in 1965, and while the Bears didn't win any championships, opposing offenses felt a certain dread playing against them.

Quarterback Sonny Jurgensen, one of the game's all-time great passers, had moved from the Eagles to the Redskins, where his targets were the likes of tight end Jerry Smith and running back

ABOVE: *Tackle Bob Lilly helped build the Dallas Cowboys' defense into an item of pride in the 1960s and 1970s.*

RIGHT: *Mel Renfro of the Dallas Cowboys and Packer Gale Gillingham watch the ball roll loose during the 1966 championship game between Dallas and Green Bay.*

LEFT: *Receiver Bob Hayes was the bullet in the Cowboys' offense. Reporters dubbed him the 'world's fastest human.'*

RIGHT: *Lee Roy Jordan, who played for Bear Bryant at the University of Alabama, was a central figure in the Dallas defense of the 1960s.*

ABOVE: *With the patience and backing of team management, coach Tom Landry built the Cowboys from a franchise loser into a championship contender.*

Charley Taylor. Another big factor in Washington was the play of running back–wide receiver Bobby Mitchell, who had come to the Redskins in 1962 after owner George Preston Marshall reluctantly dropped his opposition to black players. In 1967 Jurgensen would throw for a league-record 3747 yards. Like their namesakes, the mid-sixties Redskins didn't win the big war, but earned their reputation ambushing the favorites.

However, the main NFL challengers were Tom Landry's Dallas Cowboys, led by the guile of quarterback Dandy Don Meredith, a slinger with enough poise to hinge a career on the two-minute drill, then graduate to Lipton Tea and Monday Night Football. The 'bullet' in the Cowboys' offense was Bob Hayes, otherwise known as the world's fastest human. Meredith's other prime receivers were Lance Rentzel and Pete Gent, who would later author *North Dallas Forty*. The running game moved on the legs of Walt Garrison, Dan Reeves and Don Perkins. Tackle Bob Lilly was the anchor of the defense that featured Lee Roy Jordan, Chuck Howley, Mel Renfro and Cornell Green. A late-season, 31-30 victory over the Redskins and Jurgensen

had given Dallas its first playoff shot.

The Packers were enjoying the zenith of the greatness Vince Lombardi had brought them, with their names – Herb Adderly, Bart Starr, Jim Taylor, Max McGee, Carroll Dale, Paul Hornung, Forrest Gregg, Willie Davis, Ray Nitschke, Bowd Dowler – having become imbedded in the American consciousness. The Cowboys were just coming into their own as a franchise, finally lassoing the kind of success Texans had come to expect.

The promise of Tom Landry's first really good team nearly evaporated before 74,152 witnesses in the Cotton Bowl 1 January 1967, as the Packers scored twice to lead, 14-0, before the Cowboys had run one play. They had earned the first one on a sustained drive, but then Mel Renfro had fumbled the kickoff, Jim Grabowski scooped it up, and the Packers had the gimme touchdown they would need to survive to the championship. Not that Dallas wasn't brilliant after that, with Meredith passing and directing the ground game. The Cowboys' answer was two touchdowns of their own to even things at 14, all before the first quarter ended.

Starr reached Dale with a 51-yard bomb in the second quarter, and Dallas added a field goal by Danny Villaneuva before the half. They pulled closer with another field goal in the third. But then Starr drilled two more touchdown scores to Dowler and McGee. When the Cowboys blocked Don Chandler's conversion after the last touchdown, the Packers led, 34-20.

LEFT: *Forrest Gregg epitomized coach Vince Lombardi's winning spirit on the Green Bay offensive line. He was named to the Hall of Fame in 1977.*

RIGHT: *Quarterback Don Meredith, nicknamed Dandy Don, led the Cowboys to challenge the Green Bay Packers for the world championship in 1966.*

RIGHT: *Green Bay's Bob Jeter (number 21) upends Cowboy running back Dan Reeves during the 1966 championship game.*

ABOVE: *Green Bay quarterback Bart Starr hands off to Elijah Pitts during the 1966 championship against the Cowboys. The play went for a 22-yard gain.*

BELOW: *During the 1966 title game, Dallas quarterback Don Meredith rolls out and looks downfield.*

Meredith quickly closed the gap with a 68-yard zinger to tight end Frank Clarke, and all Dallas needed was another chance for a tie game and a shot at overtime.

They got a second chance, and more, as Meredith drove them to a first down at the Packer two-yard line with time running out. The Packer defenders hunkered down, stopping Dan Reeves for a one-yard gain, but on the next play they received help from an unexpected source. Dallas was called for offsides, and the ball was set back at the six. Three straight passes failed, and the Packers were on the way to the first Super Bowl as 13-point favorites.

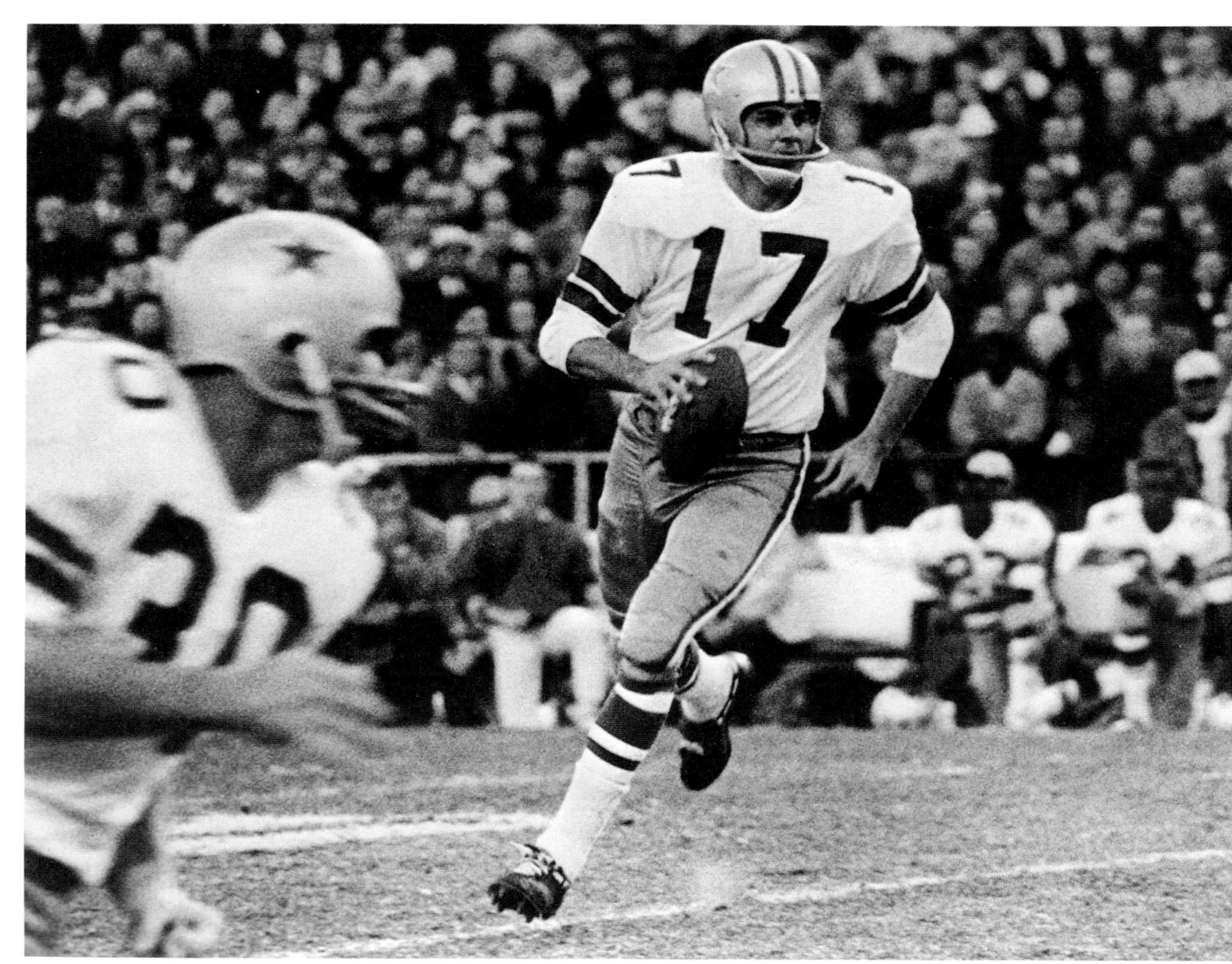

LEFT: *Green Bay coach Vince Lombardi gets a ride from the field after winning the 1966 NFL Championship. His team would go on to meet the Kansas City Chiefs in Super Bowl I.*

BELOW: *Cowboy halfback Dan Reeves scores the first Dallas touchdown in the 1966 NFL Championship.*

15
31

SUPER BOWL

Most people, including the Green Bay Packers, found the first Super Bowl more of an irritant than a game to settle a championship. The Packers had beaten the Cowboys earlier in the month, and that was all the championship they needed.

But the powers that be had forged a compromise. The leagues would merge in 1970, but a championship game, the Super Bowl, would begin immediately. The leagues would no longer try to outspend each other for talent. Instead, they would compete where football teams ought to – on the field. Thus, the first Super Bowl held some importance, more for the AFL than the Green Bay Packers.

The Kansas City Chiefs had emerged from the AFL pack and thumped the defending champion Buffalo Bills 31-7 in the playoffs. They were quarterbacked by Len Dawson, and their defense was bolstered by the great linebackers, Willie Lanier and Bobby Bell, a great defensive back, Willie Brown, and a mammoth lineman, Buck Buchanan.

To everybody's surprise, it was quite a game for a half. Although only 61,946 of the 100,000 seats in Los Angeles Memorial Coliseum were sold, the event had an audience – an estimated 60 million combined viewers from NBC and CBS, who shared broadcast rights for four years (a $9.5 million deal). A minute of advertising cost $75,000 to $85,000.

Plus there was plenty of outlandish pre-game and halftime enter-

RIGHT: *Linebacker Bobby Bell was the teeth of the Kansas City defense. He was named to the Hall of Fame in 1983.*

LEFT: *Green Bay quarterback Bart Starr hands off to fullback Jim Taylor during Super Bowl I.*

BELOW: *Kansas City quarterback Len Dawson runs the Chiefs' offense in the first Super Bowl.*

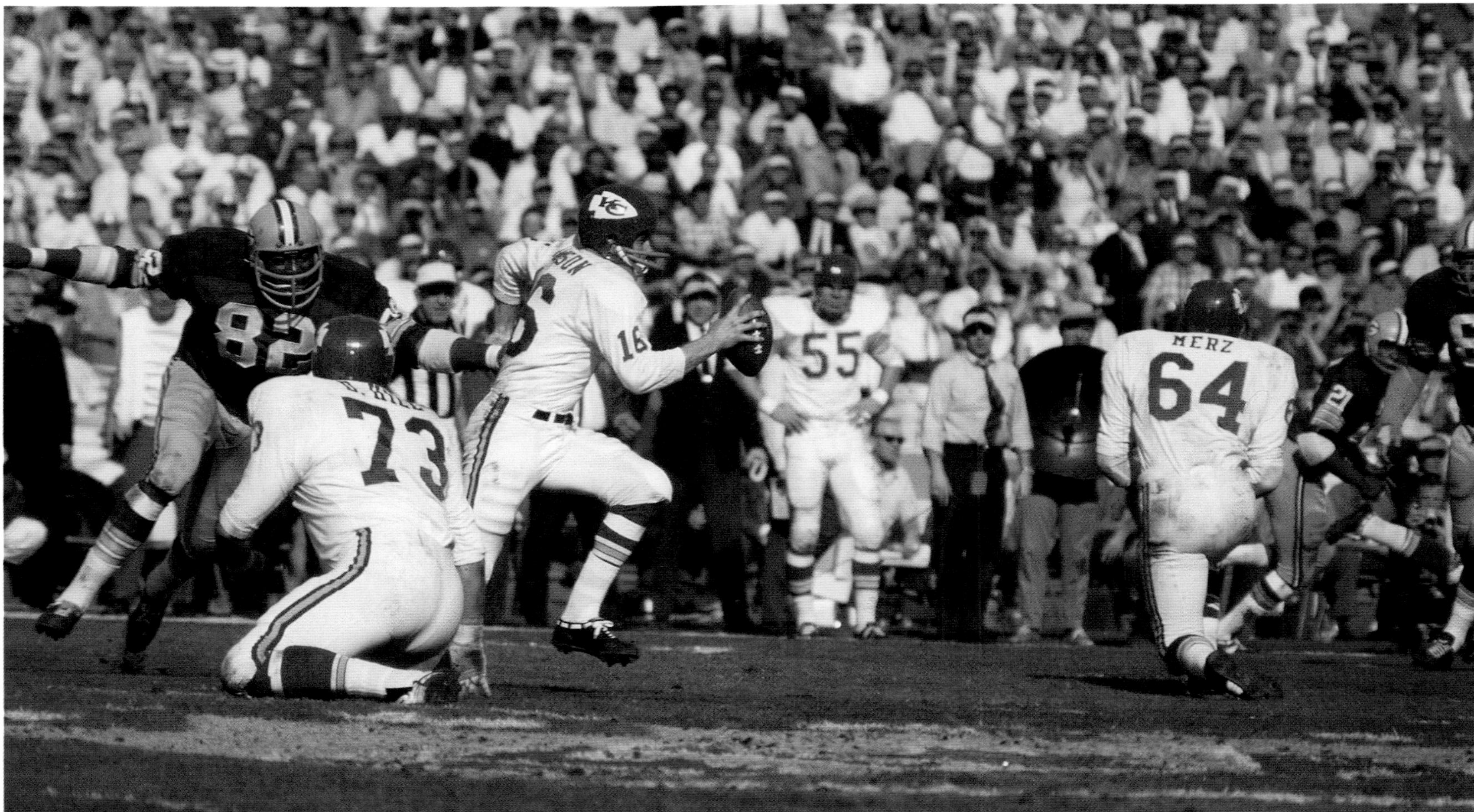

tainment, bands and dancers and batons and such. Somebody had the bright idea of releasing 4000 pigeons just before kickoff. Brent Musburger, then a Chicago sportswriter, had to clean pigeon droppings from his typewriter just as the game began.

For a while, the going proved just a bit tougher than the Packers thought it would be. Starr completed a 37-yard touchdown pass to McGee in the first quarter, and Green Bay led, 7-0. Dawson responded for the Chiefs by finishing off an impressive 66-yard drive with a seven-yard pass to fullback Curtis McClinton. The Packers came back with their own parade, with Jim Taylor rushing 14 yards for a 14-7 lead.

Before the half, the Chiefs added a field goal and took to the locker room the hope that their youth would provide the winning stamina in the second half. The young league certainly had reasons for optimism, but the triumph would come later. The 1967 Super Bowl belonged to the Packers.

LEFT: *The turning point of Super Bowl I came when Green Bay's Willie Wood intercepted a Kansas City pass early in the second half and returned it 50 yards.*

ABOVE: *Green Bay's Max McGee snares a pass on the Kansas City 20 and runs it in for the Packers' first touchdown of Super Bowl I.*

BELOW: *A happy Vince Lombardi was interviewed by sportswriters after his team captured the first Super Bowl.*

ABOVE: *The Chiefs had hoped their youth and stamina would wear the Packers down in Super Bowl I. In the end, Green Bay's power and experience prevailed.*

RIGHT: *Central to that Green Bay power was fullback Jim Taylor, shown here blasting into the Chiefs' secondary during Super Bowl I.*

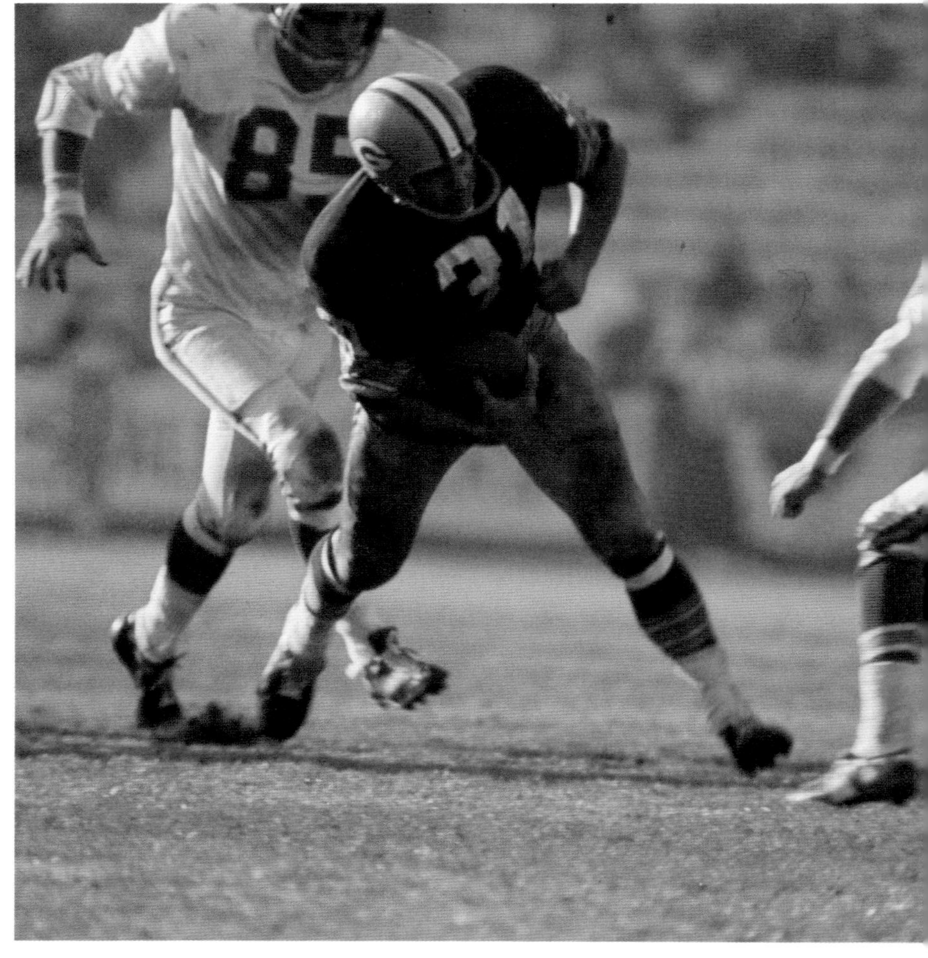

Their experience, epitomized by their efficient ground game, prevailed. First, the Packer defense opened the half with a blitz that sacked Dawson three times. Even worse, it forced him to throw an interception to free safety Willie Wood, who returned the ball 50 yards to the Chiefs' five. Elijah Pitts ran the ball over on the next play, and Kansas City's hopes visibly sagged. From there, the Packers controlled the game with two sustained, time-consuming drives for scores. It ended, 35-10.

'I just wish we were in the same conference with Green Bay,' Kansas City's Buck Buchanan said afterward. 'We have people in our league just as good or better. I don't think we got disgraced. We just got beat.'

The winning players received $15,000 each, the losers $7,500.

The two leagues held a combined draft for 1967, with the Baltimore Colts choosing Michigan State defensive tackle Bubba Smith as the first player. And Paul Brown re-entered football as part-owner, general manager and coach of the AFL's new franchise, the Cincinnati Bengals.

Otherwise, things were business as usual, with Vince Lombardi's Packers taking home another trophy.

ICE BOWL, SUPER BOWL

The AFL asserted itself a bit in the 1967 preseason, as the Denver Broncos defeated the Detroit Lions, 13-7, giving the new league its first victory over an NFL team.

But when the outcome mattered that season, Vince Lombardi ascertained one last time that he was still the fierce protector of the NFL's pride. 'The pressures of losing are awful,' Lombardi once said. 'But the pressure of winning is even worse, infinitely worse, because it keeps on torturing you and torturing you.'

Earlier in the season, it appeared that role of protector would fall to someone else. The Packers opened the season by tying the Lions, then lost games to Baltimore, Los Angeles, Pittsburgh and Minnesota to finish the regular schedule 9-4-1. The Rams and Colts, meanwhile, ran off impressive 11-1-2 records, with the Rams taking the Coastal Division title on points over Baltimore.

Los Angeles gained tremendous momentum on 9 December with a thrilling 27-24 defeat of Green Bay. Rams coach George Allen used the Fearsome Foursome (Merlin Olsen, Deacon Jones, Roger Brown and Lamar Lundy) as the front teeth of his defense. His offense was quarterback Roman Gabriel throwing to receivers Jack Snow and Bernie Casey. Another important Ram weapon was placekicker Bruce Gossett.

Still, Green Bay would have won if LA reserve linebacker Tony Guillory hadn't blocked a punt with less than a minute to play to set up a winning touchdown pass from Gabriel to Casey.

The next week, the Rams blasted the Colts 34-10 for the right to meet the Packers, the Central Division champions, in the Western Conference title game. But Green Bay ended the Rams' thoughts of greatness, 27-7, and began preparation to meet Dallas again for the NFL Championship. The Cowboys had won the Eastern crown by humbling Cleveland, 52-14.

The 1967 NFL title game was probably the most frustrating in the short history of the Dallas franchise. Certainly it was the coldest. The game time temperature at Green Bay's Lambeau Field was 13 below zero, with a dastardly windchill factor that played as the Packers' arctic twelfth man. Lombardi was said to have prayed for a deep cold spell before the game. The answer to those prayers will forever be known as the Ice Bowl.

Green Bay management had installed 14 miles of heater cables six inches beneath the surface of the field to have it warm for the playoffs. But when the temperature dropped rapidly on the eve of the game, the warming system malfunctioned, leaving the damp field to freeze as a slick glass pond. It was a truly miserable day for football. A little more than 50,000 fans suffered through four quarters of chill.

In that setting, the Packers skated to an early 14-0 lead on two Bart Starr touchdown passes. For the Cowboys, the opening was painfully reminiscent of the 1966 championship. Things turned

ABOVE: *Green Bay's Vince Lombardi has something to smile about on the sidelines during the 1967 NFL Championship.*

LEFT: *The Los Angeles Rams' Fearsome Foursome featuring Merlin Olsen (number 74), Lamar Lundy (hidden in photo), Deacon Jones (number 75) and Roger Brown (number 78).*

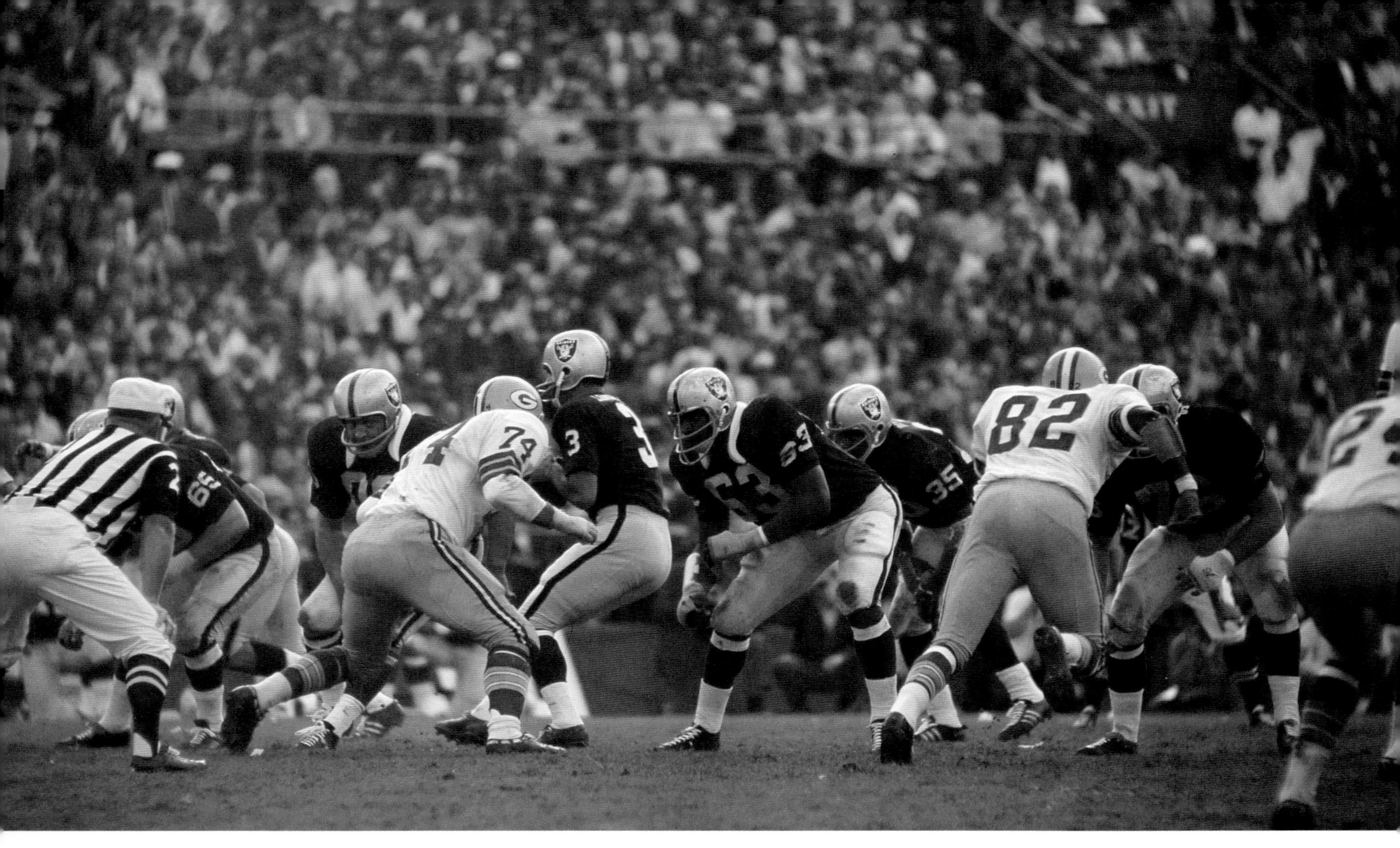

ABOVE: *In Super Bowl II, the Green Bay Packers feasted on the Oakland Raiders. Here the Packer pass rush breaks out of the blocks.*

RIGHT: *Oakland quarterback Daryl Lamonica looks into the face of the Packers' pass rush.*

momentarily worse, when Herb Adderly intercepted a pass and returned it to the Dallas 32 midway through the second period. Facing a rout, the Dallas Doomsday Defense somehow shook off the chill and smothered Green Bay's offense for the rest of the half.

With four minutes left in the second quarter, the Cowboys' Willie Townes hit Starr, forcing a fumble at the Green Bay seven, which George Andrie grabbed up and ran into the end zone for a touchdown. Dallas narrowed the deficit to 14-10 just before the half on a Danny Villanueva field goal.

The scoring was as frozen as the weather until the early moments of the fourth quarter when the Cowboys took a 17-14 lead on a 50-yard halfback option pass from Dan Reeves to Lance Rentzel. The weather Lombardi had prayed for was now lined up against him with the Dallas defense. The combination of the two worked to kill a Don Chandler field goal attempt minutes later. Then Don Meredith and the Dallas offense ran five minutes off the clock before punting to the Green Bay 32. There, with 4:54 on the clock, the Packers jump-started their offense. Between them and an unprecedented third NFL Championship stood 68 yards, the cold, and one of football's best defenses.

Afterward, in the locker room, Packer guard Jerry Kramer recalled the mood in the huddle: 'Maybe this is the year we don't make it, that it all ends. But I know every guy made up his mind that if we were going down, we were going down trying.'

In that frame of mind, the Packers started their last-ditch drive. First there was a six-yard gain by running back Donny Anderson. Then reserve running back Chuck Mercein sliced off tackle for a first down. Starr next threw to Bowd Dowler at the Dallas 42. Just as the momentum crested, the Cowboys threw Anderson for a nine-yard loss. Before the defense could celebrate, Starr answered with two quick completions to Anderson for a first down at the 30, with 1:35 left. Mercein then got open beyond the linebackers on the left, and after Starr found him with a pass, raced to the 11, where he ran out of bounds to stop the clock. On the next play, Mercein dashed off tackle for eight yards to the three.

There, on a plane of ice, the two teams played out one of pro football's classic dramas. Two rushes by Anderson netted two yards and a first down. On third down and goal at the one with 0:16 left, Starr called for a dive between Kramer and center Ken Bowman. But rather than risk a handoff, Starr made the play a keeper.

Said Kramer in the locker room later: 'He was going to go for the hole just inside me, just off my left shoulder. Kenny Bowman and I were supposed to move big Jethro Pugh out of the way. The ground was giving me trouble, the footing was bad down near the goal line, but I dug my cleats in, got a firm hold with my right foot, and we got down into position, and Bart called the hut signal. Jethro was on my inside shoulder, my left shoulder. I slammed into Jethro hard, coming off the ball as fast as I ever have in my life. All he had time to do was raise his left arm. He didn't even get it up all the way, and I

ABOVE: *Green Bay's Boyd Dowler scores the Packers' first touchdown over Cowboy Mel Renfro in the 1967 NFL Championship game.*

BELOW: *Green Bay quarterback Bart Starr dives over for the winning touchdown in the 1967 NFL Championship game.*

charged into him .... With Bowman's help I moved him outside .... Bart churned into the opening and stretched and fell and landed over the goal line.'

The Packers had won their third straight NFL Championship, 21-17, and turned their attention to the AFL's version of invincibility, the Oakland Raiders, who had finished the regular season 13-1, then obliterated the Houston Oilers, 40-7, in the title game.

Coached by John Rauch and quarterbacked by Daryle Lamonica, the Raiders were rapidly building their roughneck image. Gene Upshaw and Jim Otto were the nucleus of the offensive line. Pete Banaszak and Hewritt Dixon were the running backs, Fred Biletnikoff the primary receiver. Ben Davidson was the big name on defense.

The oddsmakers, however, weren't all that impressed and made the Packers 14-point favorites. Pity the fools who took the points. Bart Starr had a fine day passing in Miami's Orange Bowl, and Vince Lombardi had his third straight championship and two Super Bowl victories.

The gate at the Super Bowl had generated an astounding $3 million, giving pro football's business managers an inkling of the gold mine they had happened upon.

The rumors had flown the week of the game that Lombardi was planning to retire. 'It's too early for such a decision,' Lombardi told reporters when asked about it. 'I'm going to give Vince Lombardi a real hard look.' His players, however, had played the game as if it was their coach's last.

Weeks later, the team announced Lombardi had resigned as coach but would remain as general manager. That status lasted a year, until Lombardi was named coach, part owner and executive vice president of the Washington Redskins. He would coach there one season before dying in September 1970, at age 57, of lung cancer.

The 1967 season was also a landmark in that it brought the fourth and final retirement of George Halas as coach of the Chicago Bears. He was 73, the grand old man of football.

UPRISING: NAMATH, THE JETS AND THE CHIEFS

The sports world had an excuse for being caught napping in 1969. The NFL had proven its superiority, and with the dominance of the Baltimore Colts, the Super Bowl seemed a foregone conclusion. The AFL may have been enjoying its most entertaining season, with a sizzling Oakland Raiders-New York Jets rivalry. But the outcome was considered little more than a passing interest.

Still, only an NFL snob could fail to take notice of the drama, with cameras focused on the brash, charismatic Jets' quarterback, Broadway Joe Namath. First, there was the 'Heidi' game, the network gaffe that infuriated millions of television viewers but ultimately drew more attention to the raging competition in the AFL. Of course, Namath and the Jets were among the central characters, but they shared the lead with Daryle Lamonica and the perpetually dastardly Raiders. Aired by NBC, the 17 November match-up was a preview of the league championship. It was a darts match between Namath and Lamonica, an exchange of bull's eyes featuring 71 passes and 19 penalties. Stretched by the style, the game was much longer than expected, developing into a 29-29 tie in the closing minutes. Then New York added a field goal for 32-29 lead with a little over a minute left. Within seconds Lamonica pitched the Raiders to the Jets' 43 for a thrilling close. That's when NBC officials abruptly switched to a scheduled broadcast of 'Heidi,' the children's classic. Only viewers in the West, where it was 4:00 PM, were allowed to see the dramatic climax. Thousands of others in the East were outraged and immediately jammed NBC's switchboards with complaints. NBC President Julian Goodman was among the jilted fans but couldn't get a call through.

The network waited more than an hour to flash the outcome across the bottom of the screen: Oakland 43, New York 32. Lamonica had thrown a 43-yard scoring pass to Charlie Smith with 43 seconds left, then the Jets fumbled the kickoff and Preston Ridelhuber picked up the ball and scored again.

That scathing pace resumed 29 December in the AFC Championship, played in the chill, swirling winds of New York's Shea Stadium. Oakland had gotten there by winning the Western Division with a 12-2 record, then eliminating the Kansas City Chiefs, 41-6, in a playoff; the Jets had zipped the Eastern with 11 wins and 3 losses. The weather grounded both air attacks early in the championship. But Namath used his favorite receiver, Don Maynard, to work on Oakland's rookie cornerback George Atkinson. Maynard beat

LEFT: *New York Jets quarterback Joe Namath faces the pass rush of Oakland's Carleton Oats during the November 1968 game, known as the 'Heidi' game.*

ABOVE: *New York Jets quarterback Joe Namath hands off to halfback Emerson Boozer during Super Bowl III, an upset victory by the Jets over the Baltimore Colts.*

Atkinson for a 14-yard touchdown pass in the first quarter, and a short time later, New York added a field goal for a 10-0 lead. Lamonica opened up the Raiders in the second period with a 29-yard scoring pass to Fred Biletnikoff, then Jim Turner's second field goal (he had kicked a pro record 34 field goals during the season) pushed New York a little farther ahead, 17-7. George Blanda matched that moments later with a Raider field goal, and the Jets led 13-10 at the half.

Another Blanda field goal evened the score at 13 in the third, but

Namath pushed the Jets back into the lead with an 80-yard drive and a 20-yard scoring pass to tight end Pete Lammons. After Blanda kicked his third field goal to bring the Raiders within four, Namath resumed his attack on Atkinson. The Oakland corner responded with an interception and return to the New York five, setting up Oakland's go-ahead touchdown. Namath lashed back 30 seconds later with a bomb to Maynard at the Oakland six. On the next play, he threw again to Maynard in the corner of the end zone for a 27-23 Jets' lead.

Lamonica had six minutes left to work some magic. His first effort died when he was sacked at the New York 26 on fourth and 10. The second effort took the Raiders to the Jets' 24, where a fumbled lateral ended Oakland's hopes.

The Jets were headed to the Super Bowl in Miami, but that didn't matter much, according to the pundits. The Baltimore Colts, with 15 wins against a single loss, were 18- to 23-point favorites. Johnny Unitas was slowed by injuries, leaving veteran Earl Morrall as the Colts' quarterback, but that seemed to make little difference as

ABOVE: *Jets quarterback Joe Namath catching a breather on the bench during Super Bowl III.*

ABOVE RIGHT: *The Baltimore fans were sure before the game that Namath's talk of a New York victory was outlandish.*

RIGHT: *The Jet defense hampered Baltimore quarterback Earl Morrall throughout Super Bowl III, leaving the Colts with nothing more than a token touchdown.*

ABOVE: *Following the Jets' lead in Super Bowl III, the AFL's Kansas City Chiefs crushed the NFL's Minnesota Vikings in Super Bowl IV.*

RIGHT: *The leader in Minnesota's offense was tough-minded quarterback Joe Kapp.*

Baltimore humiliated Cleveland, 34-0, in the NFL Championship. The Baltimore defense was the real foundation of the squad, and just about everyone figured it would make mincemeat of Super Joe and company.

Which made Namath's mouthing off to the press in the days before the Super Bowl seem all the more preposterous. 'The Jets will win on Sunday,' he told the Miami Touchdown Club three days before the game. 'I guarantee it.' Later, he told reporters that Morrall wasn't as good as three or four AFL quarterbacks. Then he was reported to have told Colts defensive end Lou Michaels, 'we're going to beat the hell out of you.' The Colts were a little taken aback by the woofing. 'All this Namath talk isn't going to fire us up,' grumbled Baltimore's Bubba Smith.

The game had additional subplots. Weeb Ewbank, the New York coach, had directed Baltimore to world championships in 1958 and 1959, only to be let go after a .500 season in 1962. And Johnny Sample, firebrand in the Jets' secondary, had been traded by the Colts after their championships. And, in a more restrained snobbish manner, the Colts matched Namath's talk with haughtiness. Club and network (NBC had paid $2.5 million for broadcast rights) officials began planning the victory celebration in the Baltimore locker room. Colts' owner Carroll Rosenbloom went so far as to invite Ewbank to his victory party.

The Colts, it's fair to say, played as they acted: fatly overconfident. Still, they were presented ample opportunity in the first half to make the game a blowout. It just wasn't in the stars.

The Jets received and immediately established a ground game, with Matt Snell running effectively into the face of the Baltimore defense. The drive died after four minutes but it built New York's confidence. After a punt, the Colts promptly shoved their way down the field to a first down at the Jets' 19, where a pass was dropped and

LEFT: *Quarterback Len Dawson managed the offensive affairs for Kansas City and led the Chiefs to victory in Super Bowl IV.*

TOP RIGHT: *The Chiefs were only the second-place finishers from the AFL, but they soundly whipped the Vikings, the upstarts of the NFL, in Super Bowl IV.*

BOTTOM RIGHT: *The Chiefs were 13-point underdogs to Kapp and the Vikings, who had beaten Cleveland 27-7 for the NFL title. But the Kansas City defense kept Minnesota wrapped up all afternoon.*

Michaels missed a 27-yard field goal. Moments later, George Sauer Jr fumbled on New York's 12, and the Colts had another chance. Jets' defensive back Randy Beverly intercepted a Morrall pass in the end zone.

The Baltimore defense was successful in shutting down Namath's primary target, Maynard, so he threw to Sauer instead, moving the Jets on an impressive drive to the Baltimore four, where Snell ran the ball in for a 7-0 lead. Again, the Colts forged back, taking the ball to the Jets' 16 on the strength of a 58-yard run by Tom Matte. Again, the Jets prevailed, this time with Sample getting the interception in the end zone.

Still, the Colts returned to scoring position yet a fourth time just before the half, but Morrall failed to see wide open Jimmy Orr at the Jets' 10. Instead he threw to the other side of the field and suffered a third interception.

The second half opened with Unitas eager to play, but Colts coach Don Shula started Morrall again. Then Matte fumbled on the opening play, New York recovered and increased the led to 10-0 on a Jim Turner field goal. After Morrall failed to move the team a second time, Shula inserted Unitas. But the Jets had shut down Baltimore's strong ground game and defended the pass ferociously. Meanwhile, Namath was troubled by a thumb injury and replaced by backup veteran Babe Parilli, who promptly took the Jets to another third quarter field goal and a 13-0 lead.

When Turner kicked yet another field goal two minutes into the fourth quarter for a 16-0 lead, the task for Baltimore and Unitas became nearly impossible. With four minutes left, Jerry Hill scored on a one-yard dive and the NFL's dominant team avoided a shutout.

'We didn't win on passing or running or defense,' said MVP Namath, who had completed 17 of 28 passes for 208 yards. 'We beat 'em in every phase of the game. If ever there was a world champion, this is it.'

If pro football fans thought the AFL Super Bowl victory was a fluke, the Kansas City Chiefs shoved reality in their faces with a convincing 23-7 win over the Minnesota Vikings in Super Bowl IV. And the Chiefs were a second-place finisher in the AFL regular season standings.

The league had adopted a crossover playoff system, allowing the runner-up of one division to play the champion of the other.The Chiefs rode that rule to glory in 1969. Namath and the Jets won the AFL's Eastern Division, only to be knocked out of the playoffs by Kansas City, 13-6. Oakland, with a 12-1-1 record, had been the AFL's

dominant team, but the Raiders became the Chiefs' next victim, 17-7.

Suddenly, the second place team was headed for the Super Bowl. The Chiefs' offense was guided by quarterback Len Dawson and bolstered by veteran placekicker Jan Stenerud. Mike Garrett gave the ground game its wheels. The defense, with Curly Culp, Buck Buchanan, Bobby Bell and Willie Lanier, was already renowned.

Their big names didn't stop the Chiefs from being 13-point underdogs to swashbuckling Joe Kapp and the Minnesota Vikings, who had hammered their way to the NFL Championship. Kapp was described as a mediocre passer, yet he had thrown a record-tying seven touchdown passes in demolishing the defending-champion Colts, 52-14, the first game of the season. More than their offense, coach Bud Grant's Vikings were known for defense. Carl Eller, Jim Marshall, Alan Page and Gary Larsen made a very mean front four. After edging Los Angeles, the Vikings eradicated doubt and the Eastern champion Cleveland Browns, 27-7.

The site was Tulane Stadium in New Orleans, but the item of hype quickly became Dawson. He had labored for eight seasons in the AFL, throwing 192 touchdown passes in that time, more than any other pro quarterback. In 1969 he had missed six games with a knee injury, suffered through the death of his father, and then had to weather a storm of criticism about his play. On the eve of Super Bowl IV, just when it seemed he had put those things behind him, he was implicated in a news story about a gambling arrest.

The error of the story was later revealed, but in the heat of the moment Dawson's teammates and coach Hank Stram rallied around him. If the Chiefs hadn't had a sense of purpose, the press helped them find one. Kansas City's offense did its work early, and Stenerud came on to kick three field goals. That coupled with Garrett's five-yard touchdown run gave the Chiefs a 16-0 halftime lead, the same margin that had worked so well for the Jets a year earlier. It proved just as safe for the Chiefs, who rode their defense and ball control to a 23-7 win.

Around the country, the AFL owners were smiling. They were ready to merge with the NFL, and evening up their Super Bowl record with the older league made the change that much easier. It also didn't hurt that the Super Bowl gate was another record, $3.8 million.

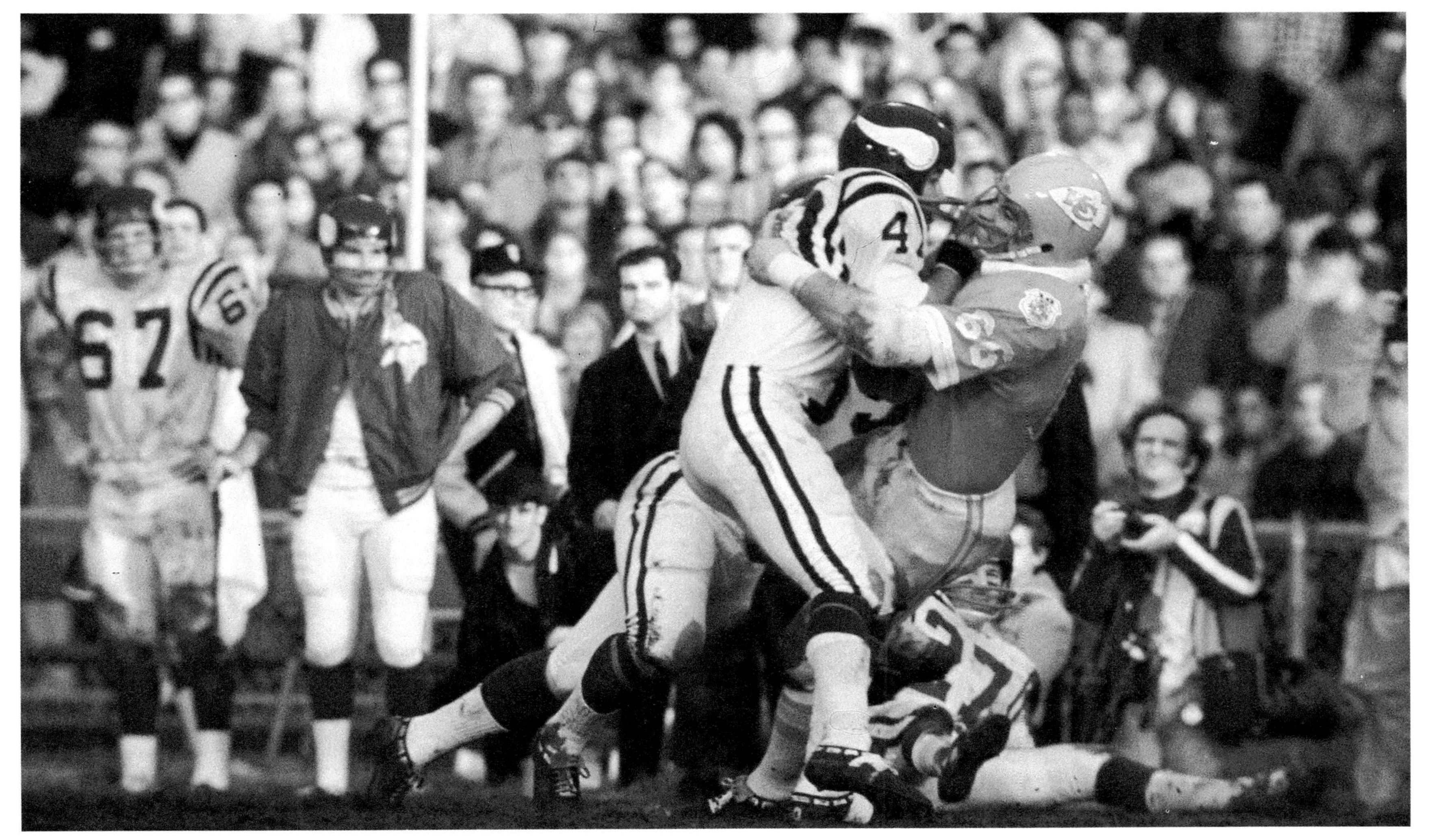

A NEW LEAGUE, A NEW DECADE, 1970-1971

COLTS, COWBOYS, DOLPHINS AND SPECTACULAR MONDAY NIGHTS

The organization of the league merger was negotiated in 1969, when Baltimore, Cleveland and Pittsburgh agreed to join the 13-member American Football Conference, which was realigned in Western, Eastern and Central Divisions.

The television industry then carved up this large, juicy bird. CBS bought the rights to all National Football Conference games, while NBC took the AFC. American Broadcasting moved into the picture with a new idea, Monday Night Football. ABC acquired the rights to broadcast 13 Monday night games each season for 1970-72. The Cleveland Browns beat the New York Jets, 31-21, setting the nation off on a new Monday night diversion, which would come to be marked by the bombast of broadcaster Howard Cosell.

The season was a great one for placekickers. Tom Dempsey kicked an NFL record 63-yard field goal, winning a game for the New Orleans Saints 8 November. Making the record even more remarkable was the fact that Dempsey was born with only half a kicking foot and only two fingers on his right hand. His foot, flattened by nature into a stub with no toes, was suited for kicking. Dempsey had kicked three field goals to keep the Saints in a nip-and-tuck race with the Detroit Lions.

But with just 13 seconds left, the Lions' Errol Mann had punched up an 18-yard field goal to give Detroit a 17-16 lead. A good kickoff return and a quick completion left the Saints at their own 45 with two seconds left, from where Dempsey worked his magic.

If the record belonged to Dempsey, the fall of 1970 belonged to ageless George Blanda, who was working his way toward becoming pro football's all-time leading scorer. Blanda had a playing career that spanned some part of four decades. In 1970 at age 43, Blanda worked come-from-behind miracles on five successive weekends to save the season for the Oakland Raiders.

Blanda first entered the NFL in 1949, when Harry Truman was president, and he retired in 1975, when Gerald Ford was taking over the White House. After 11 uneventful seasons, the Bears released him in 1959, at age 31, just in time for the birth of the newfangled AFL. Blanda was only happy to catch on with the Houston Oilers,

RIGHT: *Tom Dempsey's right foot was malformed at birth. But it proved to be anything but a handicap when he kicked a record 63-yard field goal for the New Orleans Saints on 8 November 1970.*

RIGHT: *Quarterback Roger Staubach had come from service in the navy to rescue the offense of the Dallas Cowboys. His icewater quarterbacking in close games became a trademark.*

LEFT: *Although he was aging, kicker/quarterback George Blanda worked more than his share of late-game magic for the Oakland Raiders during the 1970 season.*

where he became a star quarterback and kicker, leading his team to three championship games. Then in 1967, figuring time had caught up with the 37-year-old Blanda, the Oilers also released him. In 1968 the Oakland Raiders saw Blanda's worth and picked him up as a kicker and backup quarterback.

Oakland began uncertainly in 1970, with a 2-2-1 record after five games. Then first-string quarterback Daryle Lamonica was injured early in pivotal game six against the Pittsburgh Steelers with the score tied at 7. Blanda came in and threw three touchdown passes for a 31-14 Raider win. The next week Lamonica returned to the lineup. But with three seconds left, Oakland trailed Kansas City, 17-14. Blanda confidently kicked a 48-yard field goal for a tie.

The next week, Cleveland came to Oakland and held a 17-13 lead in the fourth quarter when Lamonica was again injured. Blanda's first pass was intercepted, setting up a Browns' field goal and a 20-13 lead. Given a second chance, Blanda drove his team to a tying touchdown, then worked them into field goal range minutes later with only three seconds left. From the Cleveland 45, he kicked a

Dallas running back Calvin Hill flies over the Kansas City defense as Chiefs linebacker Willie Lanier (63) leaps for the tackle.

52-yarder for a 23-20 win.

Miracle number four arrived with the Raiders down 19-17 to the Denver Broncos with four minutes left, when the Raider coaches inserted Blanda for a last drive. He took the team 80 yards and won the game with a 20-yard TD pass to Fred Biletnikoff. The cap on the streak came the next week against San Diego, where with seven seconds left, Blanda beat the Chargers, 20-17, with a 16-yard field goal. The Raiders won the divisional championship on the momentum of his magic.

Their season, however, ended in the AFC Championship game, 27-17, at the hands of the Baltimore Colts, who were intent on exorcising their despair over losing Super Bowl III to the Jets.

The NFC champions were the Dallas Cowboys, led by revolving quarterbacks Craig Morton and Roger Staubach and mercurial running back Duane Thomas. They eliminated John Brodie and the San Francisco 49ers in the conference title game to meet the Colts in Super Bowl V, played at Miami's Orange Bowl before 79,000.

The season had been a strange one in Dallas. The quarterback question was unanswered, and the receivers were in turmoil. Bob Hayes was benched briefly for poor performance, and Lance Rentzel was convicted on a morals charge. After nine games, the Cowboys stood 5-4, including a 54-3 humiliation by the Minnesota Vikings. But defensive leadership had rallied the team, with Lee Roy Jordan and Herb Adderley, the Green Bay great who had been traded to Dallas. Seven straight wins had put them in the Super Bowl.

The Colts had been through their changes as well, with Don Shula being replaced by Don McCafferty. But the heart of the team – linebacker Mike Curtis, quarterbacks Earl Morrall and John Unitas, tight end John Mackey – wanted badly to right their championship wrongs.

The game was a defensive struggle that rested on Curtis' fourth-quarter interception of a Morton pass. Rookie placekicker Jim O'Brien's 32-yard field goal with five seconds left gave the Colts a 16-13 win.

BELOW: *Quarterback John Unitas helped the Baltimore Colts right their championship wrongs in Super Bowl V, a 16-13 win over the Dallas Cowboys.*

ABOVE: *Quarterback Craig Morton shared time with Roger Staubach in the Dallas backfield during Super Bowl V. The game, however, rested ultimately with the foot of Baltimore's rookie placekicker, Jim O'Brien.*

RIGHT: *The Baltimore defense closed in on Morton and stopped Dallas at the right times during Super Bowl V.*

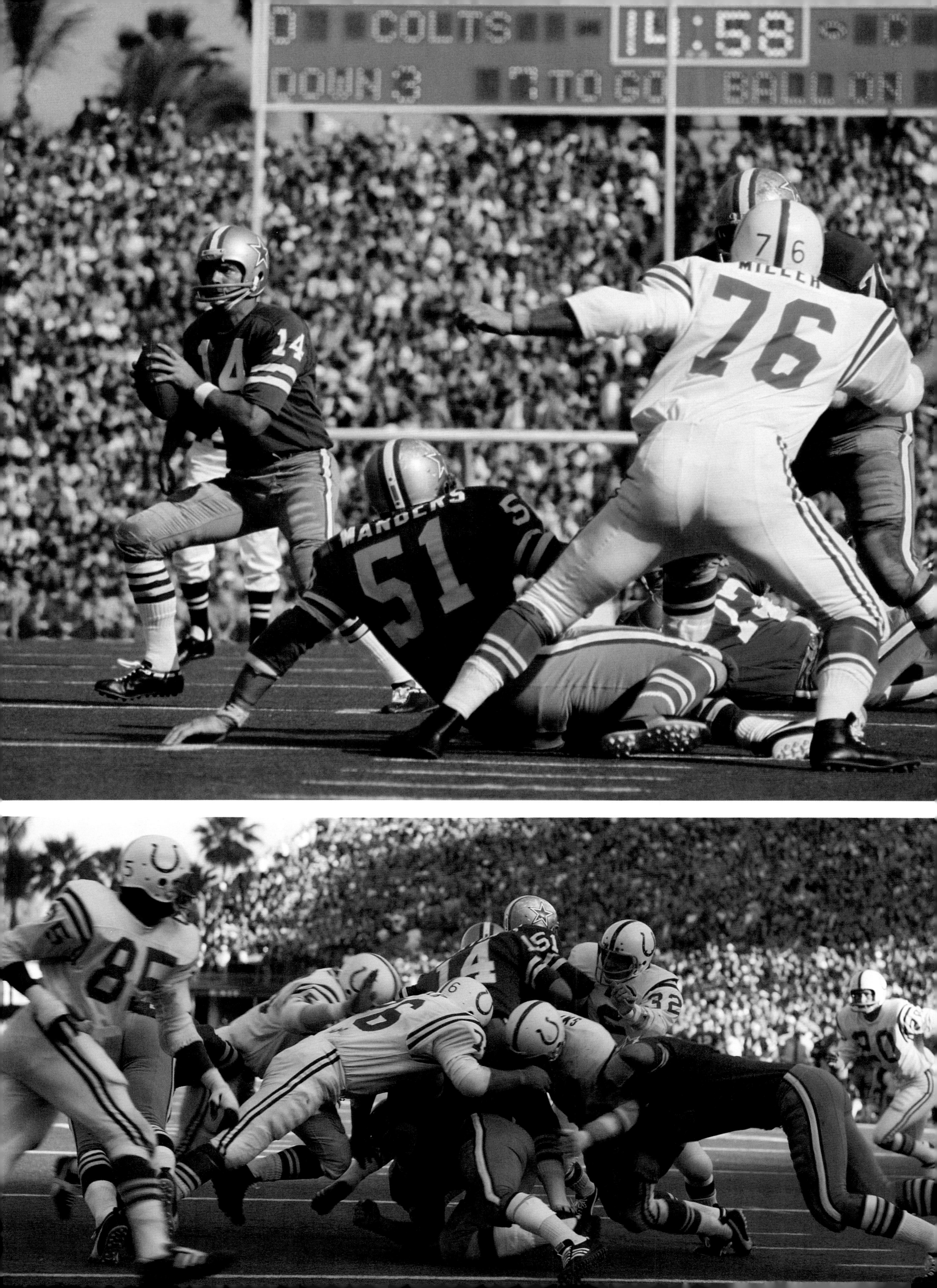
COLTS
14:58
DOWN 3
TO GO
BALL ON
MILLER
76
MANDERS
51
14

ABOVE: *Miami's Jim Kiick spins into the end zone, helping the Dolphins to a tie with Kansas City in this 1971 playoff game. The Dolphins eventually won in overtime, 27-24.*

LEFT: *The Chiefs' Ed Podolak is brought down by the Miami defense during the overtime 1971 playoff game. Podolak's memorable performance included 350 all-purpose yards.*

TOP RIGHT: *Dallas coach Tom Landry was known for an unemotional visage during the 1970s. Here he shows an unusual smile on the sidelines.*

RIGHT: *The Cowboys' Roger Staubach is sacked by Miami's Manny Fernandez during Super Bowl VI.*

For the next season, Tom Landry settled on Roger Staubach as the team's quarterback. The Navy graduate responded by leading the NFC in passing and taking the Cowboys back to the Super Bowl. There he took them one giant step farther – to their first championship. On their way, the Cowboys again turned back John Brodie and the 49ers in the NFC Championship game. As much as anything, however, the season heralded the return of Don Shula, who had shifted to the Miami Dolphins, and the startlingly quick emergence of that young franchise.

Their path to Super Bowl VI was arduous. It included the longest game in pro football history – the Christmas Day 1971 AFC playoff with the Kansas City Chiefs. The game was a kicking duel pitting Miami's Garo Yepremian against KC's Jan Stenerud. It also featured the all-star performance of the Chief's Ed Podolak, the fearsome play of Kansas City linebacker Willie Lanier, the passing of Len Dawson and Bob Griese, and the inside/outside of Miami's Jim Kiick and Larry Csonka.

After six periods of play, two sudden-death overtimes, 82 minutes, 40 seconds of regulation action, the game came down to a photo finish. The Dolphins had never beaten Kansas City in the previous six games the two teams had played. Both had finished with 10-3 records, but it appeared that Kansas City was headed for a seventh straight victory when the Chiefs scored 10 quick points. The Dolphins scored the same number in the second quarter, and the second half became a touchdown barter session, with each team trading two.

The memorable performance came from Podolak, who totalled 350 all-purpose yards – 100 rushing, 100 receiving and 150 returning kicks. But in the end, the game was decided by placekickers. The night before the game, Stenerud was named to present the AFC in the Pro Bowl, a slight to Yepremian, who had led the conference in scoring.

Stenerud had a chance to win the game with seconds left in regulation, but missed from the 31-yard line. He got a second try in the first overtime, from 42 yards out, but Miami linebacker Nick Buoniconti broke through the line and snuffed it.

When Yepremian missed from 52 yards, the game slipped into its second overtime. Weariness became the primary factor, but Csonka drew on his reserves for a 29-yard run to set up Yepremian for another 37-yard try. He calmly kicked the game winner.

Shula's bunch, however, had spent most of their magic. In the Super Bowl, the Cowboys, behind Staubach's precision passing and Thomas' 95 yards of power running, dispatched the Dolphins, 24-3. Dallas officials basked in the glow of the moment. 'This is the successful conclusion of our 12-year plan,' owner Clint Murchison said of the team's perseverance with coach Tom Landry through the franchise's first dozen years.

The Dolphins, meanwhile, had a plan of their own. The sports world wouldn't have to wait long to find out about it.

1972-1974

THE DOLPHINS DOMINATE, THE STEELERS EMERGE, THE JUICE RUNS TO GREATNESS

With the Dolphins' loss in Super Bowl VI, Don Shula became the first coach to lose two Super Bowls. Going into the 1972 season, he had a demon to exorcise. He had been the coach of the heavily favored Baltimore Colts when they were trimmed by Joe Namath and the New York Jets in 1969. The outcome had left difficult feelings between Shula and Colts owner Carroll Rosenbloom. So in 1970, Shula moved to the Miami Dolphins' struggling young franchise. While the Dolphins' quick rise confirmed his coaching genius, their loss to the Cowboys brought back a flood of doubt.

The Dolphins began training camp that next summer with a whirlwind of intensity. The high pressure system creating it was Don Shula's considerable pride. He wanted nothing less than absolute victory. Before the season was out, he would have it, watching his team dispatch 17 opponents in a row for the NFL's only perfect season.

For football fans, the Dolphins' precision was upstaged only once, on 23 December 1972, when Pittsburgh and Dallas briefly stole the spotlight. Without doubt, it was one of the NFL's strangest days. For coach Chuck Noll's Steelers, the day was immaculate, marking their first postseason win in 40 years of existence.

In Pittsburgh's Three Rivers Stadium, the first three and a half quarters of the AFC divisional playoff game between the Steelers and the Raiders were hardly memorable. The first half was scoreless, then Pittsburgh struggled to the lead with two Roy Gerela field goals in the third and fourth quarters. Shortly thereafter a young Oakland quarterback named Ken Stabler replaced Daryle Lamonica on the Raiders' last-ditch drive. With 1:13 left, Stabler, who would come to be known by the nickname 'Snake,' scampered 30 yards for a touchdown and a 7-6 Oakland lead.

It was only the second touchdown allowed by the Steelers over five games, but it appeared to be enough to beat them. With 22 seconds left, they faced a fourth and 10 at their own 40. Quarterback Terry Bradshaw dropped into the pocket to pass, realized he faced heavy pressure and scrambled right, where he stopped and blazed the ball over the middle to running back John 'Frenchy' Fuqua, who was covered by Oakland safety Jack Tatum. Whether physics or fate took over next is the question still debated in Oakland. The ball, Fuqua and Tatum came together at the 35. The two players fell, but the ball ricocheted toward Pittsburgh running back Franco Harris, who was trailing the play. Harris nabbed the ball at his ankles and raced to the end zone, where the arguments began.

Oakland players claimed the ball had hit Fuqua and bounced into Harris. The rules in those days said such a carom from one offensive player to another was an incomplete pass. The Steelers, on the other hand, argued that the ball had hit Tatum. The field referees consulted with the supervisor of officials in the press box and declared the play a touchdown, leaving the Raiders cursing amid the din of celebration at Three Rivers.

Myron Copeland, the Steelers' radio man, dubbed the play the 'Immaculate Reception.' The Raiders simply called it bad officiat-

TOP RIGHT: *With 22 seconds left in the Pittsburgh Steelers' 1972 playoff game with the Oakland Raiders, Steeler running back Franco Harris caught a deflected pass and scored the winning touchdown, a play that would be known forever as the 'Immaculate Reception.'*

RIGHT: *Harris sprints into the end zone with the winning score, beyond the grasp of Oakland's Jimmy Warren.*

LEFT: *Pittsburgh quarterback Terry Bradshaw runs the ball in the first quarter against the Oakland Raiders during their 1972 playoff game.*

ing. Fuqua, for his part, grinned and said he was remaining mum.

Three hours later, the San Francisco 49ers suffered a similar late-game disappointment. Yet they had nobody to blame but themselves. The outcome was an all-too-painful reminder of the 49ers' late-game failure in the 1957 playoffs, when they blew a 24-7 halftime lead and lost to Detroit, 31-27. Despite the ending, the game certainly started well, when San Francisco's Vic Washington ran the opening kickoff back 97 yards for a touchdown. Dallas answered with a field goal, but the 49ers turned Cowboy turnovers into two more touchdowns and a 21-3 lead.

Dallas quarterback Craig Morton finally reversed things just before the half, driving the Cowboys to a field goal and a touchdown to narrow the gap to 21-13.

Roger Staubach had spent most of the year on the bench with a separated shoulder, but Cowboys coach Tom Landry decided to play him after the 49ers scored a third quarter touchdown to take a 28-13 lead. Stauback promptly fumbled, providing San Francisco with a fifth turnover. The ensuing field goal miss by Bruce Gossett

was the difference in the game.

From that point on, Staubach ignited a scoring explosion. First, he drove Dallas to a field goal, to pull to 28-16. Then, with 2:02 left in the game, he started another drive. Only 32 seconds and 55 yards later, he hit Billy Parks with a 20-yard touchdown pass. With 90 seconds left, the 49ers led, 28-23, but San Francisco fans had good cause for queasiness.

The Cowboys tried an onsides kick, 49er Preston Riley seemed to pull it in, but Dallas rookie Ralph Coleman slammed into him, and Mel Renfro covered the loose ball. Staubach was incredibly efficient. He scrambled for 21 yards, then passed to Parks for another 19. When San Francisco blitzed on the next play, he zipped the go-ahead TD pass to Ron Sellers. The Cowboys led, 30-28. Only a perfectionist would complain that he left 52 seconds on the clock for 49er quarterback John Brodie to go to work. With three quick passes, San Francisco moved to the Dallas 22, only to have the drive stalled by a holding penalty.

The game – and one of pro football's strangest days – ended with a Brodie interception. From there, the season shifted again to Miami. The storm had gathered on opening day and started with a fury, levelling Kansas City and Houston before reaching a brief lull against Minnesota. After a narrow 16-14 win over the Vikings, the Dolphins blew past the New York Jets and San Diego, then paused to struggle with Buffalo. Again, Shula's intensity was the driving force behind a 24-23 victory. Three games, three victories later, Bob Griese, Shula's excellent quarterback, broke an ankle and had to be replaced by 38-year-old Earl Morrall.

The storm seemed to have dissipated to a squall, but with Morrall leading, Miami resumed its pace, slicing through nine straight opponents to finish the regular season, 14-0. Fortified by the 'No Name Defense,' powered in the backfield by Larry Csonka, Mercury Morris and Jim Kiick, the Dolphins ran their record to 16-0 with a 21-17 trimming of the Steelers in the AFC Championship. That set up a Super Bowl confrontation with George Allen's Washington Redskins.

It had been a nonpareil season. Csonka had gained 1117 yards, Morris 1000. The Dolphins had outscored their regular season opponents 426 to 202. But that mattered little to Shula. A loss in the Super Bowl would only make them losers again. He wanted nothing short of complete victory. As if the silent anxiety weren't enough, Rosenbloom, who had acquired ownership of the Los Angeles Rams, commented to the press that Shula would choke in the big game.

ABOVE LEFT: *Quarterback Roger Staubach led the Dallas Cowboys to a great come-from-behind victory over the San Francisco 49ers in the 1972 playoffs.*

ABOVE: *Dolphins running back Larry Csonka carries the ball during Super Bowl VII. Csonka was part of a potent Miami offense in 1972.*

RIGHT: *Another big part of that Miami offense was quarterback Bob Griese, although he missed much of the season with a broken ankle.*

RIGHT: *Redskin Bob Heinz blocks the kick of Miami's Garo Yepremian in Super Bowl VII.*

RIGHT: *Yepremian attempts to throw a pass after recovering the blocked kick, but his throw is intercepted and returned by Washington's Mike Bass for the Redskins' only touchdown.*

The oddsmakers must have believed him, for Allen's 'Over The Hill Gang,' led by Billy Kilmer, was named a three-point favorite. Washington had finished the regular season 11-3, then added playoff victories over Green Bay and Dallas. Both Washington and Miami relied on the ground game. The tomahawk in the Redskin armory was Larry Brown, who had rushed for 1286 yards in 285 carries. If opponents played the run too closely, Kilmer threw his floating butterball passes to receivers Charley Taylor, Jerry Smith and Roy Jefferson.

Griese had come back from his injury to guide the team to a late touchdown for the win over Pittsburgh, and Shula tabbed him as the starter in the Super Bowl, a decision made much of by the media.

The game, played before 90,000 at Memorial Coliseum in Los Angeles, was controlled by Miami's efficiency. After an early exchange of possessions, the No Name Defense – led by Manny Fernandez, Nick Buoniconti and Jake Scott – pinned the Redskins in their own territory.

Miami scored in each of the first two quarters, allowed a second half score off a recovery of Garo Yepremian's fumble, then settled in for a dominating 14-7 victory. Shula's doubt was finally erased, but almost immediately his thoughts turned to 1973, to sustaining perfection.

The season was just as important for Orenthel James Simpson, the Buffalo Bills' immensely talented but frustrated running back who had earned his reputation at the University of Southern California in 1967 and 1968.

LEFT: *Washington's Mike Bass leaps to intercept Yepremian's pass.*

BELOW: *Bass then streaks down the sideline for Washington's only score in a 14-7 Super Bowl loss to Miami. The victory allowed the Dolphins to complete an undefeated season, 17-0.*

The Bills, having suffered through a 1-12-1 season, held the first round draft choice in 1968. O J was the prize. Virtual anonymity was the result. The Bills had little punch on the offensive line, which was nicknamed 'The Vanishing Five.' In his first three professional season, Simpson took a beating, rushing for only 697, 488 and 742 yards respectively. His thoughts ran to quitting, or seeking to be traded. Then Buffalo hired old hand Lou Saban as coach, and he promptly announced that the offense would center on the Juice. Although the offensive line was decimated by injuries in 1972, Simpson still gained 1251 yards on 292 carries, enough to rekindle his dreams of greatness.

In training camp for 1973, Simpson confided to guard Reggie McKenzie, the stalwart on the offensive line, that he thought improved blocking would allow him to rush for 1700 yards. Why not aim for 2000? McKenzie suggested.

Such a journey would take Simpson past a major milepost, Jim Brown's single-season rushing record of 1863 yards, set in 1963. Why not, Simpson decided.

The pace was set in the first game against New England, when he rushed for a single-game record 250 yards. By mid-season, he had 1025, and speculation of a 2000-yard season started to build. In game 13, New England was again the foe, and yardage was available. The Juice gained 219 yards on 22 carries. By game 14, the last

ABOVE: *Orenthel James Simpson, known as 'OJ,' or 'The Juice,' won the Heisman Trophy at Southern California, then joined the Buffalo Bills where he struggled for several seasons behind a weak offensive line.*

LEFT: *In 1973 Simpson rushed for 2003 yards, an NFL single-season rushing record, eclipsing the mark of 1863 set by Jim Brown.*

ABOVE LEFT: *Don Shula guided his Miami Dolphins to an undefeated season and the Super Bowl title in 1972.*

ABOVE: *The Washington Redskins went to the Super Bowl on the strength of Larry Brown's running and George Allen's defensive strategy.*

LEFT: *The Washington passing game depended on quarterback Billy Kilmer. One reporter described his passes as 'floating butterballs.'*

regular season contest, against the New York Jets, Simpson needed 60 yards to pass Brown and 197 for 2000. The Bills also held slim hopes of a playoff berth (which would later die when Cincinnati beat Houston).

By the half, the Bills led 21-7, and the game's competition shifted, from team vs team to runner vs real estate. After a 25-yard gain in the third period, he needed less than 50 yards to reach 2000. The next series was the historic one. Simpson made runs of 8, 22, 9 and 5 yards, bring him to 1996. Reggie McKenzie led the next play, a gain of seven, that carried Simpson farther than any human had ever gone. After the game, Simpson gathered his offensive line in the spotlight with him. More than a decade later, the Los Angeles Rams' Eric Dickerson would rush for 2105 in 16 games, and Herschel Walker would even better that in the United States Football League's 18-game schedule.

In their quest, the Miami Dolphins fell short of another perfect season (they finished 12-2), but they still topped off the year by winning another Super Bowl trophy.

The Minnesota Vikings were the team to emerge from the NFC. With quarterback Fran Tarkenton, receiver Carroll Dale and running back Chuck Foreman, the Vikings ran to a 12-2 regular season record, then eliminated Washington and Dallas in the playoffs. Miami brushed past Cincinnati and Oakland to meet Tarkenton and company in Super Bowl VIII, played in Houston's Rice Stadium.

Shula used his power game as the Dolphins bulled to a 24-0 third-quarter lead, and coasted to the win, 24-7. It seemed the Dolphins might dominate for years to come, but a glitch developed in the grand scheme of things. The World Football League held its organizational meeting the day after the Super Bowl, and by March the Toronto Northmen of the new league had signed Csonka, Kiick and Paul Warfield to contracts. Although Csonka and Warfield played with the Dolphins in 1974, the championship atmosphere had been shattered. The WFL completed one season, then gasped and died in the middle of the next, surviving just long enough to dismantle one of pro football's truly great teams.

ABOVE: *At the heart of the Dolphins' precise ground game was the power of Larry Csonka, shown here running the ball during Super Bowl VIII.*

BELOW: *Receiver Paul Warfield provided a speedy target for Miami quarterback Bob Griese.*

THE PITTSBURGH STEELERS
A DYNASTY FROM AMERICA'S HEARTLAND

Poised at the cusp of their greatness since 1972, the Pittsburgh Steelers had been thwarted twice by the Miami Dolphins, in the AFC playoffs of 1972 and 1973. The two franchises were in a rigorous struggle to see which would emerge as the team of the 1970s. By appearing in three straight Super Bowls, the Dolphins had appeared the early favorite.

But the Miami franchise, weakened by a talent drain from the World Football League, stumbled slightly in 1974. And the Steelers, a young team brimming with ability, seized the opportunity and squeezed from it four Super Bowl championships, settling in many minds the question of the decade's dominant team.

In defense of Don Shula and his Dolphins, it should be pointed out that they did not go gentle into their goodnight. Their 1974 AFC playoff collision with John Madden's Oakland Raiders had been billed by a network PR man as 'the real Super Bowl.'

Justified, perhaps, although neither team eventually made it. It could be argued that both reached the zenith of competition that afternoon in Oakland-Alameda County Coliseum.

Both Shula and Madden had full houses, the Dolphins featuring Bob Griese at quarterback, Nat Moore and Paul Warfield at receiver, Larry Csonka in the backfield; the Raiders showed Kenny 'Snake' Stabler throwing to Fred Biletnikoff and Cliff Branch.

Moore, in his rookie season, ignited the proceedings by returning the opening kickoff 89 yards for a touchdown. The Raiders couldn't answer 'til the second quarter when Stabler tied the game with a 31-yard TD toss to Charlie Smith.

It was a margin of noses after that. Garo Yepremian kicked a field goal to give Miami the 10-7 lead at half. Stabler threw to Biletnikoff in the third to make it 14-10. Griese struck back to Warfield, but Yepremian's conversion was blocked by Bubba Smith – 16-14,

ABOVE: *Pittsburgh Steeler owner Art Rooney had suffered years of losing before seeing his franchise blossom into champions in the 1970s.*

FAR LEFT: *Oakland Raider quarterback Ken Stabler squared off against Miami quarterback Bob Griese (LEFT) in a dramatic 1974 playoff game.*

Miami. Three minutes into the fourth, Yepremian's 46-yarder stretched it to 19-14. Then with just under five minutes left, Stabler bombed 'em with a 72-yarder to Branch, 21-19, Oakland.

By the two and a half minute mark, Griese had returned the Dolphins to the Oakland 23. The Raiders were caught napping with Benny Malone's 23-yard run up the middle – 26-21, Miami. Shula knew the 2:08 left on the clock was too much. Stabler confirmed it with two quick passes to Biletnikoff, then two more to Branch and Frank Pitts. Clarence Davis then knifed inside to the Miami eight. Just 35 seconds remained. Snake burned his last time out, talked things over with Madden and receiver coach Tom Flores, then attempted a flare pass. The receivers were covered, he scrambled, and just as Dolphins defensive end Vern Den Herder pulled him down, Stabler cut loose with a desperate dead duck to Clarence Davis in the end zone.

Davis and Miami linebacker Mike Kolen wrestled for the ball, Davis won and assured himself a piece of eternity in an NFL highlight film. The Raiders, alas, went only as far as the next game, the AFC finals, where the Steelers overpowered them, 24-13.

RIGHT: *Pittsburgh coach Chuck Noll transformed the Steelers from league patsies into a powerful blend of offense and defense.*

LEFT: *The teeth in the Steeler defense began with defensive end Mean Joe Greene.*

BELOW: *The Pittsburgh defense surged and crushed Minnesota in Super Bowl IX.*

RIGHT: *The Steelers swarm and drop Minnesota quarterback Fran Tarkenton for a safety in Super Bowl IX.*

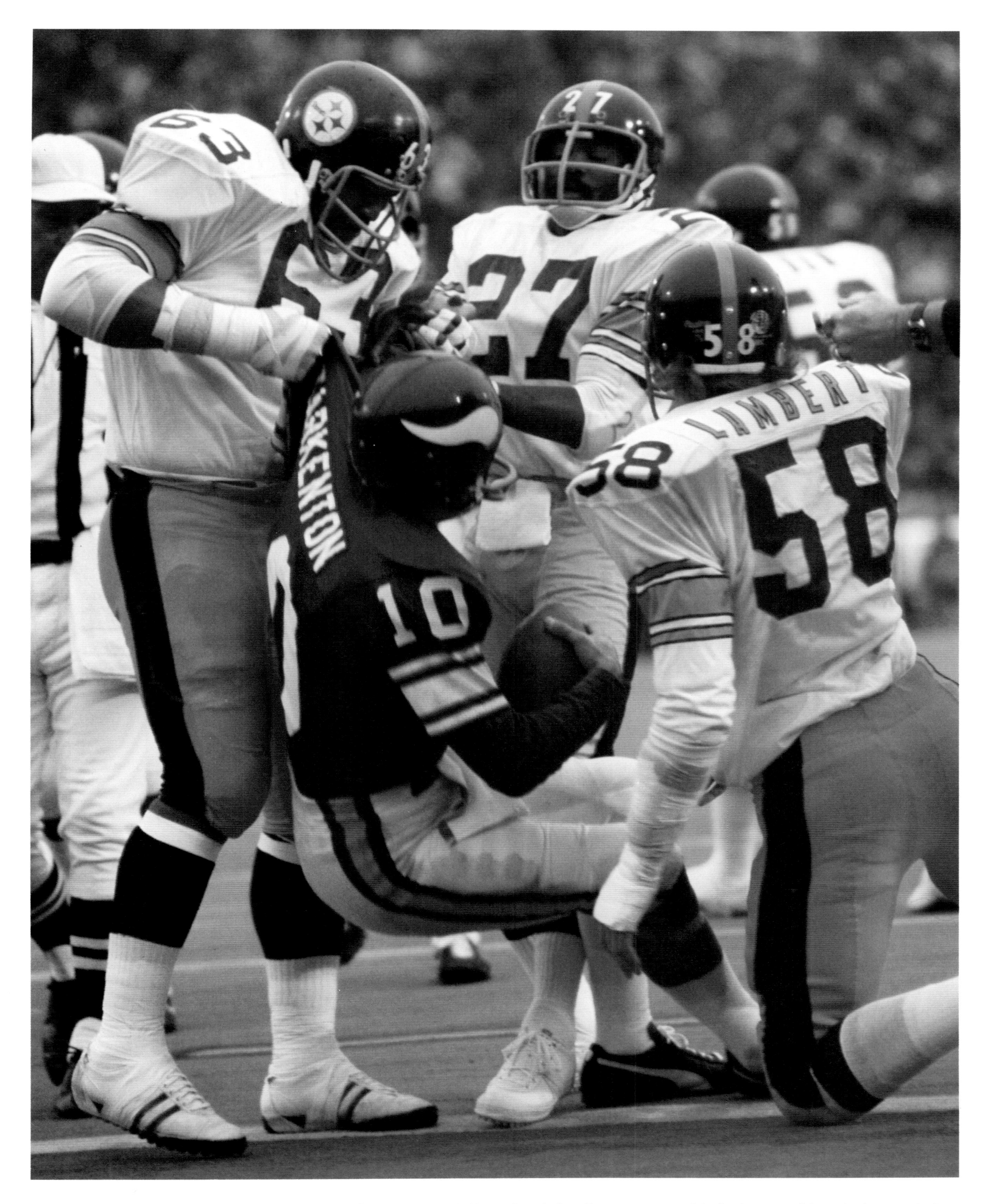

Suddenly, the moment Pittsburgh owner Art Rooney waited 42 years for had arrived. The Steelers were going to a Super Bowl. Countless times, he had anguished watching his team mired in losing seasons. The first real turnaround hadn't come until 1968, when Pittsburgh hired Baltimore assistant coach Chuck Noll to reverse the team's miserable fortunes. It took a few seasons and some brilliant and lucky draft selections. But it happened. The Steelers won four Super Bowls between 1974 and 1980, and to say they did it in 'blue-collar' fashion would be more than a bit trite. Yet there's hardly a way around it. In the age of America's great industrial decline, the Steelers became a lingering symbol of potency. They were hard, polished Pittsburgh steel, running roughshod over the competition with a defense led by Mean Joe Greene, Jack Lambert, L C Greenwood, Jack Ham and Mel Blount. The offense had a similar cast with running backs Rocky Bleier and Franco Harris and quarterback Terry Bradshaw.

The sassy style was added by receivers Lynn Swann and John Stallworth. They were mere rookies when the Steelers used their

appearance.

Also, for the second year in a row, the Steelers took the AFC title from the Oakland Raiders, the 1975 version being a slugfest that ended, 16-10. Meanwhile, Roger Staubach and the Dallas Cowboys had won the NFC title, blowing past the Los Angeles Rams, 37-7.

That momentum carried into the first quarter at Miami's Orange Bowl. The Cowboys had used Staubach and their shotgun offense to blast to a 7-0 lead. Then Swann stoked the Steelers' first scoring drive with a leaping, acrobatic catch of a Bradshaw pass at the Dallas 16. Somehow, he had retrieved the ball in midair from sailing incomplete out of bounds, then he twisted to land inbounds. Good for 32 yards, the play set up a scoring pass to tight end Randy Grossman moments later.

The teams traded an odd collection of field goals and a safety thereafter until midway into the final quarter. Holding a 15-10 lead at their own 36, Bradshaw and Swann opted for the bomb. Swann set sail, and Bradshaw lofted a fat one for him to run under. The result was another elegant passage in Swann's highlight poem: a 64-yard gamebuster for a 21-10 lead. On the downside, Bradshaw was knocked silly by the Dallas rush on the play and lost for the rest of the game.

Staubach brought the Cowboys right back with a quick touchdown pass, then got the ball back again trailing 21-17. But the Steel Curtain defense closed out the Dallas performance by intercepting Staubach's final Hail Mary attempt.

Swann, who had caught four passes for 161 yards, won the MVP trophy and the Pittsburgh legend had gained its second chapter.

The next wouldn't be written until 1978, when the Steelers staved off an AFC challenge from rookie Earl Campbell and the Houston Oilers to take their third Super Bowl crown.

defensive viciousness to subdue the Minnesota Vikings, 16-6, in Super Bowl IX. Fran Tarkenton, Minnesota's great scrambling quarterback, had brought the Vikings back for a third attempt at a Super Bowl crown. But Pittsburgh's ground game of Harris and Bleier controlled the ball, and the Steel Curtain defense took care of the rest.

By the next season, Swann and Stallworth had matured into the game's truly gifted pass catchers, which opened up the Steeler offense and helped lead the team to a consecutive Super Bowl

Campbell had set his legend in cement on 20 November 1978, against the Dolphins with 81-yard fourth quarter run. It was an incredible burst of acceleration by a leg-weary rookie on his twenty-eighth carry of the night. It froze the Dolphins in their comeback tracks. More important, it jettisoned Campbell toward the first of three consecutive NFL rushing crowns. Amazed reporters later asked Campbell how he could find such late-game strength. 'Ten more yards and I'd never have made it,' he confessed. On the night, he had gained 199 yards in 28 carries and scored four touchdowns.

ABOVE: *Super Bowl X became a wide-open all-out affair, pitting the Pittsburgh Steelers against the Dallas Cowboys.*

RIGHT: *Dallas linebacker Thomas 'Hollywood' Henderson had commented on Steeler quarterback Terry Bradshaw's intelligence before Super Bowl XIII. But it was Bradshaw who outsmarted the Cowboys and drove Pittsburgh to the title, after taking a few knocks from Henderson during the game.*

FAR LEFT: *Quarterback Roger Staubach led the Cowboys to Super Bowl X but couldn't quite get them over the championship hump.*

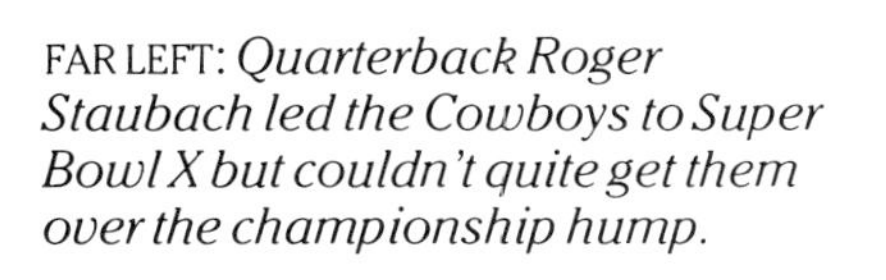

LEFT: *Houston Oiler running back Earl Campbell had an incredible rookie season in 1978.*

DUPREE
89
31
57
12
FITZGERALD
29

For three straight years, he would lead the NFL in rushing, piling up 1934 in 1980, accomplishment enough to place him among the greats.

The Steelers, however, would rule the playoffs by storming past Denver, then Houston, 34-5, in the AFC Championship. Their Super Bowl competition was their old favorites, the Dallas Cowboys.

As if the intensity for Super Bowl XIII wasn't hot enough, Thomas 'Hollywood' Henderson, the Cowboys' outrageous linebacker, stirred the coals in the days before the game, announcing to the press that Terry Bradshaw was so dumb he couldn't spell cat if you spotted him the c and the a.

Bradshaw's response?

Merely 318 yards and four touchdowns passing and the game's MVP trophy as the Steelers won, 35-31. The victory made them the first team in NFL history to win three Super Bowls. Afterward, Bradshaw basked in the locker room with a smile and told reporters, 'Go ask Henderson if I was dumb today.'

The game was hardly a masterpiece, rather a collector's item, a somewhat jazzed up reprint of Pittsburgh's 21-17 victory over the Cowboys in Super Bowl X. Having beaten Denver soundly in Super Bowl XII, the Cowboys had seemed confident the 1979 outcome would be otherwise.

Dallas took the opening kickoff and moved to two quick first downs and excellent field position at the Pittsburgh 35. There Drew Pearson fumbled on a double reverse/pass option, and the Steelers recovered at their 47. Moments later, Bradshaw hit John Stallworth with the first of his touchdown passes for a 7-0 lead. The Steeler defense then seemed to have things under control until Bradshaw was sacked toward the end of the first quarter and fumbled in his own territory. Roger Staubach quickly cashed in the gift certificate with a 39-yard scoring pass to Tony Hill.

Then in the second quarter, the Dallas defense declared Doomsday again, as Henderson and fellow linebacker Mike Hegman sacked Bradshaw and stripped him of the ball. Hegmen did the honors, running in for the score from 37 yards out to give Dallas a 14-7 edge.

Stallworth erased that minutes later when he pulled in a Bradshaw pass at the Pittsburgh 35, shook the tackle of safety Aaron Kyle and sprinted to the end zone, turning a routine pattern into a 75-yard score. Things continued to sour for the Cowboys on the following possession as Staubach threw an interception to Mel Blount. Bradshaw threw a seven-yarder to Rocky Bleier just before the half for a 21-14 Steeler lead.

The teams cooled considerably in the third, and the Dallas downslide continued. Jackie Smith, the former St. Louis Cardinal tight end who had come out of retirement to bolster the Cowboys' lineup, dropped the tying touchdown pass. Dallas kicked a field goal on the next play and trailed, 21-17 going into the fourth.

LEFT TOP: *The Steelers ran out to a big lead in Super Bowl XIII before Dallas came charging back.*

LEFT BOTTOM: *The crucial play in Super Bowl XIII came when Dallas tight end Jackie Smith was wide open in the end zone but dropped a touchdown pass.*

RIGHT: *Pittsburgh's Bradshaw passed for 318 yards and four touchdowns to defeat the Cowboys in Super Bowl XIII. He was named the game's MVP.*

Then the downslide became an avalanche. Helped by a pass interference call, the Steelers drove deep, and Franco Harris scored on a 22-yard run. Next Dallas defensive lineman Randy White, who played on the kick return team, fumbled a short kickoff. Pittsburgh recovered, Bradshaw threw 18 yards to Lynn Swann for a 35-17 lead with a little over six minutes left.

On the Steeler sidelines, the celebration began. Bradshaw saw Staubach trot onto the field and reminded his teammates that it was too early. Sure enough, the Cowboys drove 89 yards and scored to make it 35-24 with 2:27 left.

Then they recovered the onsides kick, and eight plays later, Staubach hit Butch Johnson with a four-yard pass for a 35-31 score with 0:22 on the clock.

This time, however, Bleier covered the onsides kick, and Pittsburgh coach Chuck Noll has his third Super Bowl trophy.

The next season, 1979, brought yet another Super Bowl title. The Steelers were only briefly upstaged by San Diego quarterback Dan Fouts, who passed for 4082 yards, becoming the first pro quarterback to break the 4000-yard barrier.

The playoffs became a matter of the Bradshaw Bunch dismissing Miami and Houston, which they did with relative ease. Los Angeles, led by quarterback Vince Ferragamo, and Tampa Bay, with quarterback Doug Williams, were the surprise entries in the NFC finals. The Rams won, 9-0, and provided surprisingly stiff Super Bowl opposition. They maintained a lead through the third quarter, until Pittsburgh zoomed away with the game, 31-19, on two fourth-quarter scores.

Stallworth caught three passes for 121 yards, including a 73-yard beauty for the go-ahead touchdown. But Bradshaw was named the MVP for the second year, despite throwing three interceptions.

'Winning four Super Bowls should put us in a special category,' defensive back Mel Blount said afterward. 'I think this is the best team ever assembled. They talk about Vince Lombardi, but I think the Chuck Noll era is even greater.'

'Comparisons are hard to make, but I think we're the greatest,' linebacker Jack Ham concurred.

As for Art Rooney, he had no doubts: 'This is the greatest team of all time.' One worth suffering through 42 years of losing for.

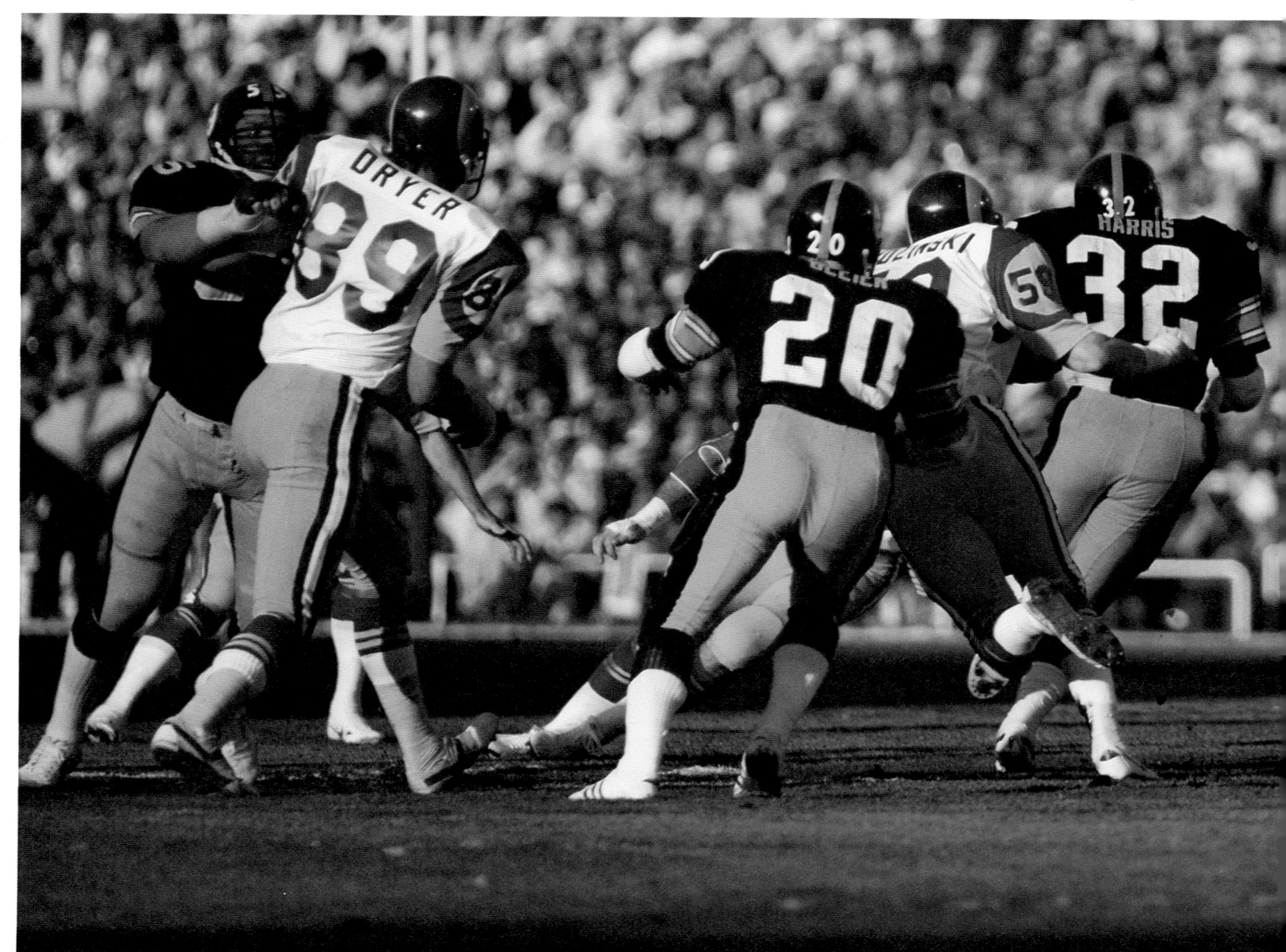

LEFT: *The Pittsburgh Steelers celebrate a touchdown in Super Bowl XIV, their fourth world championship in the 1970s.*

ABOVE: *Running back Lawrence McCutcheon was the workhorse in the Los Angeles Rams' offense, carrying the Rams to Super Bowl XIV.*

LEFT: *In Super Bowl XIV the Steelers outdistanced the Los Angeles Rams, 31-19, with a splendid mix of offense and defense.*

THE VIKINGS' FRUSTRATION
HAIL MARY

If Pittsburgh owner Art Rooney suffered through a slow, agonizing frustration watching his team lose for most of 42 years, the Minnesota Vikings anguished with a newer, more compact set of circumstances. Their agony came not at the bottom of the league, but at the top. There, some observers would argue, the pain is felt much more deeply.

Four times in the 1970s – Super Bowls IV, VIII, IX and XI – coach Bud Grant's Vikings came within one game of football's highest prize. Each time they were soundly thwarted.

'It wasn't just the score or the way they ran us around,' offensive tackle Ron Yary said after the Oakland Raiders whipped Minnesota 32-14 in the eleventh Super Bowl (1977) and last Viking appearance. 'I don't know how you can play in four of these things and lose them all. Not only lose them all, but play bad football. I don't know how or why it happened, but for the first time in all the years that I've been playing football, I'm embarrassed.' The ultimate expression of Minnesota's playoff misfortunes came not in a Super Bowl, but in the 1975 playoffs. The 1975 Vikings were their usual veteran, balanced selves. Having compiled a 12-2 regular season record, they were eager to return to the Super Bowl for a third straight year and secure the trophy.

Their first obstacle in the playoffs was a young Dallas wild card team, laced with rookies and carrying a 10-4 record into the game at

ABOVE: *Linebacker Thomas 'Hollywood' Henderson was a vital part of the Dallas defense until cocaine abuse sidetracked his athletic career.*

LEFT: *The passing of Dallas quarterback Roger Staubach eventually did in the Minnesota Vikings in the 1975 playoffs.*

RIGHT: *The efforts of placekicker Toni Fritsch were a key part of the Dallas machine in the 1975 playoff drive.*

Metropolitan Stadium in Minneapolis.

A cynic would have said that the up-and-down Cowboys didn't have a prayer. The day, of course, would prove differently. The Cowboys, in fact, had several prayers. Their late-game miracle would provide the NFL with a Ave Maria for posterity.

The Vikings recovered a fumbled punt in the second quarter and used the field position to take a 7-0 halftime lead. Dallas evened things up with a third-quarter drive, then took the lead on a Toni Fritsch field goal just minutes into the fourth quarter.

Facing the challenge of the season, Fran Tarkenton pulled the Vikings together for a 70-yard drive in 11 plays. Brent McClanahan powered in from the one to make the game 14-10, Minnesota.

Faced with a similar challenge, the Cowboy offense fizzled and punted with about three minutes left. The answer would lie with the defense, which had been bolstered with a crop of rookies – Danny White, Herb Scott, Bob Breunig, Thomas Henderson. The telling moment came as Minnesota faced a third and two at the Cowboy 47. Tarkenton eschewed the dive for a rollout. Dallas safety Charlie

ABOVE: *The Cowboys' Roger Staubach beat the Vikings with a 'prayer' in the 1975 playoffs.*

LEFT: *Dallas receiver Preston Pearson caught the Hail Mary pass, sinking Metropolitan Stadium in Minneapolis into an eerie silence.*

Waters blitzed and dropped him for a three-yard loss. Reluctantly, the Vikings punted.

The Dallas offense again fizzled. The last hope hinged on a fourth and 16 situation at their own 25. Roger Staubach and receiver Drew Pearson decided to fake a post pattern and angle for the sideline. The momentum of the pass probably would have carried Pearson out of bounds for an incompletion. But he was bumped by cornerback Nate Wright, and the official ruled Pearson had been forced out of bounds.

With 37 seconds left, Dallas had a first down at the 50. When the next pass fell incomplete, Pearson said it was time to work on Wright long again. The pass was short, bringing Pearson back from the end zone to catch it. As he moved to the ball, Wright fell, or as the Vikings claimed, he was knocked down by offensive interference. Pearson caught the ball at the five, clutched it to his waist, then felt it slipping away as he fell into the end zone. With the ball pinned awkwardly at his hip, Pearson glanced around for penalty flags.

There was none, only the dead silence of Metropolitan Stadium. The play became enshrined as 'Hail Mary,' and has become over the years one of the game's hallowed moments. Tarkenton suffered an even larger loss later, when he learned his father had died of a heart attack watching the game on television.

The Vikings in their four Super Bowl appearances made more money than any team from 1970 to 1977. They would have traded a great portion or all of it for a world championship trophy.

THE MID 1970s

OAKLAND TRIUMPHS, DALLAS GETS ANOTHER

Pro football found its stride in the second half of the 1970s. Game attendance had been weakening since 1973, but the league opened two new franchises in 1976 – Seattle and Tampa Bay. With that, a gate draw that had been hovering around 11 million fans per year zoomed off toward 13 million. The television ratings continued their upward trend as well, lifting with them the league's contracts with the three major networks. The Super Bowl moved from averaging just over 80 million viewers to more than 100 million by the 1980s.

A Harris Sports Survey in the mid 1970s reported that 70 percent of the nation's sports fans said they liked pro football, while only 54 percent showed an appreciation for baseball, which had long billed itself as the 'national pastime.'

The league signed what was described as the largest TV contract in history in 1977. That same year, the league owners signed a five-year collective bargaining agreement with the players union that put $55 million into the players' retirement fund.

On the field in 1976, the Oakland Raiders blasted to a 13-1 regular season record behind Ken Stabler's 2737 yards passing and Mark van Eeghen's 1012 yards rushing. After a close game against New England in the playoffs (the Raiders needed two fourth-quarter touchdowns to win, 24-21), John Madden's bunch dethroned the reigning Steelers in the AFC Championship, 24-7.

Figured to be a close game, their Super Bowl match-up with Minnesota proved to be a mere formality. Oakland won, 32-14, giving owner Al Davis the prize he had labored 13 years to win.

Davis had come to the lowly Raiders in 1963 after a stint as an assistant coach with the San Diego Chargers. In one year, he turned miserable losers into a second place finisher, earning AFL Coach of the Year honors for himself. Through the succession of coaches who followed him – John Rauch, then Madden – Davis had exerted

RIGHT and BELOW RIGHT: *The Oakland Raiders ran past the Minnesota Vikings in Super Bowl XI to win their first championship.*

ABOVE: *The snap in the Raider offense was provided by quarterback Ken Stabler, who threw for 2737 yards during the 1976 season.*

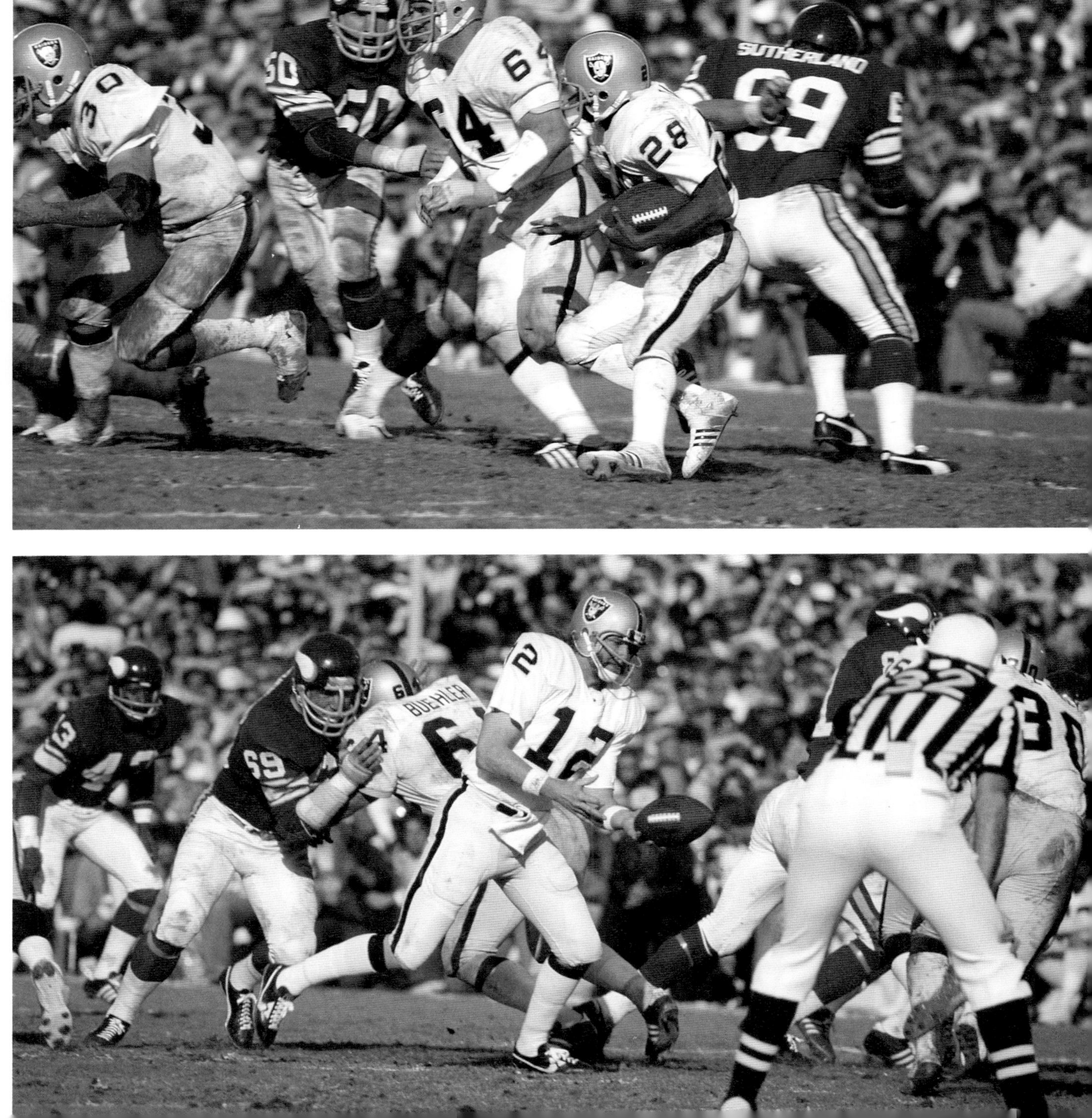

his considerable will in molding a fiercely competitive club. Madden had won six division titles before finally breaking through to the Super Bowl.

Though he had battled the NFL as commissioner of the AFL, and would later fight the league and win the right to move his team to Los Angeles, Davis enjoyed a moment of peace with NFL Commissioner Pete Rozelle following the Super Bowl win. 'Your victory was one of the most impressive in Super Bowl history,' Rozelle told Davis.

Clarence Davis had rushed for 137 yards, and Fred Biletnikoff had won the MVP award with four catches for 77 yards, but the day more than any other Super Bowl had been a team victory. 'They can't say any more that we don't win the big one,' Madden told his players.

The next season, 1977, was marked with milestones. Chicago Bears great running back, Walter Payton, set the single-game rushing record 20 November against Minnesota with 275 yards in 40 carries. Two weeks later, the league played its 5000th game.

On Christmas Eve, fans were given a thrill for a present, as the Raiders fought through a double sudden-death overtime to keep their string going in the AFC divisional playoffs against Bert Jones and the Baltimore Colts. Tight end Dave Casper caught only four passes in the bullet-riddled afternoon, but three of them were for TD's, including the 10-yard winner in the sixth period of play.

By any standards the game had a wild pace, with the teams matching big play for big play. Oakland running back Clarence Davis opened the scoring late in the first quarter with a 30-yard touchdown run. Baltimore strong safety Bruce Laird countered in the second with a 61-yard interception return to tie the game, then the Colts took a 10-7 lead just before half. The third period was just minutes old when Casper caught the first of his three scoring passes, an eight yarder. The scoreboard lights hadn't quit flickering before Baltimore's Marshall Johnson returned the ensuing kickoff 87 yards for a 17-14 Colts lead. Moments later, Oakland's Ted Hendricks blocked a punt, setting up another scoring pass from the Snake to the Ghost, this time for 10 yards and a 21-17 Raider lead.

The fourth quarter became a matter of touchdown trading. After Bert Jones worked a Baltimore drive, Ron Lee scored from the one. Oakland responded similarly, with Pete Banazak getting the one-yard plunge for a 28-24 Oakland lead. John Madden went crazy on the sidelines over the next 78 seconds as Jones rushed the Colts back down the field to another touchdown, a 13-yard run by Lee, for a 31-28 Baltimore lead with half the quarter to play.

Facing an uncertain end, Baltimore suddenly became tentative, and Stabler was anything but. With a hair under three minutes left, the Raiders got the ball back at their 30. By the two minute warning,

ABOVE: *Ken Stabler passed the Raiders to a thrilling defeat of Baltimore in double sudden-death overtime in the 1977 playoffs.*

they had advanced to their own 44, where Madden called Ghost to the Post (Casper on a post pattern). The Colt secondary forced the path of the play to be altered from the left side of the field to the right, but Casper changed course and arrived just in time to pull Stabler's pass in over his shoulder, a picturesque catch for a 42-yard gain.

Three plays later, with 30 seconds left, the Raiders faced a fourth and one at the Baltimore five. Madden considered going for the win but didn't want to hinge his season on one play. He opted for the tie and a shot to win in overtime. He sent in nervous Errol Mann, who kicked the game-tying 22-yarder. Regulation ended at 31 all.

The scoring whirlwind died in the first overtime, then the Stabler-Casper routine resumed in the sixth period. Efficiently the Raiders moved downfield, where Casper went to the corner of the end zone and pulled in the 10-yard game winner.

Their hopes of another special season died the next week in the AFC title game against the upsurging Denver Broncos, led by the veteran Craig Morton. Denver ran out to a 20-3 lead, but Stabler finally found the Raiders' pulse in the fourth quarter with two touchdown passes. A little more time, and they might have won it.

BELOW: *The veteran thrower Craig Morton took the Denver Broncos to the Super Bowl by defeating Oakland in the AFC Championship game.*

Such words were blasphemy in Denver, where Broncomania was raging. The Broncos had earned their place in the big event by beating Pittsburgh and Oakland in the playoffs.

Meanwhile, in the NFC, the Cowboys had added to the Vikings' woes by beating them, 23-6, in the title game. With Roger Staubach, the Dallas passing game was as impressive as ever. But the Cowboys had a new edge in their backfield with rookie back Tony Dorsett, their number one draft choice out of Pittsburgh. He had contributed immediately, gaining 1008 yards his first season, and the Cowboys had turned in an impressive 12-2 record. The Super Bowl hype was built around the two old Dallas quarterbacking foes, Morton and Staubach, coming face to face. The real difference, however, turned on Dallas' formidable 'flex defense,' featuring Ed 'Too Tall' Jones, Harvey Martin, Jethro Pugh, Randy White, Hollywood Henderson, D D Lewis, Bob Breunig, Charlie Waters and Cliff Harris.

Played in the Louisiana Superdome, the game was the first Super Bowl held inside. The Cowboys quickly lowered the roof on Denver. Under heavy pressure, Morton threw first one interception, then another, which Dallas converted into scores, and the rout was on, ending 27-10.

The Cowboys had their second world title.

Roger Staubach wouldn't have a greater moment until the 1979 season, when he led a wild comeback to knock the Washington Redskins out of a post-season berth.

Staubach called Dallas' 35-34 come-from-behind win over Washington in December 1979 the most exciting game he ever played as a Cowboy. Better than four Super Bowls. Better than six NFC Championship games. Better, even, than Hail Mary.

Going into the final game of the 1979 season at Texas Stadium, both Washington and Dallas had 10-5 records. If the Redskins won the game, they had the NFC East title. If they lost, their season would end, because the Chicago Bears had a points advantage for the wild card spot.

The Redskins powered and finessed their way to a 17-0 second-quarter lead, seemingly enough to put the game away. Even Staubach had never come back from such a deficit. Quarterback Joe

LEFT: *The Dallas offense was making regular trips to the Denver end zone, and hammered the Broncos 27-10 in Super Bowl XII.*

ABOVE: *Quarterback Roger Staubach ran the Dallas offense to near perfection in coming back to beat the Washington Redskins in December 1979.*

RIGHT: *A late touchdown pass to Tony Hill allowed the Cowboys to beat the Redskins in 1979 and knock them out of the playoffs.*

LEFT: *The Cowboy defense smothered Craig Morton in Super Bowl XII.*

Theisman had sneaked for one score and passed 55 yards to Benny Malone for another, and Mark Moseley had kicked a field goal.

The Cowboys didn't act like dead men, however. They calmly put together a scoring drive midway through the period, and then as time wound down, they added another, albeit a bit more frantically. With 0:09 on the clock, Staubach threw Preston Pearson a 26-yard touchdown pass. In Redskin retrospect, that was the killer.

It set the stage for the Cowboys' third-period drive to give them the lead, 21-17. Just as Redskins fans were about to get numb, Washington awakened with another 17-point outburst, beginning with a one-yard scoring plunge just moments into the fourth period, and Washington had the lead again, 27-21.

With just under seven minutes left, Riggins worked his big, lumbering magic, a 66-yard touchdown run, setting up a seemingly insurmountable 34-21 lead. Washington's final challenge was the clock. The offense and defense worked together to chew it up.

But with about three minutes left, running back Clarence Harmon fumbled, Cowboy Randy White recovered. A mere 40 seconds later, Staubach threw a 26-yard touchdown pass to Ron Springs.

On the next series, the Redskins found themselves facing third and two at their own 33 with 2:27 left. Out of magic, big Riggins was dropped for a loss by defensive end Larry Cole, and Washington punted.

Trailing 34-28 with 1:47 on the clock, Staubach had a loaded shotgun and two timeouts left. Bad dream time for the Redskins. He used 60 seconds to get to the Washington eight. On the next play, he lofted the ball to Tony Hill in the corner of the end zone, just beyond the reach of defensive back Lemar Parrish. Rafael Septien's extra point was the winner, 35-34.

Staubach graciously left the Redskins 39 seconds to work a miracle. It wasn't enough, of course. Roger Staubach had a sweet, sweet memory for his old age.

OPENING THE 1980s

SAY HEY TO THE BAY

Just as Philadelphia had emerged suddenly to usher in the 1960s, they made an abrupt appearance in the 1980 Super Bowl, moving mostly on the wits of coach Dick Vermeil and the arm of veteran quarterback Ron Jaworksi.

Unlike their 1960 edition, the Eagles failed to win the championship. That, of course, would fall to the Oakland Raiders, the first Wild Card team to win its way to the championship. Things, however, had changed for the Raiders. Ken Stabler had been traded for Dan Pastorini, and coach John Madden had retired to become a CBS TV analyst, giving the reigns over to his assistant, Tom Flores.

The year, however, belonged to Oakland backup quarterback, Jim Plunkett, the one-time Heisman winner out of Stanford who had won AFC Rookie of the Year honors in 1971 with New England, then drifted into anonymity. He would have remained there if Pastorini had not suffered a fractured leg in a loss to Kansas City the fifth game of the season.

Plunkett took over from there, driving the Raiders to an 11-5 record and a wild-card spot in the playoffs. There, they hammered Houston, 27-7, then eased by Brian Sipe and Cleveland, 14-12, and played a grand game against favored San Diego and Dan Fouts for the AFC title.

With Plunkett's passing and the running of Kenny King and Mark van Eeghen, the Raiders ran out to a 28-7 first-half lead. Fouts finally jumpstarted his offense, but the Oakland defense, led by Ted Hendricks, Lester Hayes and John Matuszak, got a 34-27 win.

LEFT: *Coach Dick Vermeil led the Philadelphia Eagles to a resurgence in 1980.*

ABOVE: *Running the Philadelphia offense was quarterback Ron Jaworski. He took his team all the way to Super Bowl XV.*

The sports world had figured the Dallas Cowboys would be Oakland's Super Bowl opponent after Tom Landry's team had whipped the Eagles badly at the close of the regular season.

But in the chill of Philadelphia's Veterans Stadium, running back Wilbert Montgomery chugged his way to 194 yards rushing. The defense, led by end Carl Hairston, shut down Dallas in the second half, and the Eagles won, 20-7. However, Plunkett and the Raiders quickly established who had the magic in the Super Bowl. He completed 13 of 21 passes for 261 yards and three touchdowns to win the MVP honors and the game, 27-10.

'I can't say enough about him,' Flores said of Plunkett to the locker room crowd of reporters. 'He met every challenge this season with style and class. He has great competitive spirit and deserves all the credit in the world.

'His career has had a lot of ups and downs. During the bad years he took all the criticism and never said a word.'

The Oakland Raiders would be followed as world champions by the San Francisco 49ers in 1981, bringing another Bay Area team to the top of pro football.

In fact, the playoffs leading to Super Bowl XVI were filled with surprises and thrills, with players suddenly emerging as stars.

The first-round AFC playoff between Miami and San Diego in the Orange Bowl on 2 January 1982 put some juice into the television ratings, although the playoff ramifications were almost nil, because the winner, San Diego, never made it to the Super Bowl.

Never mind that. From start to finish, the Dolphins and Chargers played a classic, packed with the range of emotion and heroics.

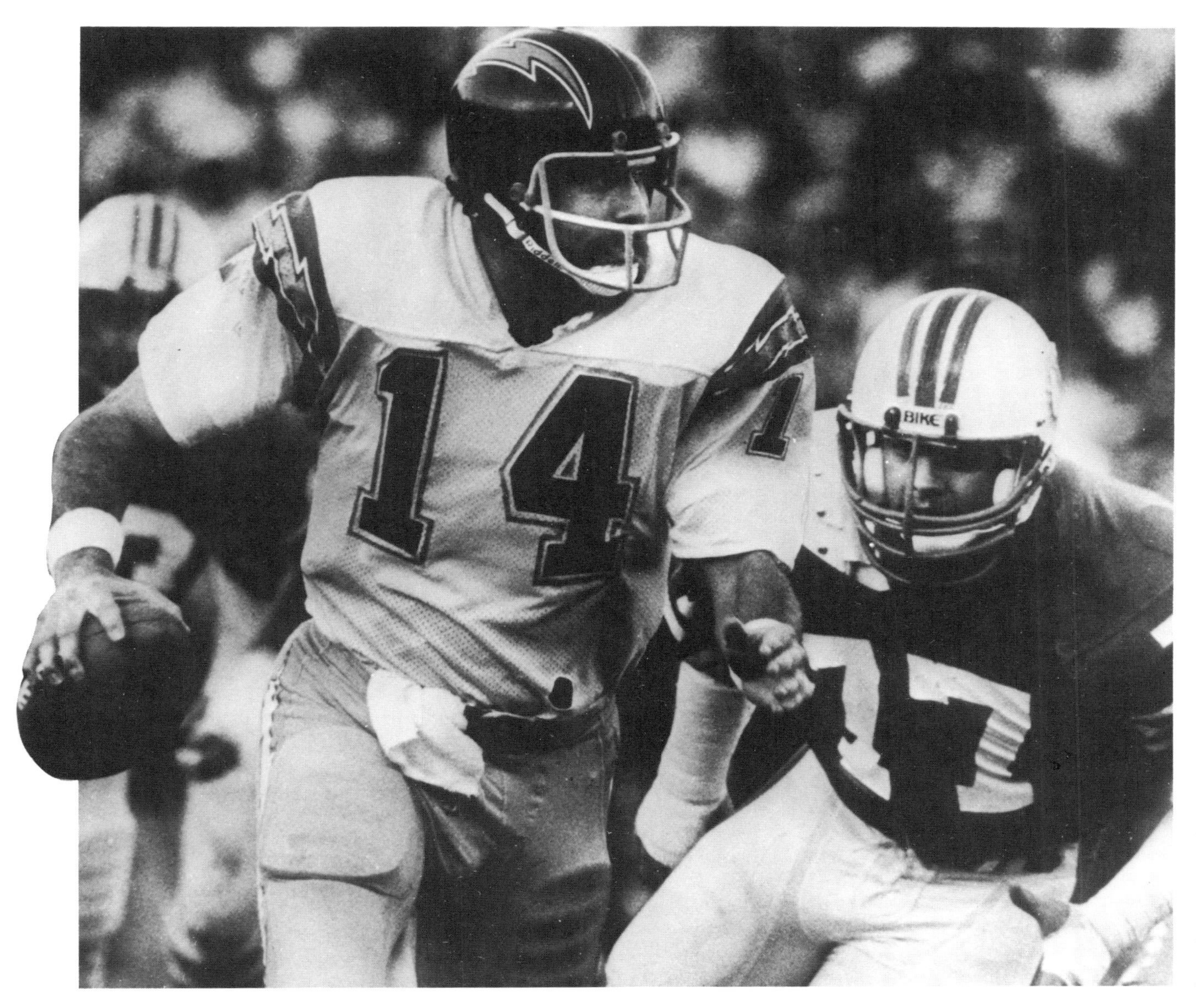

LEFT: *Quarterback Dan Fouts pushed the San Diego Chargers to a big lead in their January 1982 playoff game with the Miami Dolphins.*

BOTTOM LEFT: *Quarterback Jim Plunkett rescued his sagging career by taking the Oakland Raiders to the championship of Super Bowl XV.*

BELOW: *San Diego tight end Kellen Winslow put on one of the great performances of all time as the Chargers beat Miami in their January 1982 playoff match.*

From the cool comeback of Miami's veteran benchwarmer, Don Strock, to the cramp-ridden theatrics of San Diego tight end Kellen Winslow, this was a game of extremes. Highs, lows. Peaks, valleys. What began as a blowout ended as a death match.

Charger quarterback Dan Fouts began the game by driving his team into field goal range, where Fred Benirschke booted a 3-0 lead. Then, to San Diego's glee, the Dolphins made every conceivable mistake. First, Wes Chandler returned a punt 56 yards to put the Chargers up 10-0. Next, the Dolphins let the ensuing kickoff bounce

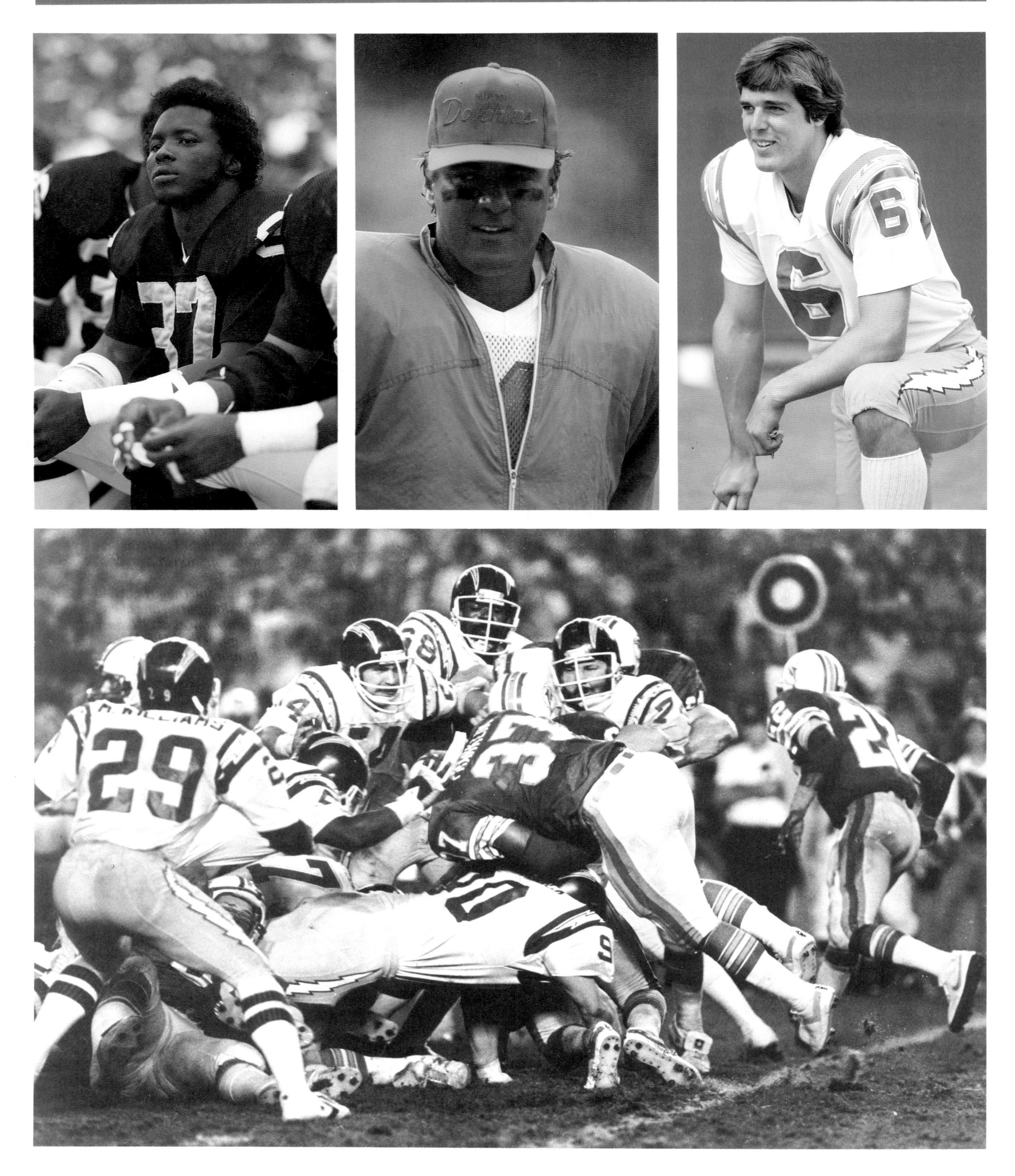

around until the Chargers fell on it. A quick drive led to a Chuck Muncie run for another TD and a 17-0 lead.

That didn't seem enough, so Miami quarterback David Woodley, threw an interception. Four plays later, Fouts threw a short one to James Brooks for a 24-0 lead. Finally, as an act of mercy, the first quarter ended.

And Miami coach Don Shula decided veteran backup Don Strock was the man to try the comeback. Strock provided a much-needed transfusion of calm by driving the Dolphins to a field goal. On the next possession, he drove them again, finishing the job the second time with a one-yard TD pass to Joe Rose.

Leading 24-10, the Chargers sensed something, so with 30 seconds left in the half, they tried a 55-yard field goal instead of punting the ball deep. They missed, giving Strock one more chance. The Dolphins had reached the 40 with six seconds left, and Shula decided it was time to flicker a few fleas. Strock threw 15 yards to receiver Duriel Harris, who, as tacklers closed in, turned and lateralled the ball to running back Tony Nathan. He streaked to the

FAR LEFT: *A key element in the Oakland Raiders' success of 1980 was corner back Lester Hayes.*

MIDDLE LEFT: *Substitute quarterback Don Strock led Miami to a miracle comeback against the Chargers in January 1982, only to see his team fall short.*

LEFT: *After missing a key field goal, San Diego's Rolf Benirschke finally kicked a winner to beat Miami in their January 1982 playoff.*

LEFT: *Miami fullback Andra Franklin runs into the forward wall of the San Diego defense in the AFC playoff classic on 2 January 1982.*

RIGHT: *San Francisco quarterback Joe Montana was able to shine in the 1982 playoffs.*

BELOW: *Montana's favorite target was receiver Dwight Clark.*

end zone as time ran out, bringing the Dolphins to within a touchdown at 24-17.

If the Chargers entertained thoughts that the comeback was only a bad dream, Strock woke them up at the outset of the second half by driving the Dolphins to the tying touchdown. He finished the job off with a 15-yard toss to Rose.

Fouts and the Chargers finally shook off their disgust at the close of the period with a go-ahead touchdown, a 25-yard pass from Fouts to Winslow. Strock's answer was a 50-yard touchdown pass to tight end Bruce Hardy that sapped any momentum the Chargers hoped to regain. The San Diego fortunes sagged further when Miami's Lyle Blackwood intercepted Fouts' pass on the first play of the fourth quarter. A fine 12-yard run by Tony Nathan gave Miami a 38-31 lead. Not bad for a team once down by 24. Not good enough, however.

The Dolphins came right back for the jugular, driving deep into Charger territory with the clock dying. But then, at the San Deigo 18, rookie fullback Andra Franklin struggled to get more yardage and fumbled.

Showtime for Kellen Winslow. For the television cameras, he emerged as the weary hero, shrugging off cramps and injuries, rising from a prone position on the bench to re-enter the game and lead his team to victory. Dramatics aside, Winslow turned in one of the great athletic performances of modern football history.

He made several key receptions in the Chargers' 10-play drive to tie the game, and each time it seemed, the Dolphin defense would

BELOW: *The 49ers broke Dallas hearts in the 1982 playoffs.*

ABOVE: *San Diego's Charlie Joiner caught a pass to set up the winning field goal in the Chargers' 1982 AFC playoff defeat of Miami.*

TOP RIGHT: *Ken Anderson guided Cincinnati into Super Bowl XVI against San Francisco.*

RIGHT: *The San Francisco defense tightened up on Anderson in Super Bowl XVI, and gave 49er coach Bill Walsh his first championship.*

punish him. After a bout with cramps and exhaustion, he came back into the game with the ball on the Miami nine. He went to the corner of the end zone, and the Miami defense seemed to go with him, which allowed Fouts to throw to James Brooks for the score.

Tied at 38, the game still held 58 seconds in regulation. So Strock started again, only to throw an interception, which the Chargers returned in the form of a fumble, recovered by Miami's Tommy Vigorito at the San Diego 48. Given a second chance, Strock quickly moved the Dolphins into winning field goal range at the Charger 25.

Enter Kellen Winslow again, to the marvel of the broadcast crew working the game. The best leaper on the team, Winslow seemed the perfect choice by San Diego coach Don Coryell to bolster the field goal defensive unit. Winslow blocked Uwe von Schamann's kick – with his pinkie finger, as he explained later.

The result was overtime, and a freaky one at that. San Diego won the toss and marched the ball to the Miami nine, where Benirschke unexplainedly shanked his field goal attempt.

Time for Strock again. Using the craftiness one can acquire from a decade of being Don Shula's backup quarterback, Strock took his team back to the San Diego 25. Uwe von Schamann lined up again, only to have the nightmare repeated. The 34-yard attempt was blocked, this time by defensive end Leroy Jones.

The Chargers then moved to a miserable situation, third and 20 at their own 45. Enough being enough, it was time again for Kellen, who caught Fouts' pass well short of the first down yardage but bulled his way there. Moments later, Benirschke finally ended the thing, 41-38, with a 29-yarder. The numbers for both sides were suitably impressive. In three quarters, Strock had completed 28 of 42 passes (67 percent) for 403 yards and four touchdowns. Fouts connected on 33 of 53 for 433 yards. And Winslow? A mere 13 catches for 166 yards.

Despite the Dolphins' and Chargers' best efforts, the best entertainment of the post season was Show Montana.

The San Francisco 49ers had the surprise of the NFC in 1981. Coach Bill Walsh had glued together quite a unit with an assortment of draft picks, free agents and trades. Finishing 2-14 in 1979, they surged to 13-3 over the 1981 regular season. The backbone of the team was an unsung defense, but the star of the show was quarterback Joe Montana. Since his college days at Notre Dame, he had shown a knack for comin' back.

The playoffs that year offered ample opportunity to showcase the abilities of both facets of the 49ers' game – the unsung defense and Montana's come-from-behind, late-game heroics. In the end, both got their just rewards: Super Bowl rings.

Montana's big moment came against the Dallas Cowboys in the NFC Championship game played at Candlestick Park 10 January 1982, although trivia buffs will recall he threw three interceptions that day. The two teams jumped back and forth until Dallas took a 17-14 lead just before the half on a Tony Dorsett sweep.

Things remained that way until the middle of the third quarter,

when Cowboy quarterback Danny White threw an interception, which the 49ers used to set up the go-ahead touchdown, 21-17. Early in the fourth, Dallas tightened things up to 21-20 with a Rafael Septien field goal. Then rookie running back Walt Easley fumbled for the 49ers, the Cowboys took over at midfield and four plays later White threw tight end Doug Cosbie a 21-yard touchdown pass for a 27-21 lead.

Montana was known as a confidence man, but he promptly deflated the 49ers' tires by throwing an interception on the next possession. Time for the San Francisco defense, which stopped the Cowboys' eat-the-clock plans and forced them to punt.

Show Montana got the ball back at the 49er 11-yard line with 4:54 left. Montana and Walsh wisely used the ground game to eat up the Cowboys' prevent defense. If they showed signs of tightening, Montana drilled a quick one to his primary receivers – Freddie Solomon and Dwight Clark. The moment of truth came at the Dallas six on third and three with 58 seconds left. Montana was to look for Solomon in the left of the end zone, but the primary receiver was covered, and the Dallas rush, led by 6-foot-9 Ed 'Too Tall' Jones, was bearing down. So Montana exited to his right, bought just enough time, and lofted a high one, just as the Dallas boys crashed in. Dwight Clark, 6-foot-4, waiting at the back of the end zone, leaped up and grabbed the ball. Beautiful catch. Highlight films. History. The works. Ray Wersching's conversion kick put the 49ers in the Super Bowl, 28-27.

The unlikeliest of Super Bowl opponents – San Francisco and the Cincinnati Bengals – had the unlikeliest setting – the Pontiac Superdome.

This time, the San Francisco defense took center stage. Not that Montana and Clark and Solomon didn't do their part.

The game was simply won in the first three quarters on key defensive plays, particularly a goal-line stand in the third when Cincinnati quarterback Ken Anderson was leading his team back from a 20-0 deficit. After scoring a touchdown to narrow the lead to 20-7, Anderson completed a big pass on his next possession to Cris Collinsworth at the 49er 14. The Bengals then changed weapons to big fullback Pete Johnson and battered to a first down at the three.

Johnson then picked up two yards to the one, where the Bengals tried him again, this time over left guard. SF lineman John Harty stopped him for no gain. Anderson then tried a pass, but was unable to find any open receiver in the end zone and had to settle for running back Charles Alexander at the one. Linebacker Dan Bunz hit him high and wrestled him down for no gain The Bengals went again to Johnson on fourth down, but the 49er defensive line wasn't in the mood to give ground.

From the momentum of a tremendous goal line stand, San Francisco went on to win its first Super Bowl, 26-21.

The Bay Area had introduced the eighties.

STRIKE

THE REDSKINS EMERGE

An estimated 110 million television viewers had seen San Francisco and Cincinnati battle in Super Bowl XVI. The popularity of the sport had bulged, and with it, so had the league's revenues.

The players union figured on pulling in some of that cash when the five-year agreement with the league ended in 1982. The owners and the players went round and round about the money issue without reaching an agreement. Finally, at midnight 20 September, following a Monday night game between Green Bay and the New York Giants, the players went on strike.

Through October and most of November, the nation's couch potatoes searched the dial on Sunday afternoons for something to watch: Ronald Reagan movies, college division games, old westerns – anything.

Finally, the players and owners reached an agreement 17 November, and play resumed three days later. The 16-game schedule was shortened to nine games, and the Super Bowl became a tournament with 16 teams getting a shot.

The finals, Super Bowl XVII, in a strange, offbeat year became a collision of monikers. The Killer Bees versus the Hawgs and Smurfs. Sounds like a bad Japanese horror flick. Rather, it was good old hard-nosed football, with a dash of Walt Disney.

The Killer Bees were the Miami Dolphins' stinging defense, named because many of the starters – Lyle and Glenn Blackwood, Doug Betters, Bob Baumhower, Kim Bokamper, Bob Brudzinski – had last names starting with B. The Hawgs were the Washington

RIGHT: *Quarterback Joe Theismann and coach Joe Gibbs guided the Redskins to Super Bowl XVII in the strike-shortened 1982 season.*

LEFT: *The Packers and Redskins leave the field after their 20 September 1982 game. The next day, the players in the league went on strike.*

BELOW LEFT: *Coach Don Shula returned his team to the championship round for Super Bowl XVII.*

BELOW: *The Redskin offense triumphed over the Miami defense, known as the Killer Bees, in Super Bowl XVII.*

Redskin offensive linemen, dubbed such because they averaged 270 pounds and grunted opponents out of the way. The Smurfs were the Redskins' diminutive receivers, Alvin Garrett and Charlie Brown.

The game was billed as a rematch of the 1973 Super Bowl. After a decade, Don Shula was still the Dolphins' coach. But the Redskins had a new leader, Joe Gibbs, a purveyor of the passing game who instead came to rely on the run for the 30 January Super Bowl in Pasadena.

The reason for Gibbs' favoring the run was 32-year-old John Riggins, Washington's blend of power and speed at fullback. Riggins, a former University of Kansas star, had sat out the 1980 season over a contract dispute. His comeback in 1981 had been a slow one. But he had been a major factor in the Skins 8-1 regular season record in 1982.

By the playoffs that year he was peaking and told Gibbs he should run the ball plenty. The coach listened, and in three playoff wins Riggins carried the ball 98 times for 444 yards, an average of more than 30 carries and 114 yards per game.

BELOW: *A late-game run by Washington's John Riggins delivered Super Bowl XVII for the Redskins.*

ABOVE: *The Miami offense, run by quarterback David Woodley, gave Shula an early lead in Super Bowl XVII.*

In the Super Bowl he would surpass that, teaming with the Hawgs to become the battering ram that broke down Miami's defense.

The Dolphins scored first on a 76-yard bomb from quarterback David Woodley to Jimmy Cefalo. Washington answered with a Mark Moseley field goal. Miami then drove to a first down just inside the Washington 10, but the Redskin defense turned nasty. On fourth down, Uwe van Schamann kicked a field goal for a 10-3 lead. Theisman laced together a series of deceptive plays on an 80-yard drive, completed by a four-yard scoring pass to Garrett with just over two minutes left in the first half.

With the score tied at 10, Miami's receiving team struck back, freeing Fulton Walker on the return for a 98-yard touchdown. It was the only time that a kickoff had been returned for a touchdown in a Super Bowl. Washington rushed back down the field in the closing seconds of the half but ran out of time on the Miami 16 trailing 17-10.

In the third quarter, Moseley kicked another field goal, bringing the Redskins to 17-13. The Washington defense continued to dominate, holding the Dolphins' offense to almost nothing. It was the Miami defense that nearly put the game away with two minutes remaining in the period. Theisman was attempting a pass from his own 18 when Bokamper rushed in and tipped the ball. The big nose tackle was poised to catch the tip and run in for a score when Theisman alertly jumped in and knocked the ball away.

The fourth quarter would belong to Riggins and the Redskins. They were driving into Dolphin territory and faced a fourth and one at the Miami 43. Washington ran Riggins left and used a man in motion to draw cornerback Don McNeal away from the coverage area. Miami was in a six man line, and when McNeal realized the vulnerability he attempted to regain his position. But he slipped and was unable to get more than a hand on Riggins, which of course wasn't enough to stop Big John. 'Riggo's Run,' as the play became known, went for 43 yards and the go-ahead touchdown.

Ten minutes were left, and the Redskins used them running Riggins right at the Dolphins. They ate up the clock and digested another touchdown for a 27-17 victory, Washington's first championship since 1942.

Riggins had finished with 166 yards on 38 carries, which was MVP material and pretty near Hawg Heaven.

SURPRISE, SURPRISE 1983-1984

The football world can be forgiven for thinking the Washington Redskins were a lock to repeat as Super Bowl champions. They had given pro football some of its more thrilling moments in running to a 14-2 record during the 1983 season. They scored 17 points in the final six minutes to overtake the Los Angeles Raiders, 37-35, 2 October in Washington's RFK Stadium. Their Monday night games were even more exciting, if less productive. The Redskins lost two, 31-30, to Dallas, and 48-47 to the Green Bay Packers, a masterpiece of a game that featured a winning kick by Jan Stenerud. Stenerud had kicked field goals for the Kansas City Chiefs for 13 seasons, until just before the 1980 season when they released him. He bounced through tryouts with several teams before settling with the Green Bay Packers.

For three years, Stenerud led the league in kicking percentage, making better than 80 percent of his field goal attempts. By the 1983 season, Stenerud, a Norwegian, needed just 19 field goals to break George Blanda's NFL record of 335.

As the season progressed, he added three-pointers in the best possible way – helping his team to win. In the first game against Houston, he kicked two, including one in overtime to give the Packers a 41-38 victory.

ABOVE RIGHT: *Jan Stenerud made the 1983 season a record breaker for the Green Bay Packers.*

RIGHT: *Miami quarterback Dan Marino broke into the NFL and almost immediately began setting records.*

FAR RIGHT: *The Chicago Bears' Walter Payton established a new standard for excellence in rushing.*

Two games later, Stenerud defeated the Los Angeles Rams, after running back Eric Dickerson fumbled, giving the Packers the opportunity to kick a 36-yarder for a 27-24 win.

With 54 seconds left against Washington, he knocked up a 20-yarder, his second field goal of the game, for a 48-47 Green Bay victory. Later in the season, Stenerud would defeat the Chicago Bears on the game's final play with a 19-yarder, then break Blanda's record against Tampa Bay with four field goals, taking his career total to 337.

The Redskins didn't so much break records as they did the LA Rams' backs, 51-7, in the first round of the playoffs, which only served to increase the talk of invincibility. A narrow win over the 49ers, 24-21, in the NFC Championship the following week quieted the talk some.

Still, Theisman's troops were rated a three-point favorite against the Raiders, who had throttled the Pittsburgh Steelers, 38-10, then repeated the act, 30-14, against the Seattle Seahawks of Chuck Knox in the AFC Championship.

To say the least, Super Bowl XVIII left the Redskins stunned and elicited comparisons to their 73-0 loss to the Bears in 1940. It wasn't quite that bad. But it was bad. Raiders' classy back Marcus Allen rushed for a Super Bowl record 191 yards, and the LA defense, led by Howie Long, Lyle Alzado, etc., wrapped up the Washington offense for a 38-9 win.

'We're the Slaughterhouse Seven,' Long said of the Raiders' front defense. 'We never had a hog that tasted so good.'

While 1983 had been the season for smashing silly Redskin hype, 1984 in the NFL rapidly developed as a time for smashing records, any kind of record – passing, rushing, receiving – and most of the big ones fell:

*The Chicago Bears' Walter Payton bypassed Jim Brown's record for career rushing yardage of 12,312 yards. By season's end, Payton had 13,309 and was well on his way beyond 15,000, a territory uncharted.

ABOVE: *The Los Angeles Raiders flexed their offense and crushed the Redskins in Super Bowl XVIII.*

BELOW: *Defensive end Lyle Alzado led the demoralizing Raider defense against the Redskins.*

*Miami quarterback Dan Marino threw for 48 touchdown passes, blowing right by Y A Tittle's single season total of 36, and passed for 5084 yards, becoming the first player to go beyond 5000 yards.

*Mark Clayton, Marino's prime target, caught 19 touchdown passes, breaking the record of 17 set by Don Hutson, Elroy Hirsch and Bill Groman.

*Los Angeles Rams running back Eric Dickerson beat OJ Simpson's single season rushing record of 2003 yards (in 14 games) by piling up 2,105 in 16 games. Simpson's record for combined yardage, 2243 all-purpose yards in 1975, also fell to Dickerson by a single yard, 2244.

*In the receiving department, Washington's Art Monk caught 106 passes, breaking Charley Hennigan's record 101 catches for Houston in 1964. And Charlie Joiner of San Diego claimed the lead in career receptions, finishing with 657, well ahead of Charley Taylor's 649 catches.

*The Bears' defense set a record with 72 quarterback sacks. Defensive end Richard Dent had 17 and a half sacks to lead the team.

*The San Francisco 49ers set a record of regular season wins by going 15-1. The 49ers also showed the sports world a thing or two in the Super Bowl by shutting down Miami's grand passing attack, regardless of its records. The Dolphins zipped by Seattle and Pittsburgh in the preliminaries, running up 76 points in two games. The 49ers, meanwhile, knocked off two developing teams, the Chicago Bears and New York Giants, to make the meeting at Stanford Stadium.

ABOVE: *The Rams' Eric Dickerson rushed for 2105 yards in 1984, breaking OJ Simpson's single-season rushing record.*

ABOVE RIGHT: *Mark Clayton of Miami set a new record for receiving touchdown passes (19) in 1984.*

RIGHT: *San Diego's Charlie Joiner set a record for career receptions in 1984, with 657.*

ABOVE: *The Chicago Bears' defense clobbered their opposition in 1985.*

Unfortunately for the Dolphins, Joe Montana and the rest of the San Francisco team tired quickly of hearing how great Miami was in the pre-game hype.

With three second-quarter touchdowns, the 49ers sealed the Dolphins' tomb and went on to bury them, 38-16. A profoundly disappointed Marino had thrown for 318 yards but also had two crucial interceptions.

Montana, ever the Golden Boy, completed 24 of 35 attempts for 331 yards and three touchdowns, enough for everybody's MVP award. The San Francisco ground game, balanced between backs Wendell Tyler and Roger Craig, contributed 211 yards to the cause.

Bill Walsh, the 49ers' coach, had his second Super Bowl championship, and the people who had been calling him a genius suddenly found themselves amidst a chorus of 'Amens.'

BELOW: *The 49ers' quarterback Joe Montana signals a touchdown during a goal-line crunch in Super Bowl XIX.*

MIDDLE LEFT: *Quarterback Joe Montana picked the Dolphins apart in Super Bowl XIX. His primary receiving target was his roommate, Dwight Clark.*

LEFT: *The San Francisco ground game in the 1984 regular season was bolstered by Roger Craig.*

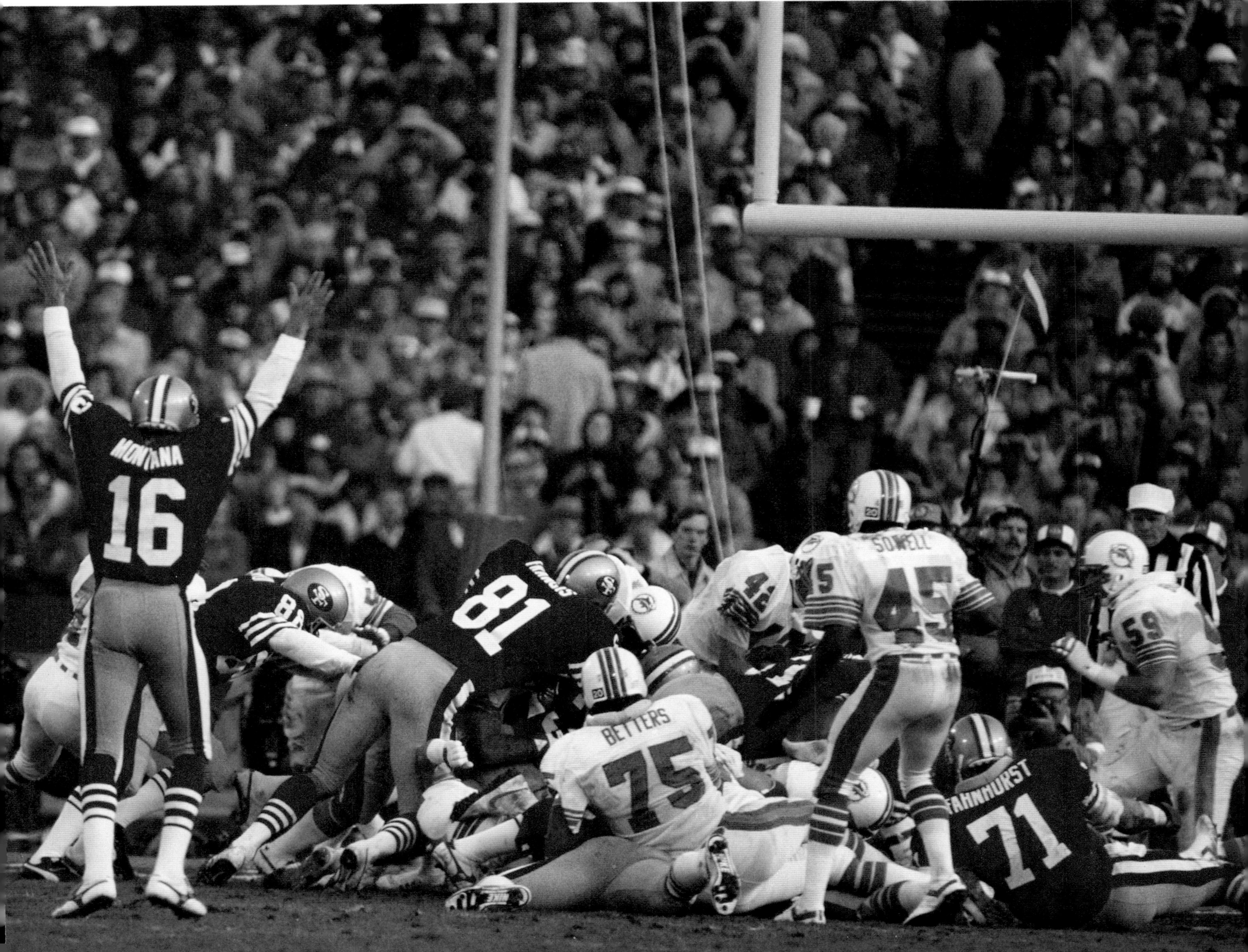

BACK TO THE BASICS

Lest pro football stray too far from its roots with high-tech passing offenses and fancy formations, the game underwent a back-to-the-basics movement in 1985 and 1986. Nothing could be more fitting than having two of the NFL's oldest franchises, the Chicago Bears and New York Giants, lead the charge.

The most fundamental of all basics, of course, was a snarling defense, armored by a corps of linebackers, safeties and defensive ends who routinely broke legs, wills, spirits, game plans or anything else that got in their way. Certainly, these defenses were paired with beautifully efficient offenses, but make no mistake, the alpha and omega of the Bears' and Giants' success were their defenses.

The Bears, the Super Bowl XX champions, were a curious mix of dastardly characters and sweetly silly stage hounds. The road show was led by William 'Refrigerator' Perry, the monstrous defensive tackle (his weight ranged between 310 and 350 pounds) and sometimes fullback out of Clemson whose size and gap-toothed grin made him an overnight folk hero and media-money machine spewing out endorsements with down-home South Carolina ease. The popular, sensational figure was punk-rock quarterback Jim McMahon, a Brigham Young star whose sunglasses, headbands and general outrageousness belied the little-believed truth that in his private life he was a family man. His mouth irritated coach Mike Ditka, but he had an arm and a knack for winning. So he was tolerated. Then there was the incomparable yardage machine, Walter 'Sweetness' Payton, who had led the NFC five times in rushing since 1977, giving the Bears' offense a battering ram component. Other names cropped up with regularity – wide receiver Willie Gault, safety Gary Fencik.

Fortunately, the team had some quietly efficient defensive players who tended to be the serious types. Otis Wilson, Mike Singletary and Wilber Marshall were the game's best linebackers. Richard Dent, Steve McMichael and Dan Hampton completed the defensive line.

Somehow the team clowns convinced its more respectable members to join a bit of video-age PR called 'The Super Bowl Shuffle.' The video, plus the blizzard of posters, books and other endorsements, all generated huge numbers of dollars, almost as huge as the points generated on the field. The Bears finished the season 15-1 (losing only to Marino and the Dolphins), then chilled the Giants, 21-0, and the Rams, 24-0, in the playoffs.

The New England Patriots of former Baltimore great Raymond Berry featured running back Craig James and revolving quarterbacks Steve Grogan and Tony Eason. They surprised Miami in the AFC Championship, 31-14. But the Bears made a meal of them in the Super Bowl, turning the game into a 46-10 rout. Still, it was the most-watched program (probably because of the Chicago sideshow) in television history, with 127 million viewing and another dozen million or so catching it on the radio.

Chicago's odd road show seemed a sure fire bet as repeat champions for 1986, but McMahon's shoulder was injured, and the rest of the team seemed to be tripping over egos distended by all the

ABOVE LEFT: *William 'The Refrigerator' Perry gained overnight notoriety as the Bears' noseguard and occasional fullback.*

ABOVE: *During the 1985 season Chicago linebacker Mike Singletary earned the reputation as one of the best defenders in the league.*

LEFT: *Linebacker Wilber Marshall (58) and defensive end Richard Dent (95) were two of the reasons the Bears crushed the Patriots in Super Bowl XX.*

BELOW: *Chicago quarterback Jim McMahon (9) pitches to running back Walter Payton (34) in Super Bowl XX.*

bloated media attention. As a quarterback replacement at mid-season, Ditka brought in diminutive Boston College Heisman trophy winner Doug Flutie, who had played with the New Jersey Generals of the recently dispatched United States Football League. With little time to learn the Chicago offense, Flutie struggled, and the Bears rolled over and died under the weight of the Redskins in playoffs.

The real team of 1986 was the Giants, similar to their predecessors in that when they grinned their defensive grin, the fangs were nasty linebackers. Lawrence Taylor out of the University of North Carolina had shattered Joe Theisman's shin on Monday Night Football during the 1985 season, which added to his already established reputation as the most vicious player in the league. There wasn't a

RIGHT: *Where the Bears left off with crushing defense, the Giants picked up. Here linebacker Harry Carson (53) crunches a New Orleans Saint.*

LEFT: *Chicago quarterback Jim McMahon led the Bears to Super Bowl XX but was injured during much of the 1986 season.*

BELOW: *Chicago management acquired quarterback Doug Flutie late in the season to replace McMahon, but the Heisman Trophy winner from Boston College struggled in the playoffs.*

quarterback in the game who didn't see Taylor blitzing and think of the sickly snap of Theisman's playing career. The Giants offered that kind of intimidation.

The New York defense, however, was much, much more than Taylor. It was a phalanx of great linebackers, notably Harry Carson, Carl Banks and Gary Reasons. The offense wasn't bad either, with little Joe Morris, giving coach Bill Parcells a great ground game, and Phil Simms, who overcame fan discontent to prove he was a great quarterback.

The 1986 season became one display of power after another. The only distraction was the team's habit of sneaking up behind Parcells at the close of each victory and dumping an icy cooler of Gatorade over his head. In the playoffs, the defense peaked, mauling Joe Montana and the 49ers in the first round, 49-3, then humiliating the Redskins in the title game, 17-0. The Super Bowl, the Giants' first championship appearance since Y A Tittle and 1963, became a matter of subduing quarterback John Elway and the Denver Broncos.

ABOVE: *The Denver Broncos played their way into Super Bowl XXI with a dramatic overtime win over the Cleveland Browns in the AFC Championship game. Here Rich Karlis boots the winning points.*

RIGHT: *Quarterback John Elway had led the comeback against the Browns in the AFC Championship, but the New York Giants corralled the Bronco offense in the Super Bowl.*

The Broncos had made it to the big game with a magical 98-yard fourth-quarter drive against the Cleveland Browns to tie the game at 20. Elway had worked his team up the field and threw the tying touchdown pass with 0:39 left. In overtime, Rich Carlis kicked the winning field goal.

Their magic settled into the Rose Bowl turf sometime in the first half of the Super Bowl. Showing his ability was mixed with moxie, Elway scrambled and tossed his way to a 10-7 first-quarter lead, then continued to power the Broncos with sizzling passes. Their momentum stalled in the second quarter, however, as Carlis missed two field goals and Elway was sacked for a safety. Denver held a 10-9 halftime lead, but New York's offense turned the field into a freeway in the second half.

For the game, Phil Simms completed a record 22 of 25 passes, spraying completions around the Giants' receivers and running-backs, to Phil McConkey, Mark Bavaro, Stacy Robinson, Joe Morris and others. With that, Simms took the MVP trophy, and the Giants took the Super Bowl, 39-20. 'He quarterbacked as good a game as has ever been played,' Parcells told reporters afterward. There were plenty of witnesses to agree with that assessment: more than 100,000 in the Rose Bowl stands, more than 120 million watching on television from 60 countries around the world.

Pro football had traveled far since the days of Jack Cusack and Curly Lambeau, when starting a franchise required a $500 line of credit and a bag of dreams. Stoked by millions in television revenues, the business of football approaches the centenniel of its birth, marked by Pudge Heffelfinger's $500 appearance in Pittsburgh in 1892. Its dreams for the future could run to an international format, with teams in London or Paris or even Moscow. Perhaps, pro football's bicentenniel will celebrate intergalactic competition, with a scoreboard in the stars.

A bit ambitious for a game of yards? Maybe. But only maybe.

INDEX

Numbers in *italics* indicate illustrations

Picture Credits

The Bettmann Archive, Inc.: pages 10 (both), 11, 12 (both), 13 (both), 14 (left), 15 (bottom), 16, 17 (both), 20 (top), 21 (top), 26-27, 27 (above), 28 (both), 31 (top), 39 (bottom), 43 (center), 46, 50-51, 51 (below), 58 (below right), 76 (top), 80 (bottom), 85 (bottom), 101, 107 (top right), 108, 109, 144 (bottom), 162 (bottom), 175 (bottom right), 180.
Chicago Bears: page 81 (right).
Dallas Cowboys: page 167 (left).
Focus on Sports: pages 146, 169, 172, 173 (bottom), 176 (both), 178 (both), 182 (all three), 183 (both), 184, 185 (both), 186 (top), 187, 190-91 (all three), 193 (both), 196 (both), 197, 200 (top), 201, (all three0, 202 (both), 203 (all three), 204 (all three), 205, 206 (both), 207 (both), 208 (both, 209, 210-11 (all three), 212 (both), 214 (both), 215 (all three), 216-17 (both), 218 (both), 219 (both), 220 (both), 221 (bottom left), 222 (top three), 223 (both), 224 (below), 225 (both), 226 (bottom), 227 (both), 228 (both), 229 (all three), 230 (both), 231 (all three), 232-33 (all four), 234-35 (all four), 236 (both), 237, 238 (both).
Library of Congress, page 26.
Pro-Football Hall of Fame: pages 14 (right), 15 (top), 19 (both), 20 (bottom), 21 (bottom), 22, 23, 24, 25 (both), 29 (both), 30 (both), 31 (bottom), 32 (left), 33 (right), 34, 35 (all three), 36, 37 (all three), 38 (both), 39 (top), 42, 43 (top), 44 (both), 45 (center & bottom), 49 (below), 53 (both), 54 (both), 55 (both), 56 (both), 57, 58 (above & below left), 59 (both), 60 (both), 61 (all three), 63 (top & bottom), 64 (bottom), 65, 68 (left), 70 (top), 72 (top), 73 (bottom), 76-77, 81 (left), 82, 83 (both), 84, 90 (bottom), 91 (top), 92 (bottom), 93 (top), 96 (all three), 105 (bottom), 113, 116, 117 (both), 119 (top), 120, 121 (both), 122 (both), 123, 126, 129 (top), 130, 133 (bottom), 137 (top), 138, 144 (top), 145, 147 (bottom), 150 (bottom), 155 (right), 157 (top), 159 (top), 161 (left), 154 (top right), 165, 166 (top right), 167 (right), 168 (top), 173 (top), 177 (bottom).
Stanford Sports Information, Stanford University: page 52 (right).
University of Illinois: page 47.
UPI/Bettmann Newsphotos: pages 32 (right), 33 (left), 43 (bottom), 45 (top), 48 (below), 48-49, 51 (above), 52 (left), 62-63, 64 (top), 66-67 (all 30, 68 (right), 69 (both), 70-71, 71 (top), 72 (bottom), 72-73, 74-75 (all four), 77 (top), 78-79 (all three), 80 (top), 85 (top), 88, 89, 90 (top), 91 (bottom), 92 (top), 93 (bottom), 94-95, 97, 98-99 (all three0, 100, 102-03, 104, 105 (top), 106-07, 107 (bottom), 110-11 (all three) 112, (both), 114 (both), 115 (all three), 118 (both), 119 (bottom), 124-25, 126-27, 128 (both), 129 (bottom), 131 (both), 132, 133 (top), 136, 136-37 (bottom), 139 (both), 140 (both), 141, 142-43, 147 (top), 148-49, 150 (top), 151 (both), 152 (both), 153, 154 (both), 155 (left), 156, 157 (bottom), 158 (both), 159 (bottom), 160, 161 (top right & bottom right), 162 (top), 163 (both), 164 (left & bottom right), 166 (top left & bottom), 168 (bottom), 170-71 (all four), 174-75, 175 (top), 177 (above), 179 (both), 181, 186 (bottom), 188-89, 192 (both), 194, 195 (both), 198 (both), 199 (both), 200 (bottom), 213, 221 (top & bottom right), 222 (bottom), 224 (top), 226 (top).